BORN or BRED?

Martin Bryant: the making of a mass murderer

Other great titles from Fairfax Books:
What the Mother Knew by Edmund Tadros
The Scarlet Thread by Maurice Gurvich and Christopher Wray
Flirting with Finance by Virginia Graham and Anneli Knight
Learning From Legends Business by John Eales
The Age Good Food Guide
The Sydney Morning Herald Good Food Guide
The Age Cheap Eats
Plus a great range of lifestyle, finance, sport and leisure books.

To find out more about these titles and other great offers please contact either
The Age Store on 1300 656 052 or www.theageshop.com.au or
The SMH Store on 1300 656 059 or www.smhshop.com.au

Copyright © 2009 Fairfax Media Publications Pty Limited,
1 Darling Island Rd Pyrmont NSW 2009

All rights reserved. Other than as permitted under the Copyright Act, no part of this publication may be reproduced, stored in a retrieval system, or transmitted, in any form or by any means (electronic, mechanical, photocopying, recording or otherwise) without written permission of the copyright owner.

All opinions expressed in *Born or Bred* are those of the authors and not intended as an endorsement by Fairfax Media, its divisions, employees or products. The views, people and events featured in *Born or Bred* are not necessarily endorsed by Fairfax Media.

The Sydney Morning Herald is a registered trademark of Fairfax Media Publications Pty Limited
The Age is a registered trademark of The Age Company Ltd

Publisher Fairfax Media Publications Pty Limited

Authors Robert Wainwright and Paola Totaro

Editor Shane Brady

Photographers Dallas Kilponen, Roger Lovell, Andrew Meares, Bruce Miller, Jason South, Rick Stevens, Angela Wylie

For design or production enquires, contact Peter Schofield on (03) 9601 2149
For copyright or marketing enquiries, contact Caroline Lowry on (02) 9282 3582

Printed in Australia by McPherson's Printing Group
ISBN 978-1-921486-09-8

BORN or BRED?

Martin Bryant: the making of a mass murderer

ROBERT WAINWRIGHT & PAOLA TOTARO

To our parents

Rae and Arthur, Mariella and Paolo

The beginning of all possibilities

Contents

Key Locations	7
Introduction	8
Finding Carleen	11
Jamie	21
Spiders up the Wall	30
Aftermath	39
Maurice	46
A Bouncing Boy	53
Early Signs	62
The Arsenal	71
The Convict	76
Eliza	83
Carnarvon Bay	90
High School	96
Silly Marty	102
A Family Myth	110
The Story Changes	114
Lawn Mower Man	119
The Man in the Hat	124
The Fortune	132
You're Looking for Me	140
Helen	148
Taurusville	155
A Lawyer's Brief	162
Copping	170
Call the Police	178
All Alone	184
The Truth	192
Money and Guns	200
The Final Descent	208
Through His Eyes	220
The Lawyer	229
The Psychiatrist	238
Beyond Bryant	252
Behind Bars	264
The Cafe	270
The Car Park	277
The Toll Booth	282

The Authors

Robert Wainwright has been a journalist for 30 years, rising from the grassroots of country journalism in Western Australia to become a senior writer with *The Sydney Morning Herald*. His career has ranged from politics to crime, always focusing on the people behind the major news of the day. He was a Walkley Awards finalist in 2004. This is his fourth book, after *Rose: The Unauthorised Biography of Rose Hancock Porteous* (2002), *The Lost Boy* (2004) and *The Killing of Caroline Byrne* (2009).

Paola Totaro is the European Correspondent for *The Sydney Morning Herald* and *The Age*. Before her posting to London, she was Editor of the Saturday *Sydney Morning Herald*. Paola has held some of the paper's most senior positions in her 26-year career, including editing News Review, heading the *Herald's* State Political Bureau and leading the Education and Urban Affairs teams. In 1992, she co-edited the first *Herald Guide to Schools* book. She has just been elected to the management committee of the 140-year-old Foreign Press Association of London.

Key Locations

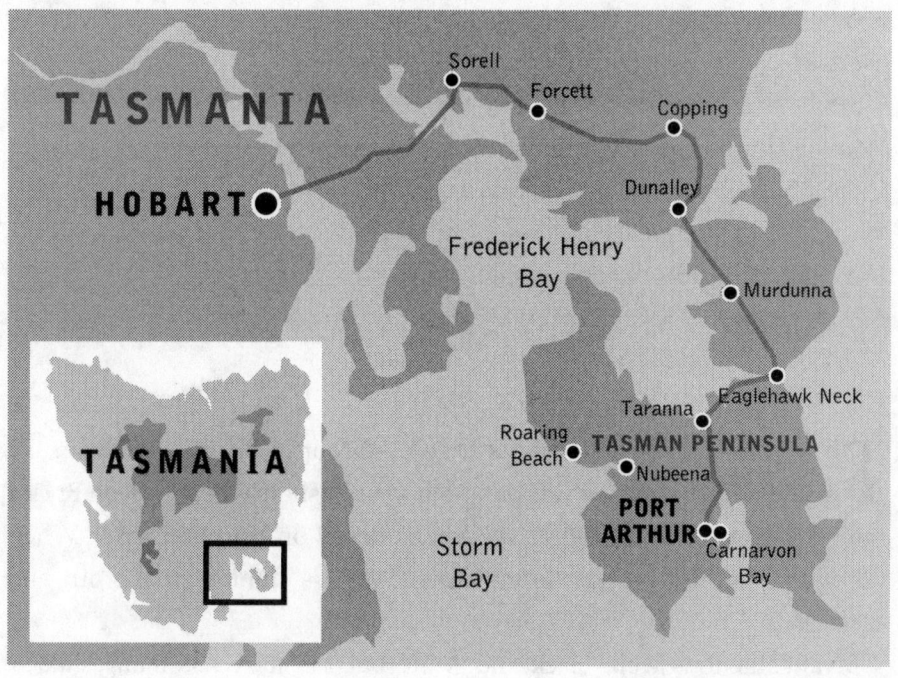

Introduction

This project began as a chance to tell the Martin Bryant story from the inside. *Martin My Son* was our pitch to publishers when Carleen Bryant agreed to work with us to produce a book based on her manuscript. When she withdrew, the project turned instead into a hunt for the truth and answers.

Bryant's actions were black and white but his story has many shades. In the midst of the frantic media coverage in 1996, aspects of his life were misinterpreted or simplified. Apart from coverage around the 10th anniversary in 2006, there have been few attempts to revisit, in a meaningful way, one of the world's most senseless and horrific massacres.

Part of this is due to the attitude of the Tasmanian Government, which has made concerted efforts to all but erase the event from history. In 2001, the Government took the unprecedented step of passing legislation exclusive to Bryant. This effectively blocked the dissemination of any information about the man himself, and we were informed that any requests would be met with a non-negotiable "no comment":

"While reasons are numerous, among them the fact that media was revisiting the event annually was creating enormous distress for the victims and many families of the victims both in Tasmania and nationally," an official email stated.

Our experiences have been vastly different. Yes, there are many people who understandably want to forget and move on. Others though have taken the opposite view. Some have even forgiven as part of their personal approach to healing. Nobody we have approached has refused to talk, and a number of the families of victims have co-operated with media in talking about the event and their subsequent lives. Police who investigated the case have given interviews in recent years.

As you will see, this is not a book that simply recounts the event. You cannot ignore what happened but we have deliberately placed the chapters on the killings at the back of the book to give readers the choice of avoiding graphic violence.

This book is an attempt to delve beyond what we think we know about crime, to place events in context and to provide an answer not only to why this horror might have unfolded but what possibilities we now have, thanks to neuroscience and greater understanding of the human psyche, that might give us a chance to prevent a recurrence – or at least lessen the chances of such an event happening again.

The recent case of the 17-year-old boy who gunned down 15 people, seeking revenge for his loneliness, in Germany is a case in point.

World renowned psychiatrists who deal with the burgeoning problem of mental health in young people encouraged us to tell this story – not only to dispel primitive notions of "evil" but to focus attention on the fact that preventing and treating mental illness in young people is society's greatest insurance against violence.

This is a story that crosses generations, families and class – and shows that just as truth can be stranger than fiction, tragedy can strike us all.

CHAPTER 1
Finding Carleen

The mobile phone text message arrived on the morning of departure, late but to the point: *Wrest Point Casino cafe. Buffet lunch. 12.30. Okay?*

As the flight from Sydney banked through high cloud, a glimpse of Hobart emerged from the early winter mist. First, a fortress of eucalypt-shrouded mountains, then the deep, cold green of the Derwent River, its serpentine grace spoiled only by the high-rise casino tower perched awkwardly on one arm.

Less than two hours later, inside Wrest Point's overheated innards, we anxiously scan the faces of a predominantly elderly crowd. Could that be her jostling for cutlery? Or over there, piling roast beef on to a plate from a steaming bain-marie? How to peer inquisitively into the faces of total strangers? Is that an echo there of that haunting, blue-eyed stare? One woman dressed in a lilac jumper, dark jeans and a bob of ash-blonde hair seems slightly familiar. Dare we ask straight out: "Are you *his* mother?"

Daunted by the crowd milling around the buffet we duck and weave, stealing sidelong glances and sharing quizzical looks. Finally, at the far end of the dining room, we spot two 60-something women at a table framed by a panoramic glass wall. Their profiles are reduced to silhouette by the river glare outside but it is clear they are chatting intimately, their heads close together. We hover, undecided when the clatter of plates interrupts their conversation and, as one woman turns to face the disturbance, the artificial light illuminates her face. Now, there is no doubt. Here is the same long, pale face. The very same straight nose, modulated lower lip and slightly quizzical, sideways set to the head. Her complexion is infused with more colour than his unforgettable, albinoesque pallor and her hair, too, is different, a disciplined bob of tightly permed coils that is the antithesis of her son's strange, white waves. But the steady, blue-eyed gaze she turns on us is enough to dispel all doubt.

We have found Martin Bryant's mother.

Twelve years earlier, Carleen Bryant's only son had been convicted of shooting dead 35 men, women and children. No single gunman anywhere in the world has killed so many people. Martin Bryant did not deny his crime but neither did he ever explain it. He pleaded guilty and, with no need for a trial, there was no opportunity for the expected 200 witnesses assembled by the Crown to air their accounts of the massacre.

What might have triggered this strange young man's murderous spree remained a mystery, locked inside his mind. Sentenced to 35 lifetimes in Risdon Prison, Martin Bryant lives in the jail hospital, his gruesome record unchallenged. And now his mother finally wants to talk, but to say what? That she had come to terms with having raised a mass murderer and to tell what it was like, or to protest his innocence as a victim of some unlikely conspiracy to bring down society?

As we sit down to begin the first of what we hope will be numerous conversations, Carleen Bryant is palpably, visibly anxious. We introduce ourselves nervously, shake hands stiffly and chat about the flight, about the weather, about anything except the elephant in the room. Carleen's friend Joan speaks for her at first, breaking the ice and explaining how the pair met. She has no qualms about mentioning the unmentionable. As a kind of mentor, she has encouraged and facilitated Carleen's increasing need to tell the family's story.

"We met in a friend's kitchen," Joan begins. "There were quite a few people there, and we were chatting away. I remember talking to Carleen and thinking that something had happened in her life, feeling instinctively that there was some pain there. I said to her: 'What has your life brought you?'

"You could have heard a pin drop. Nobody said a word. There was silence. Then Carleen piped up brightly and said: 'My husband died early,' and it was almost as if the people around us breathed a sigh of relief. I didn't know about Martin, I had no idea at that time."

Joan's experience says much about Carleen's life post-Port Arthur. Hobart is a small town in every way, even the spires of its cathedral remain the tallest silhouettes in the city. But Martin Bryant's crime registered large on a global scale. And everywhere she goes, Carleen lives with the terror that she will be identified. A decade on, she keeps largely to herself, has forged a handful of close friendships with people in her local parish, and confines social interaction to church functions where she feels safe and protected.

"What about your own family?" we ask.

At the mention of siblings, her body stiffens and she is on guard again: "Did you read my brother's letter? The one I photocopied for you?" she asks sharply.

The letter is written in a neat, tight European-style cursive, seemingly an innocuous note from brother to sister. Its contents are anything but, imbued with an icy outrage. A long forgotten debt elicits a written pledge for repayment followed by an announcement that her brother and family are moving interstate. Then, the brutal point:

> *Regarding Port Arthur, I wish to advise that I hold you and your family responsible for my present predicament ... I do not believe that you appreciate fully the legacy which your son has delivered to this family and the fact that we will endure his evil doings for as long as we all shall live. In some respects I am happy that you have found solace in the Lord, however that is small compensation for what the remainder of the family is left to endure – no matter for whom you pray, never include me! The only other time I will sight you will no doubt be at our mother's passing. From this day on I do not acknowledge your existence nor will I converse with you.*
>
> *Michael*

In this family, the crime of the son has been laid squarely at the feet of his mother. Not only must she live with the tragedy wreaked on innocents by her only son but the magnitude of his crime has meant that his mother must endure a lifetime of inescapable, searing shame.

Carleen's rejection at the hands of her brother illustrates that while she has said very little publicly, she too is a victim. Her social exile is total and self-imposed, an earthly purgatory where carefully built denials provide her with her only refuge. Indeed, in the mind of his mother, it is simply not possible to accept that the six-pound boy she gave birth to, the blond-haired toddler who loved the sea and spent idyllic holidays fishing, swimming and later scuba diving near the family's holiday cottage behind Port Arthur, could possibly have returned to the very same place as a young man to embark on his final, infernal spree.

And just as in the aftermath, Tasmania, and indeed the nation, asked itself what could possibly have sparked a fury so deadly that Carleen has been driven to tell her own life story and expel at least a few of her demons. It is as if her own family's seemingly unremarkable journey can somehow dispel any lingering suggestion that her son's monstrous actions might bear a relationship with something in his past.

It took 10 years for her to start, a confluence with the anniversary of the killings. As the inevitable media coverage reignited public debate, Carleen finally sat down at a tiny kitchen table and began, painfully, to handwrite what would eventually become a 15,000-word draft:

> *For as long as I have been able to remember, I have never been a confident person. From my childhood to becoming an adult, I was always self-conscious. Writing is not something that comes easily to me and I certainly didn't consider it possible to complete this story ...*

Carleen's memoirs paint a picture of yet another idyllic, if much poorer, childhood spent on the land in semi-rural bliss. Hidden inside her own, cheerful words is another world full of an unimaginable suffering – one barely acknowledged and often defiantly denied, which began with an alcoholic father's threat to throw his wife and newborn daughter from the car on the way home from hospital, to the suicides of both a first love and a much-loved husband. One which ended with an only son imprisoned for mass murder.

....

Tasmanian caravan parks are all but deserted by June each year. When Carleen invites us to visit her home, it is clear that even the sunniest, windless day cannot erase the frightening prospect of enduring a bitter winter in a caravan. Yet she is unruffled.

Her camper van is parked neatly towards the rear of the park, close to the shower block and laundry and out of sight of the main road. There's a jaunty awning attached to the specially converted 1985 Toyota van, and a bike leans against the gas bottle. The ageing Ford sedan parked behind is what she uses to drive around town rather than disengage her home every time she needs to run an errand.

Here, Carleen keeps the sum of her possessions. She owns a house on the other side of the continent where her daughter Lindy lives. Carleen insists she is not hiding, and nor does she struggle to make ends meet. Living frugally is her choice.

Inside the van, it's a tight squeeze – cosy if you want to be positive. There is a meticulously made bed at the end of a narrow walkway, a small fridge and custom-made kitchen cabinets not dissimilar to a small yacht's galley line one side of the van. A tiny shower recess and laundry are hidden neatly on the other side, and groceries are stored tidily in a box in the boot. A small black-and-white TV provides a connection with the world.

Like any home, trinkets and keepsakes have their place on the walls but there are no family photographs. It is unlikely Carleen is hiding her connections as visitors are so few and far between. Rather, it seems that the constant reminder is too difficult. The small sitting area at the front is home to a table where she writes or eats.

Pull back the set of curtains and the van's windscreen is revealed. Her dining chair swivels 180 degrees and clicks into place to become the driver's seat. Pulling up anchor can take just a moment.

"I can go whenever I want," she says.

It's clear the abandonment by immediate family hurts deeply. Just as her brother railed against the shame wreaked by Martin's crime, she too rails against any suggestion that her living conditions are the result of anything but her own life choice. She remains furious that a magazine article described her camper van as "just a caravan".

Carleen rarely visits her son. Her first contact visit in eight years occurred only a few weeks before our first meeting. For much of the first decade, her weekly telephone calls were ignored by a man who, by all accounts, has continued to withdraw into a shell, fattened by ice-cream and inactivity.

Very occasionally, he would agree to a visit during which she was forced to bang on the Perspex screen between them in an attempt to hold his wandering attention.

On this last, unusual visit, mother and son sat knee-to-knee in a bare room with two officers stationed in a corner. The visit lasted less than an hour, and just as she has always done, Carleen did most of the talking.

"I talked about everything and nothing. It didn't matter really. It was more about being together," she says without conviction.

"But did he say anything? Anything at all?" we coax.

"Not really. He never says much. Never has. But I know he was happy to see me because he hugged me as I was leaving."

The Crown decided it wanted to spare a grieving Tasmania from yet another revisiting of the bloody scene. The distress of a long-running court case and the agonising evidence of a potential 200 witnesses was simply too much to ask the community to bear.

The strategy, however, threw up a strange side effect. In its humane efficiency, the lack of a trial created a vacuum of information, which was immediately filled – and continues to be fed – by conspiracy theorists. There are a handful of obsessives who insist Martin Bryant is either totally innocent or was the fall guy in a plot hatched to justify the then Howard government's subsequent reforms to the nation's firearm laws. Others say it was the work of unnamed terrorists. None of it is worth canvassing here.

In the terrible decade since, Carleen Bryant continues to shelter with the inane writings of the conspiracy theorists. Despite our blunt rejection of the possibility that her son is innocent, she says she still wants her story to be written, lifting the lid for the first time on the inner workings of the family.

Her own memoirs venture only tentatively into the events of April 28, 1996, but acknowledge her son's fragile mental condition in the weeks before the massacre:

> Being Martin's mother, I had the experience and insight to tell when he was agitated. Over the years, if someone or something was putting pressure on him this is how he would react. His stress showed in the agitation I could clearly see. After Martin came back from the last trip, I noticed that he was very restless, agitated and worrying about something. There was not the usual pleasant welcome when I visited. He

would ask how long I intended to stay. I wondered why he was behaving in this manner.

She refuses to go any further.

"That's your business," she declares, offering only that while she accepts Martin was there on the day, somehow he was not responsible.

"He was in the Seascape [guest house] but was not supposed to come out alive …" Her explanation trails off.

Does she remember where she was when she heard the news about the murders?

"Of course I do," she snaps. "I was out shopping. I saw it on a TV."

"He was with me the night before. He had dinner with me …"

....

Carleen Bryant is agitated and on the phone. She has spent the past fortnight reading and re-reading our proposal for the publishers, and the words had become disturbing. The more she read, the more they pushed and poked and prodded. Words pricked like pins. Paragraphs cut and sliced her life into raw slivers.

We can imagine her at the tiny table inside her van, under a flimsy light. Alone, to interpret words and phrases that dance and pivot like her chair, which swivels to become the driver seat of her getaway vehicle. She must have felt like starting the engine and racing off on one of her mainland jaunts. Anything to escape being Carleen Bryant.

What do the words really mean? Why is she being described in such detail, with a long, pale face, straight nose? Albinoesque. Like Martin. Is it really necessary? And it isn't accurate. What is this "sideways set" to the head? Doesn't that suggest "criminality" or guilt?

Carleen is offended. Her anger is clear over the phone.

A new letter arrived. The covering note was polite but guarded, pointing out that many corrections need to be made to our manuscript. It concluded:

> *This was simply meant to be a biography of my life, not a rehash of public perceptions of Martin's guilt. Just remember he never had a trial.*

Carleen's anger had risen as she read through the document, particularly on the question of her son's guilt. He had been persuaded to plead guilty by his lawyer, John Avery, she cried. He had been persuaded to change his story. Martin had always denied ever being in Port Arthur that day.

Under pressure, the thin layer of acceptance had crumbled. No longer was her son perhaps in some way involved, but merely a victim of some absurd conspiracy plot. He was never there, there was no link to the weapons, and there were no fingerprints or DNA.

Assumes guilt, she wrote underlining a sentence which asked if her son's attempts behind bars to kill himself were an indication that he might now understand the suffering he inflicted: *Not the reason. Guilt was never proved in court. The decision was based on Avery's persuasion to plead guilty.*

She had told us a few weeks earlier that his protest was against being shifted from the prison hospital back to the general prison population. Prison officials had relented.

In an email sent through a friend, she had opened up for the first time to the possibility that her son may have committed the murders. It was penned as if to be printed in a book:

Martin Bryant's suicide attempts in Risdon Prison have at least two diametrically opposed possible explanations. They may be due to Martin having at last accepted that he was responsible for the multiple deaths of which he was accused. If in fact he was the gunman on the 28th April 1996 at Port Arthur he may have finally remembered deeply repressed memories of that day and that burden was too much for him to carry for the rest of his life in gaol. An equally valid reason could be that he was finally able to piece together the reasons for his physical scars from the Seascape fire and his inability to recall any of the events at Port Arthur that day. If in fact, the so-called Port Arthur conspiracy theory is even partially correct, then let us consider the implications. Many people over the past 10 years have done what it would appear the then DPP, Damian Bugg, did not do i.e. examine all the evidence including a number of eyewitnesses who gave a completely different but consistent description of the gunman which would have at least raised doubts when compared with a photo of Martin Bryant taken a matter of days before the massacre. Also, the almost farcical police interview with Martin at which the court-

appointed lawyer did not even bother to attend, thus denying the accused a witness independent of the police. If, in fact, Martin Bryant was not the gunman but was intended to be a scapegoat to be found incinerated along with guns which could not be used to provide forensic evidence in Seascape Cottage, then as a 29-year-old condemned to spend the rest of his life in prison for a crime he knew he had not committed, suicide would appear the only logical way out.

A few weeks later, she notes matter of factly that a prison doctor had diagnosed Martin with a form of autism known as Asperger's syndrome. It gives her a medical reason for his abnormal behaviour as a child.

Of course, it does not explain his actions as an adult: people with Asperger's are not potential mass killers.

Carleen's greatest concern, however, is her daughter Lindy, Martin's younger sister. We had hoped she would also co-operate and provide another, until now hidden voice, but Carleen sees it another way: *Assumes, suggests family dysfunctional from a mere public opinion of an accusation.*

"You can forget about talking to Lindy," Carleen says during a subsequent phone call. "Why do you need her anyway? I can tell you everything you need to know."

•••••••••••••••••••••••••••

The final email is succinct and, frankly, not surprising. Carleen Bryant has withdrawn from the project. The decision is not negotiable, she insists through Joan, and she feels the better for it.

This book is not what Carleen Bryant had in mind because more often than not it challenges her world view. It is not written to justify her son's conviction but to explore the person – and the family – of the man who killed more people as a lone gunman than anyone else in the world.

What made Martin Bryant? Why did he do what he did?

Could such a crime have been prevented if he were better managed as a child? Or was it as an adolescent, growing into adulthood when he needed help from society? Can we learn anything from the behaviour of a young man that might teach us to respond differently?

Martin Bryant's guilt is not in question: he confessed both directly and indirectly, initially to police during an interview when he pointed to himself and said "me", and later to his lawyer, John Avery. He also confessed to the psychiatrists who assessed whether he was fit to stand trial. His first lawyer, David Gunson SC, disqualified himself when he was told Bryant wished to plead not guilty – suggesting Bryant had confessed to him, too.

Compiling Martin Bryant's story has led us to several other lives, previously unknown men and women who were the young man's forebears, family that created his genetic make-up and whose life experiences influenced, generation by generation, the behaviours of those to follow. There were also the extraordinary stories of those who, through a quirk of fate, indirectly influenced or directly shared key parts of his life.

None are culpable, no one could have known what this boy would choose to do with his life. Theirs are ordinary lives surviving often extraordinary circumstances. They are tales Australian both in struggle and success.

CHAPTER 2
Jamie

"Jamie?" Terry McCarthy tries to drain the anxiety from his voice as he answers the phone. He has to be in control, if that is possible. There are lives at stake.

"Yes, that's correct." The formality of the reply at the other end of the line sounds ludicrous in the circumstances.

"It's Terry. How are you?"

The voice, slightly high-pitched, eager and childlike, brightens, as if greeting a friend: "How are you, Terry? I'm all right."

The police negotiator relaxes a little. It is the gunman: "You're OK are you?"

Jamie's voice turns to steel, the fragile trust gone in a moment: "Pretty damn quiet. I mean, are your boys creeping up on me or something? Two hundred metres away from me and bang, bang, bang, they'll go for me."

McCarthy is taken aback. Somehow the guy has spotted the Special Ops Group still hiding outside the cottage in the dark. Their last conversation had ended in anger an hour before so any mistake could have devastating consequences.

"I gave you an assurance that wouldn't happen, and I guarantee it won't happen, OK?"

Jamie has moved on: "And can that guarantee with the helicopter?"

The bloke is back on the chopper. He has just murdered dozens of innocent people – 30 or more, according to the body count – and is holding at least three people hostage in the cottage, yet all he wants is a helicopter ride. It is a ride he is never going to make but McCarthy has to stall.

"Well, I can't guarantee anything in relation to the helicopter. I still haven't been told what the situation is with us getting one for you but, ah, we're certainly trying to do something for you. Do I have a guarantee from you that you will allow Rick and David to leave?"

"That's right. I'll keep Sally, um, as hostage."

McCarthy struggles to find words to keep Jamie calm but not indicate approval to taking Sally Martin, owner of the Seascape guest house with her husband, David, as a hostage. The other guy – Rick, he keeps saying – is actually a man named Glen Pears, who'd been shoved in the boot of a car at gunpoint at the Port Arthur service station a few hours earlier: "Well, I'd prefer you didn't keep anyone, Jamie, but, um, you know, er, you're the man that's making the decisions."

It seems to satisfy Jamie, at least for the moment. He is in charge, and he knows it: "I'll tell you what man, yeah ... things are gonna work out well for me. What's the time by you?"

"Well, I have the time at one minute to seven."

"Oh. One minute to seven ... that's all right so that's OK. Good."

McCarthy wants to lead the conversation back to the hostages. He has to take the emotion out of the conversation, draining his own anger at what has just happened at Port Arthur, what might have happened to his own family, his own children.

"Now, Jamie, we were talking earlier on about Rick and the fact that you kidnapped him at Fortescue Bay."

"That's correct. Yeah."

"You talked about his wife ... Do you know anything about his wife?"

"I know how high up in things she is."

McCarthy is perplexed: "How high up? What do you mean by that, Jamie?"

"In work; higher than what you are. The intelligence and everything, university and everything."

Jamie is showing his own intellectual misgivings. To him, success is measured by a university education, not by professional achievement.

This man hates himself.

"I'm more interested in this helicopter ride."

Back to the helicopter. McCarthy stumbles to find another excuse to stall. "I need to find out a lot of information … flight plans … first of all we've got to get a machine that is able to fly at night."

"Of course." Jamie is listening. Perhaps he will soften his deadline.

"You've set this time at 11.30 to midnight is making it very, very difficult for us …"

"Oh well, I can change it to a later date."

"Well, what time would you like to …"

Jamie sighs, the details are trivial: "Early in the morning … daybreak … about seven."

McCarthy can see another opening, perhaps wide enough to end this identity game:

"Now you've given me your name as Jamie. We both know that that's not correct. Are you prepared now to give me your correct name?"

"Not really, no. I …"

So he confirms it is an alias: "Why not?" Jamie mulled it over: "I'll tell you what, right, at seven o'clock in the morning I'll give you my passport number."

His passport? What is the bloke playing at?

"Have you got your passport there?"

"Um, in the glove box. I've got a photocopy of it in my wallet but I want you to guarantee that you'll have one in the morning early."

"Well, look, uh, I can't guarantee anything until you start, you know, start playing it straight with me."

Jamie laughs quietly, McCarthy's threat impotent. He tries again: "You're not playing it straight with me so it's difficult for me to go and convince the people that have to be convinced that you're genuine … I really do want to help you here but you're not making it very easy for me to help you because you're not telling me anything. OK?"

"Yeah." Noncommittal.

"… and I really do want to sort this out so that nobody is hurt. OK? I really wanna do that, and everybody here wants to do that."

"I want my ride, man."

The words are petulant, threatening, objecting to Terry's prodding.

"But if you won't co-operate with us …"

"I wanna helicopter." Jamie has descended into a tantrum, like a child.

"If you won't give us some simple information. There's not a lot we can do for you, Jamie."

There is a pause. He is thinking now: "That's true, that's true." The voice has calmed.

It is like riding a mad roller-coaster. McCarthy needs to get the conversation back to the hostages. Are they still alive? Details are still scarce, given the scale of the carnage down there.

"Now, you know this is a significant sort of er, er incident that's occurred today. The fact that you've kidnapped someone and you've, got, you know, you've got hostages in this cottage."

"Um ..."

"We're treating it very, very seriously but it sounds to me like perhaps you're not."

The child is still petulant: "Well ... well, I've missed out on a lot of rides on these helicopters. Don't you understand that?"

McCarthy tries to respond but Jamie cuts him off: "I missed out on one about four years ago. I was going to buy one for $95,000. It was advertised in *The Mercury*. I'm very upset about that."

"I'm sorry," McCarthy soothes. The guy has just given another hint. He is a local.

"You can buy a helicopter. I've got the money. Don't you understand? I've got the money, I've got all the wealth ..."

Suddenly his rant ends. So will the call. Jamie has had enough: "What I'll do is I'll phone you back up at twenty past eight."

McCarthy isn't expecting it: "No, well that's too late ..."

"I'll give you some more information. Goodbye." He is gone, the silence filled by STD beeps.

McCarthy sits back, sweating from the concentration. It had been his third conversation with the gunman since 3.20pm on a Sunday – April 28, 1996 – that will never be forgotten. Jamie isn't his real name but to challenge him on his identity might endanger the hostages – if they aren't already dead. The best guess is they are dealing with a strange young man named Martin Bryant. Checks are being made. In the meantime, he has to play it cool, keep up the contact, keep him on the line for as long as possible.

At first, Jamie appears calculating, issuing his demands for a helicopter with a precision that suggests great planning. Now, McCarthy is not so certain. The conversation wanders from complete control and manipulation to childlike responses ranging from a desire to be liked or even a clumsy approach to make friends, to raw anger, threats and puerile tantrums. He admits little and yet is now offering his passport as proof of his identity.

How life can change in a moment. At lunchtime that day, McCarthy had been lounging on the couch, watching his brother John on television playing AFL for Fitzroy against Brisbane. His three-year-old son was at his parents' house and due to be picked up later.

He was called into the Hobart headquarters just before 3pm: there had been a mass shooting at Port Arthur, the convict settlement 90 kilometres from the city, and the gunman was almost certainly holed up in a guest house near the scene. There was no time to drive down there. The phone had been isolated and the experienced negotiator was needed to establish contact while a team assembled on the ground.

Even after eight years in the job, McCarthy was not prepared for the next few hours; the absurdity, the terrible waste.

When he gets home, exhausted, after midnight, he goes to hug his son and cries in the arms of his wife.

....

"Hello." Jamie is back.

"Are you happy now?" McCarthy asks, confident the Special Ops guys have pulled back to the main road.

"Oh, I'm right next to the hostages. Yeah, of course I'm happy. Yeah."

"You're right next to the hostages?"

"Yeah."

"Have you fed them? I know you were cooking a meal for them earlier on …"

The response is strange:

"I've moved one of them anyway. I've actually moved one of them, transport one of them …"

"What? From where they were in the double bed?"

"Yeah, that's right."

"They're now with you, are they?"

"Yeah. I've actually transported the female, Sally."

Jamie describes his captive as if she is an alien. The woman must be petrified – if she's still alive, that is. The others listening in are having their doubts. There are no background noises at all. The house behind Jamie is deathly silent. And what is this word "transported"? It sounds like he was carrying a body.

McCarthy persists: "Right. Sally. So Sally's with you now?"

"That's correct."

"Is she able to talk to me?" This is critical, the only way of knowing if anyone was alive.

"No, well I've got her up here on the couch so …"

"Right. Well, can I chat to her for a moment …"

Jamie sees through the ruse: "Hey, hey, hey, hey, I'm just wondering when this helicopter's gonna arrive. Is it still gonna be in the morning?"

McCarthy has to respond: "Well we're working on that but, as I said, I still need some real information … you talked about a passport earlier; that you had a copy in your wallet."

"That's right, yeah."

"Now if you don't want to tell me your name that's fine but how about giving me your passport number and we can do a check on that?" He holds his breath.

"I think it's HO24967, if I can remember it, 'cos I travelled quite a lot overseas. And most, um, travel agencies know me around town, around Hobart, I should say so."

"Right. HO24967."

"Yeah, I think that's the number but …"

"You haven't got your wallet?" It was like dealing with a scatty teenager.

" … most of the travel agencies, er, they'll know me."

So Jamie won't identify himself yet admits it is an alias and then gives away his identity with a passport number. Unless it is false, of course. It seems he can't decide if he is hiding from his crime or wants to be known, lauded for it.

"Obviously, the travel agencies deal with a lot of people, Jamie, so it's difficult for us to go there and say, 'Look, we're talking to this man and he says that he does a lot of business with you.' No doubt they'd have a few clients that probably do a lot of business with 'em."

Jamie insists: "Yeah, just let them know I've got blond hair and they'll know me, if you don't know how much of a character I am. I'm, I'm 28 years old."

"You're 28?"

"Yeah, and I've got blond hair and I'm slim."

"Uh huh."

"I'm, well, always well dressed and they'll know … if you can get in touch with them you can get all information on who I am and where I live and …"

"Well you could just as easily tell me that." McCarthy is challenging but Jamie won't bite. It is cat and mouse, but their roles keep changing. "Jamie, what significance is it now whether you tell me your name or not?"

"I'm resting. I'm happy here with the hostages. I mean, they're completely safe. I've cooked them something to eat and …"

"Well, are you prepared to allow me to, ah, have a quick word with Sally, just, er, to see how she's feeling."

"Um, ah yes, she's half asleep anyway."

"Half asleep?"

"Yeah."

"I'd imagine she'd be very, very frightened. She's an elderly lady."

"She'll be fine. I mean they could eat well. I've taken them to the toilet …"

"It sounds like you're taking good care of them, there's no doubt about that … and I'd like to thank you for that."

The notion of pandering to this madman is galling but McCarthy has no choice. The bloke is still edgy about the Special Ops guys. He can't see them but that doesn't stop the threats. There is gelignite upstairs, he says, ageing Chinese-made sticks stored by his hostage. And he is prepared to use them.

"I'll blow them up, too, with that so I'll blow myself up if it has to come to that …"

"I don't think it needs to come to that does it?"

Jamie is mumbling. He is back on the helicopter, and wants a guarantee it will be there in the morning: "I'll phone you back up in an hour."

McCarthy tries to keep him on the line: "Before you go …"

He is gone again.

••••••••••••••••••••••••••

"Jamie?" McCarthy asks in hope more than anything. Maybe the hostages have overpowered the guy and are calling to say they're safe.

"Yeah, that's correct." Hope dashed, replaced by this stilted dance of recognition.

Confirmation of Bryant's identity has come through since their last conversation. His yellow Volvo had been abandoned at the site. Witness accounts put him at the scene; a young man well known for his strange behaviour as much as his striking appearance. Seemingly harmless, now they know differently with more than 30 dead and dozens injured. What are they dealing with? A well-prepared killer, a haphazard simpleton or something in between? What are his motives, and what will he do next?

"It's Terry here. Everybody well?"

"Everything's fine, yes." The voice is cold.

"I just want to clarify two other points in relation to the helicopter."

Jamie listens.

"You were talking about having Sally in front with you but there's only two seats …"

"Well, she can sit in the back and I'll sit where the pilot is at the front."

"Right you'll sit up the front. Now are you planning on taking firearms with you?"

Jamie considers the question: "No, not really."

"Sorry?" McCarthy isn't expecting the reply. Isn't this guy going to take one of his guns?

"I'm actually gonna have the knife. I've got a really good knife."

McCarthy plays it steady: "OK."

Jamie is explaining: "When I let Sally in the back, I'm gonna actually have it next near the pilot's ribs."

"Why do you want to do that?"

"Precaution. To make sure that everything's gonna go all right … I hope they're not going to try anything."

"Look, I can assure you that we are not going to try anything. We don't want to see anybody hurt, particularly you … and, ah, we don't want to endanger anybody's lives."

The threat remains.

Jamie's next words are chilling: "It's not only, um, dying, it's the pain that people can inflict."

"I don't want to see anybody suffer any pain. Do you?"

"No, I don't."

"Right. OK. Now are you going to, are you going to lead Sally in front of you when you walk out?"

"Yeah. I'll have the knife to her ribs or throat. She's actually gonna sit in the back. I'm gonna sit in the front and have this knife near the ribs of this pilot."

"Well what assurances do I have from you that you're not going to hurt either Sally or the pilot?"

"Do you want me to throw the knives out now? I don't wanna use a firearm … just this cunting knife … It's about 15 inches long. A stainless-steel combat knife."

"OK." Jamie is getting agitated again. McCarthy has to calm him down.

Jamie changes the subject: "Yeah, what time do you make it?"

"Just after nine."

"Just after nine? Let's make it 10 o'clock, all right? Bye."

"All right. Before you go, before you go, just one last thing. Ya there? Jamie are you there?"

Beep, beep.

The line is dead.

CHAPTER 3
Spiders up the Wall

What does a person take from childhood to adulthood? How do experiences, good and bad, shape an individual, their view of the world and place in society?

The childhood of Carleen Marion Cordwell – for that is the real Carleen Bryant – was defined by hardship: life was a battle, financially, emotionally, physically. She was taught early to be grateful for everything, even the smallest kindness. Despite upheaval, constant moves, familial violence and at times, sheer cruelty, the young girl – and the adult woman – refused to sheet home blame and adopted the detachment needed to survive. Her resilience was learned from the women of the family – her mother, Freda, grandmother, Eva, even a half-sister, named Joyce. The men, by contrast, were often troublesome and sometimes worse, damaged psychologically by war, perhaps, or the seemingly endless need to reinvent themselves to survive on meagre finances. Carleen's maternal grandfather, George Trevor Hutton, had always struggled. A 21-year-old labourer near Devonport at the top of Tasmania when Freda was born in 1908, he finished his working days at the Electrolytic Zinc Company on the banks of the Derwent near Hobart at the bottom of the island.

It was Carleen's father who had the most impact on his daughter and undoubtedly shaped her psyche. During his life, Arthur Albert Cordwell was a farmer, private investigator and railway worker. In his will, written many years later, he described himself as a carpenter although there seems little to indicate he turned a piece of timber other than to drive a ragged fencepost into the ground.

Carleen, born with a heart defect – part of my heart missing, as she describes it – grew up hearing stories of Freda's childhood in Tasmania's north coast hinterland. North Motton, 20 minutes by car from Devonport, was a semi-rural hamlet of a few hundred people at the time and remains that way. It was named like so many Australian towns, after an English village, and settled in 1859 to grow potatoes, its soil enriched by weathered basalt deposited by volcanic activity 400 million years before. Little has changed in the past century.

The Huttons were a small family by the standards of the early 1900s. George and Eva had only two children – a son and a daughter – and managed to live in the relative comfort of a rough, three-room cottage. That was until a maternal aunt died. Eva now had to cook and clean for two families. When travel between two houses, mostly by foot, became too much, the two families simply merged. Suddenly, there were seven people in a cottage of similar size. This was the way as families moved and evolved or as death and financial circumstance altered in a harsh world. Freda now slept on a couch rather than a bed, and she and her siblings walked everywhere. If she was lucky, the family had access to a horse and cart, particularly when the Great War broke out and the men went off to France.

The fact that Carleen, a generation later, would know details of where and how her mother slept and the miles she had to walk to and from school each day reveals the use of stories to suppress the little girl's complaints or to demonstrate just how grateful she should be for her own childhood. There seem to be no stories of her mother's childhood happiness, other than a retelling of the day Freda and her brother, Reg, hurtled down a hill on a billycart. Reg, who was at the wheel, lost control and his sister was thrown into a barbed wire fence, lacerating her leg. The scars remained as a physical reminder until she died in 1998 at the age of 90, although the psychological scars of her grandson's deeds would have cut much deeper.

After she left school, Freda worked as a maid for a man named Captain Cannon, and there is a Cannon Street in North Motton, suggesting the family was well-to-do. There, she kept house, milked cows and tended the captain's wife and two children. Freda may have been poorly paid but the family were respectful of their staff, and her memories were of a kind, inclusive environment.

It wasn't until 1934, at the relatively mature age of 26, that she met and married Carleen's father. The relationship with Arthur Cordwell appears to be one of utility rather than romance. He was already in his 50s, five years older than her own father in fact. Married once already, he had sired four children – three sons and a daughter named Joyce, who was roughly the age of the woman he would marry. Freda Hutton, housemaid, would make a good carer as much as a wife – a chattel, an unpaid worker.

The marriage was unhappy and violent, at the very least psychologically. In her darker moments, as if to share the burden – or perhaps because of what Carleen had already witnessed as a child – Freda would share her secrets and fears with her eldest daughter.

Nothing was hidden, even the day her husband drove his wife and new baby daughter home from the hospital and threatened to throw them both from the car. The demands of a second family were clearly a burden but, as a staunch Catholic, he could do little about it, and three more children followed, two daughters, Margaret and Helen, and a son, Michael.

Carleen's account of her childhood is memorable for its focus on minuscule detail and its brushing aside or omission of reality, tragedy and hardship. Her memories are exact about events but displays of emotion are rare. She felt the impact of a difficult childhood, her parents' tumultuous marriage and a flawed, neglectful father; it is there still in her anxiety and unease in social situations. And yet her writing is stoic, glossing over the sadness, hinting only that it may have been much, much worse:

> *The marriage was not to be a happy one because Mum soon discovered that Dad was an alcoholic. There was never any physical abuse, but there certainly was mental abuse, which was humiliating and degrading.*

Perhaps Arthur Cordwell's problems could be blamed on what he saw at the Western Front in the latter stages of the Great War. His records held by the National Archives run to 17 pages, describing not only where he went and those he served with but also those he left behind.

He was a 33-year-old married farmer from Sandy Bay, on the southern outskirts of Hobart, when he enlisted in July 1917 and shipped out from Melbourne aboard the HMAT A32 Themistocles a month later. What prompted him to enlist so late in the war is not clear but his papers say he received an extra two shillings above the standard eight shillings a week. The handwritten document also records his physical description – tall for a man of his era at a touch over five feet 10 inches, lean at 171 pounds, with a "fresh" complexion, fair hair and grey eyes – his future grandson to a tee.

Cordwell's tour of duty seemed unremarkable, if nine months in France as a gunner with the 12th Battalion could be described in such a way. He returned aboard the cargo ship, City of Poona, in March 1919. Although his only physical injury was a septic toe, Cordwell was clearly a damaged man.

A year later, his 17-year marriage to Sarah Lavinia Briers was in difficulty and became the subject of a maintenance order in 1920. It is not clear if Cordwell left his wife or if he was widowed when she died in 1935, about the time he met and married Freda Hutton. He had certainly left the farming life, and tried his hand at being a private investigator but apparently stuck his nose where it was not wanted and lost his job. At least that was the explanation given to Carleen, presumably by her mother, without further detail. By the time he married Freda he was working for the Tasmanian Railways Department.

In May 1940, at the outbreak of World War II, Cordwell tried to enlist again. By now he was describing himself as an agent, living in West Hobart with his wife and young daughter, Carleen, but it seems clear Cordwell wanted to escape to a place where his identity was unquestioned. His attempt lasted two weeks, according to war records which show that Private Cordwell re-enlisted on May 14, was promoted to Lance Corporal the next day and then discharged on May 26 on "compassionate grounds" because of his age.

Carleen, the eldest of four children by the marriage, was born in 1938. There was now a large family – sons and daughters, half-brothers and sisters, cousins and second cousins. At times she felt like Joyce Cordwell's daughter rather than her half-sister. It was a small comfort in a childhood otherwise dominated by the frequent upheaval created by an increasingly dysfunctional and itinerant father.

The family settled in Montrose, one of a string of dowdy suburbs that follow the Derwent towards its source in Lake St Clair north-west of the capital. The family shuffled between rented accommodation, first as a family unit and then in a home they shared with Nan and Pop Hutton, who had followed the family to southern Tasmania.

The suburb is dominated by St Paul's, the Anglican church on the high side of Main Road, which, as the name suggests, was the road which connected the city's north road through suburbs such as Moonah, Glenorchy, Goodwood, Chigwell, Elwick, Berriedale, Claremont and Austins Ferry until the Brooker Highway was built. It takes a few moments to drink in the view across the Derwent from the front steps of the sandstone structure, which has survived time far better than the decrepit graveyard behind. There, the few surviving headstones stretch back deep into the city's colonial past while the expansive panorama in front encouraged parishioners to return each week to give thanks for the natural beauty of their lot in life.

The church would leave a significant mark on Carleen, looming large from the family house across the road, slotted between two shops – Peacock's shop on the left and Lowe's on the right.

The position, next door to a grocery store, was a bonus for a family with no car. Seven-year-old Carleen often shopped for her mother, using food ration cards for tea, butter and sugar. There was little money in the early years after World War II, not enough for Christmas presents one year. Instead, a neighbour chipped in to help Freda put new bodies on the girls' old dolls. Clothes, too, were often hand-me-downs from friends, the family poor but often just managing.

There were happy memories too; friends, such as Cynthia next door with whom she remains close. They went to Glenorchy Primary and had the freedom of a 1940s childhood, playing in the bush and riding bikes without fear, or brakes. There was also death, such as the day she and a group of friends, including the son of the local minister, were walking home from school. When they were opposite St Paul's where the boy lived, he ran across the street and was hit by a truck. The tragedy remains a vivid, traumatic memory.

Life changed again when Carleen was nine. The family moved further into the Tasmanian hinterland to Westerway in the Derwent Valley, 50 kilometres from Hobart, where they lived in a cottage on half an acre of land.

She remembers the masses of lupins of every shade, the lush hop fields and the tourists who would stop to admire them on their way to and from the nearby Mount Field National Park where the last wild thylacine was captured in 1933. It was beautiful but an existence of self-sufficiency. Her mother grew vegetables and kept a cow, and water had to be pumped to the house from the Tyenna River.

By the age of 12, the family had moved again, to Bridgewater on the northern outskirts of Hobart. Her father's drinking had now descended to such a level that he often sat in a room by himself drinking from flagons. He slept when he wasn't drinking, leaving Freda to raise the family alone and pay the mortgage.

She worked at the hotel opposite the house, tucked beside the causeway that connected the village to the main road into the city. Freda cooked at the pub during the day before rushing home in the evening to feed her own children. Carleen's reminiscence of the family's proximity to the pub swings between "convenience" for her mother to "amazement" that she was able to manage despite a husband who was now out of control. Often it was left to the children to turn on the oven to cook a prepared meal.

The memories are sparse but telling for a child, particularly for one who lacked any confidence and would spend her life fighting chronic shyness:

> *We would ask Dad for money to buy toothpaste, but he would simply tell us to use salt. When he was away we would go into his room for any coins but there were very few there. One year my father gave me a new bike for my birthday. I still remember the brand name, it was an Atlantic, and none of the neighbour's children had one. I was so proud of that bike. But not long after, Dad decided to sell it. The reason he gave was that too many were riding it and it was too dangerous on the road, but it was safe on a small side street near the Bridgewater Bridge. I assumed he wanted the money to buy more wine. Taking that bike away from me broke my heart.*

Arthur Cordwell was now in the grip of an alcoholic psychosis, imagining spiders crawling up and down the walls of his room. Freda had had enough and wanted him out but he refused until she agreed to pay him out – a financial settlement that forced her to go back to the bank to extend the mortgage. Then, at last, he was gone.

Some years later, he reappeared fleetingly, at least in official records. In August 1956, during a moment of painful regret, Cordwell wrote to the army.

The brief letter, in neat hand, remains on record, the blue ink faded slightly:

> Dear Sir,
> Sorry that I am so late asking you for some medals. Please asking if you would be good enough to forward same to me.
>
> Yours faithfully,
> AA Cordwell

He got a reply a fortnight later. Typed and blunt. Yes, records showed he had been awarded the British War Medal and the Victory Medal. There was a receipt for both, signed by him at a ceremony in 1922. If he wanted copies, it would cost him £1-2/2.

There is no indication that Cordwell, who was now 72, alone, tortured and living in Bellerive on the eastern bank of the Derwent facing the city, followed up the offer and received his medals.

Certainly, he got no satisfaction and when he died a decade later, on March 19, 1966, aged 82. It seems that in death Freda forgave her husband, at least publically, describing him as "dearly beloved" in the funeral notice. But they would be buried apart, he in the Catholic section of the Hobart cemetery – a family outcast as his grandson would become, although for very different reasons.

························

Carleen did not like school. She fled Brighton High School as soon as she turned 16, unlike one of her sisters who would later be head girl. Although her memoir names a few neighbourhood friends, there was no mention of school life – no friends, no sports, no teachers, no recollections beyond the image of the priest's son killed on the way home. It seems there was nothing in school for a young woman who, by her own admission and stilted writings, struggled academically and even more with self-confidence.

The outside adult world beckoned as a different proposition, particularly in the 1950s when employment was plentiful. Everyone seemed to have a job. It seemed so easy to become an independent adult, earning a wage, a future and respect. There was always a second job if the waitress's wage was not enough.

Carleen followed her mother and grandmother into a career of service, working alongside Freda in the local pub where she made friends with the owner's daughter. She had found a place in life – and her first relationship.

Through friends she met a man named Arthur Gangell, 10 years her senior, who had spent 12 years in the armed forces and had just returned from the Korean War. The couple fell in love, or so the teenager believed. It would not have occurred to her that she was again following in her mother's footsteps into a relationship with a man much older, a father figure also shaped by war who too would prove incapable of offering the love she craved. No, Carleen was impressed by his manners and gentlemanly demeanour – never swearing around ladies – and his job as a supervisor at the Electrolytic Zinc Company where her grandfather worked. Arthur appeared to be a man with a financial future, not only a man with a steady, well-paying job but a budding entrepreneur who bred and raced greyhounds. His pride and joy was a dog named Joker's Call, which would win a significant race in Tasmania, although Carleen took little interest and could not recall the event other than it was a championship.

It would, ultimately, be a shattering experience for a young woman who was, on her own reflection, very naive. She tells the story of the day she ran into the hotel calling for her mother to separate two greyhounds Arthur had locked in a shed to mate. The howling from within convinced her that the dogs were tearing each other apart. Freda sent her home, her daughter's innocence perceived as an embarrassment.

In 1960, the couple announced their engagement but it would go no further after Arthur was sprung shortly after at the local drive-in having a dalliance with a student teacher. He tried to dismiss the incident as innocent – "helping her with her maths" – but the romance was over.

Carleen tried to forget the affair by working harder. She was well established in a new job at a print and textiles factory, testing samples in the laboratory, and worked at a hotel in Swansea during her holidays to pay off her first car, a Morris Minor. At other times, she earned extra money by taking work waitressing in a local cafe.

It gave Carleen her first taste of independence and the ability to occasionally escape the boredom of small town life where the only entertainment was a weekly film night in the old, cold hall. She and a friend named Joan would "save" their weekends and, once a month, drive to Hobart for the week where Freda Hutton had returned to live. The only stipulation was that they had to be back in time for the Saturday night arrival of tourist buses. One night, in their rush to get back in time, Carleen rolled her car on the narrow gravel road into Buckland, and Joan was badly injured. It would be the first of a number of car accidents.

On another occasion in a new car – an FJ Holden – she almost ran off the causeway at Bridgewater driving home late one night after delivering textile samples to the factory owner, Claudio Alcorso, an Italian immigrant whose love of the arts would, years later, lead him to establish the Australian Opera Company.

Arthur Gangell re-entered her life in 1962, briefly and tragically. He had married the teacher from the drive-in, and the couple now had a baby son, but Arthur was still unhappy. In early September, Carleen agreed to meet him at a Hobart hotel to hear his tale of woe. It was a strange conversation, she would recall. He regretted the dalliance and losing Carleen but there was no attempt to rekindle the relationship.

It was more an ending and an explanation to clear the air. Then a strange remark, one that Carleen would later wish she had taken more notice. Arthur told her that if anything happened to him, he had left something for her in his office. After that they parted company.

On September 22, a fortnight or so after their conversation at the Talbot Hotel in New Town, Arthur Gangell gassed himself sitting in his car at home. He was driven by something far deeper than personal unhappiness or a failed relationship with Carleen Cordwell but the horror was nonetheless real, and she could not help but wonder what part she had played. Like the mystery item left in his office, Carleen never found out, or even suspected, what his reasons might have been.

The Talbot Hotel would figure again in her life more than three decades later, just as fleetingly and with far more dire consequences. This time it would involve a son she was yet to bear.

CHAPTER 4
Aftermath

Sergeant Michael Dyson bangs on the front door of the modest flat-topped bungalow at No.7 Maritana Place, Berriedale, a northern suburb of Hobart. Seconded from protective security to the major incident room as an intelligence liaison officer, he bangs again, louder; there was no time for niceties.

It is after 10pm on April 28, 1996, but those inside are still awake, the lights ablaze. Two colleagues – constables Clayton and Russell – stand beside him. It is the most serious assignment in their short careers. A tall woman with tight, ash-blonde curls answers the door. She is, clearly, his mother.

"Do you have a son named Martin Bryant?" he barks, the urgency clear in his voice. The woman peers into the blackness, shivering against raw nerves and the autumn chill that comes after dark.

"Yes," Carleen Bryant replies hesitantly. "Why?"

Sergeant Dyson answers the question with his own: "Does he own and drive a yellow Volvo with a surfboard strapped to the roof?"

"Yes."

Carleen is outside now, unsure what to do. She can barely make out the features of her interrogator, which only adds to her fear. What is this all about and where is Martin?

In truth, the appearance of Sergeant Dyson comes as no surprise to

Carleen, rather a confirmation of the anxiety pricked a few hours earlier as she watched the evening television news reports of the massacre at Port Arthur.

Among the pictures is Martin's car, or what looks like it, apparently abandoned by the side of the road near Port Arthur. The reporter is describing it as belonging to the gunman. She can't see the number plate but the familiar surfboard is perched on the roof-rack, as it always was. He never took it off to surf, as far as she knew.

After the news, Carleen rings Martin's girlfriend, Petra Wilmott. The three had had dinner the night before at Carleen's house, before the young couple headed out to a couple of nightclubs. Petra had stayed with Martin overnight, as she frequently did since they met two months earlier, but left in the morning to head back to her parents' home at Nicholls Rivulet, 30 minutes south-west of Hobart.

"I'm worried. I can't reach Martin," Carleen tells the young woman when she comes to the phone. "He's not answering at home. It looks like his car at Port Arthur, and they say it was the gunman's car."

Petra has seen the news as well. She is scared too, and agrees to come back to Hobart and stay the night with Carleen for company, in the hope that Martin will show up at some stage. Her dad will give the young TAFE student a lift.

Carleen seems to have calmed down by the time Petra arrives. It is now after 8pm. There is no need to worry, Carleen assures her. Martin has probably gone to Melbourne. He's taken off before without saying anything. He loves going to the zoo. He'll probably ring in the morning to say things are OK. Either that or turn up in a day or so and wonder what all the fuss is about.

Petra hopes Carleen is right.

"Should we go over to the house and check? He might be there," Petra suggests. Maybe the phone isn't working or he's fallen and hurt himself.

Carleen dismisses the idea: "No, we'll just wait here. Martin doesn't like people snooping through his things."

So they sit there waiting for something to happen, neither woman brave enough to voice their worries aloud: is Martin a victim or could he be … no, the thought doesn't bear repeating aloud.

The police themselves are still uncertain. There have been numerous telephone calls during the afternoon, raising the name as a possible suspect,

Martin Bryant, the strange young man who has voiced hatred of David and Sally Martin. But it isn't enough to be certain. They need something more concrete. Even the discovery of Martin's passport in the glove box of the yellow Volvo isn't enough. It isn't until 8.30pm, when the car's registration is confirmed – Bryant does not have a driver's licence – that police act.

Now, Sergeant Dyson stands on Carleen Bryant's doorstep voicing a horror beyond words, a notion seemingly impossible but one that she knows, if she reaches down far enough inside, she knows could be true.

Her son, her blond boy, is accused of murder, no, murders. Multiple killings. In cold blood.

She would later write of the moment:

> *My world was being attacked by information that made no sense. Numbness and disbelief gripped me and I was in such a distraught state I had no idea how long my questioning continued.*

The interrogation would last hours. First, the three officers take the women to Bryant's house in Clare Street in New Town, on the western fringe of the city centre. They drive in silence, lost in their own thoughts about what lies ahead. The street is quiet as they pull in front of the big, square white house. Television screens flicker in a few windows but most houses are darkened, their occupants asleep early on a Sunday. Within days this neighbourhood will become a gruesome magnet for those wanting to look and peer, gawk at where the seemingly inhuman has come from the staid and suburban. Steady lines of traffic will build and snake, slowing past No.30 before accelerating away in disbelief.

Mainland and international media teams will be far less subtle, parking their vans outside as reporters and cameramen venture into the property to look through windows and question neighbours about the young man who has amused and endeared a few and scared many more. One crew will even be accused of breaking into the house to be the first to publish photos of Martin Bryant, the whites of his eyes digitally enhanced to turn his naturally vacant gaze into a demonic stare. Despite condemnation and an apology, the doctored photograph is still being published a decade later.

Tonight though, it is dark and profoundly lonely as Carleen reluctantly unlocks the back door and sets off the alarm, the piercing siren shattering the quiet. The group steps into the kitchen. It is a clutter, the remains of breakfast still on the sink. A pile of photographs lies scattered on the table, most snapped in recent months with Petra as they glowed in the first flush of their 10-week relationship. There are photographs of them in the town of Richmond where they'd been on an outing just three days earlier. They show happiness, or so it seems at least. Above all, they show what the man who left them there craved most: normality.

Martin Bryant had placed the pictures there deliberately. He wanted people to know not only what he had done but, in his simplistic way, wanted to influence how the world would see and interpret him. His actions make clear that he has contemplated the possibility of being killed.

Sergeant Dyson phones the incident room. This has to be handled carefully, with proper procedure. Find out who owns the photographs and ask their permission first before selecting the best in terms of identification, he is told. Then get one of the constables to bring the photo and the women, if they agree, back to headquarters for formal interviews. A warrant to search the house, particularly for weapons, will be arranged after they'd gone.

"Do you know who owns the photos?" he asks the two women after ending the telephone conversation, the still blackness outside accentuating their surreal surroundings.

"Me and Martin," Petra replies.

"Can we borrow one? You'll get it back. We need it for ID."

The young woman nods blankly. Carleen's silence is read as consent.

The two constables lead them back to the car while Sergeant Dyson waits alone for the warrant. It arrives at 12.30am, and the methodical search begins. In the kitchen pantry, on the top shelf, he finds two empty handcuff packets alongside wrapping for a Smith and Wesson revolver and spent cases for .308 and .223 calibre bullets. There are more in a locked cupboard under the stairs on the ground floor. Inside he finds a plastic grocery bag containing several hundred rounds of .308 rifle ammunition and two rifle cases.

The search stops while a locksmith is called to open a safe in an upstairs bedroom. Inside is more ammunition and personal papers including what amounts to the last will and testament of Martin Bryant. Sergeant Dyson leaves everything where he has found it. He has enough to call in the CIB. The detectives will handle it from here.

The initial search yields only a small part of what is scattered through the house. Three searches over the ensuing week will uncover an arsenal of weapons, ammunition and paraphernalia, showing not only the extent of Bryant's firepower and his intent but his inability to organise his plans. It shows too, perhaps, a desire to be caught.

Firearms and ammunition are found in hidey holes throughout the house – inside the pantry or plastic bags in the cupboard, above the stove, and even inside two pianos, one in an upstairs bedroom and the other in a front room. One rifle has even been left in the hallway, but only because he knew he wasn't coming back – dead or alive. Police also wonder if the house and its scattered contents indicate anything about the gunman still holding them at bay inside the Seascape guest house. Some rooms in the house have only a few pieces of furniture; others are so cramped and piled high with rubbish they can hardly move as they hunt for clues.

The list prepared by Sergeant Gerard Dutton of the ballistics department says it all:

- A box containing 649 .308 calibre cartridges.
- A box containing 658 .308 calibre cartridges, a Daewoo shotgun booklet, one box of 12-gauge cartridges.
- An ammunition box containing 16 .223 calibre cartridges.
- An ammunition box containing 20 .308 calibre cartridges.
- Australian Automatic Arms self-loading rifle, serial number SAR020236, minus the magazine. Found in the hallway.
- A .308-calibre cartridge case. Found in a container on a shelf above the stove in the kitchen.
- An ammunition box containing 20 .308 calibre cartridges. Found in a paper bag inside a piano in an upstairs bedroom.
- A telescopic sight mount in box marked Suitable for AR-15/M16. Found in a paper bag inside a piano in an upstairs bedroom.
- A leather ammunition belt containing 30 .223 calibre cartridges. Found in a paper bag hidden in an upstairs bedroom.
- Forty-four .223 and 11 .308 calibre cartridges. Found in a paper bag inside a piano in the lower right front room.
- An empty detachable box magazine. Found in a paper bag inside a piano in the lower front right-hand room.

- An ammunition box containing nine .223 calibre cartridges and empty ammunition boxes. Found in a paper bag hidden in the lower front right room.
- A wooden tea box containing 48 .308 calibre cartridges. Found in a paper bag inside a piano in the lower right-hand front room.
- A plastic bag containing 41 .223 calibre cartridges. Found in a paper bag inside a piano in an upstairs bedroom.
- Three .223 and one .308 calibre cartridges. Found in a paper bag inside a piano in the lower right-hand front room.
- Three ammunition boxes containing 55 .223 calibre cartridges. Found in a paper bag inside a piano in an upstairs bedroom.
- An ammunition box containing 20 .308 calibre cartridges. Found in a paper bag inside a piano in an upstairs bedroom.
- An ammunition belt and 22 .308 calibre cartridges. Found in a paper bag inside the piano in an upstairs bedroom.
- Three ammunition boxes containing 48 .223 calibre cartridges; and three ammunition boxes containing 44 .308 calibre cartridges. Found in paper bags hidden in the lower right-hand front room.

They have their man. Now it is a matter of ending the siege at Seascape.

••••••••••••••••••••••••••

Between 4am and 6am at Seascape, there is a lull in the shooting. Freezing SWAT teams crouched behind trees and in wet ditches around the property can't tell if the man inside is sleeping or just watching and waiting for a false move. Like everything else in this bizarre and terrifying day, nothing makes sense.

During the night the bloke has been moving from room to room as if trying to create the impression of being many rather than one. He has obviously found weapons and ammunition inside the house because he is shooting a number of different guns – more than 150 shots, they count – moving all the time, sometimes crawling from one room and position to another, turning lights on and off to confuse his whereabouts. He was even outside at one point, and always stood back slightly from the windows so as not to present an easy target. It is textbook stuff, as if out of a magazine or manual, but clumsy, too. Still, a man like this is dangerous not only because of the array of weapons but his obvious intent to kill.

Not that they are returning fire. It is too risky, either being shot at themselves or being the cause of the hostages being killed. And that presents another problem: are any of the hostages alive? There is no way of knowing for certain but most guess they are already dead. There have been no noises in the background during the telephone conversations between the gunman and Terry McCarthy during the night, no hint of human activity, and he has been reluctant to let the negotiator talk to any of the three.

Still, there is no sense taking chances, and even Ian Sale, the Hobart psychiatrist working with them, can't rule out at least one hostage still being alive. Command has contemplated storming the house on several occasions but decided against it. It would unnecessarily endanger the police officers, and something would happen soon enough. This guy is so unpredictable. He has asked for nothing but a helicopter ride and even identified himself by his passport. Why he did what he did and what he wants are a mystery.

Things change quickly after first light. Just after 7.30am there is a series of shots followed 10 minutes later by the sight of smoke curling from an upstairs window facing the bay. Within minutes the flames are visible, licking at the window frames. Ammunition can be heard exploding through the house as the fire spreads. Someone inside, presumably the gunman, is hurling furniture against the windows. An assault on the house is again ruled out.

Within 10 minutes, the fire has taken hold on the ground floor. The whole building is alight, and ammunition can be heard exploding as the heat and flames spread. Whoever has been moving around is now downstairs. More shots ring out; no one quite sure if they are aimed outside or inside. By 8.15am, most of the house is ablaze. The gunman has to come out, perhaps with hostages. The teams prepare.

At 8.25am, the gunman appears. Or is it one of the hostages? The police can't be sure through the smoke. The man staggers from the building, dressed in black with his shirt on fire. He disappears in the whirl of smoke. They wait. A minute later he reappears, naked now, the burning clothes torn from his body. He falls to his knees and writhes on the ground in agony. They swoop, binding his legs and arms.

It is 8.37am. The siege is over but the horror has just begun.

CHAPTER 5
Maurice

Carleen Cordwell met her future husband in April 1965. She had accompanied a friend and her husband who were inspecting a farming property for sale at Sandy Bay just south of Hobart. It was, coincidentally, the same neighbourhood her father had left to go to war half a century before – although then with a different wife and family.

Maurice Bryant was a 36-year-old English immigrant from the town of Dunston near the industrial city of Newcastle-upon-Tyne, not far from the Scottish border. Carleen's recollection is slightly confusing, suggesting Maurice was selling a property he owned although there are no records to back this up. Neither does his early life in the bleak industrial landscapes of northern England suggest that farming was in his blood.

It was more likely that he was employed as an agent to sell the property. Maurice spent an hour or more showing off the place to the prospective buyers, chatting about its features and history to the interested couple, but all the while he was struck by their companion, a tall, shy woman with pale blue eyes and tight blond curls. As they were leaving, his conversation changed tack: there was a dance that night at the nearby Rapid Club. Would Carleen like to accompany him?

Although taken aback – not at his tone but the unexpected interest – she accepted. If the invitation was a surprise then his proposal of marriage the next day must have floored her. Perhaps swayed by his dancing abilities – she recalled it primly as a very enjoyable evening with a good continental band – she accepted. The speed of their union seemed at odds with her earlier and limited experience of men but, as with her mother, there seems to have been a sense that opportunity was at play. How many chances of marriage does a girl get, particularly when she is in her late 20s and still living with her mother?

Five months later, on September 4, they were married at St Paul's in Montrose, the church high on a hillside overlooking the Derwent where she had been baptised and, as a young child, watched the minister's young son die beneath the wheels of a truck. It was a small affair as Maurice's family were all back in Britain.

His was not a happy tale either, a childhood – like his new wife's – imbued with loss, unhappiness and trauma. In 1936, when he was seven years old, Maurice had found his mother lying on the pantry floor of their terrace home. Thinking she was playing with him, the young boy leaped on her back for a horse ride. But this was no game. Ellen "Nellie" Bryant was dead, a victim of tuberculosis, they told the distraught boy.

His mother's death – and the terrible way he discovered her – was a cataclysmic event for a little boy and, as science now tells us, left an indelible imprint on his brain that would shape his moods and personality for the rest of his life. His father, Thomas, bereaved and left to raise Maurice and his three sisters – Ellen, Elizabeth and Jane – alone, would struggle with his own demons: life in Newcastle-upon-Tyne was tough, money was short and the world was again careering towards another war.

Maurice, like so many English children living in the big cities and towns, ended up being evacuated as a young teenager to the relative safety of rural England. Alone, separated from his siblings and his dad, he was sent to stay with a farming family from a village outside the market town of Bishop Auckland. A child who had already lost his mother in terrible circumstances was again coping with loneliness, among kind strangers, but strangers nevertheless.

The struggles continued into manhood. With no money or opportunity to continue an education in postwar Britain, the young Maurice joined the army, where he spent a year mostly stationed in Germany, finally returning to the streets of Dunston to take up a job as a wood machinist in the same sawmill as his father. There seemed little prospect of escaping the red-brick confines of Collingwood Terrace, where his parents bought a house shortly after they married. It was a classic two-up, two-down with a toilet and coalhouse at the bottom of the small concrete yard; tiny for a family of four children. It was in a busy part of town, virtually alongside the community centre and across the road from a pub, the Tudor Rose. The Imperial Cinema was around the corner in the main shopping precinct.

It was also a short walk to the banks of the brown Tyne, a river once so valuable as a source of fresh salmon that its access had to be controlled by government to lessen disputes among fishermen. But industrialisation and the rich veins of coal converted it to a serpentine ribbon of muck coiling beneath the shadows of the old colliery and dwarfed by the enormous straiths, or steel-piped docks, for the coal ships.

Across the river lay the city of Newcastle-on-Tyne with its old Roman forts and evocative remnants of Hadrian's Wall. But it was little compensation for a young man who had now seen a glimpse of the world beyond his small-town origins and liked what he saw.

In the end though, it was a family dispute that helped push him out of the family home.

Maurice would later describe his credentials as being a trained cabinet-maker, and when, on April 5, 1951, he chose to roll the dice and buck against more disappointment and bad memories, he left his father and sisters to join the thousands of postwar migrants who paid £10 to sail to Australia. One million would arrive over three decades, lured by promises of jobs, houses and optimism. Very few "£10 Poms" would taste the sunshine and then choose to go back.

Mr M. Bryant of 9 Collingwood Terrace, Dunston-on-Tyne, Nr Newcastle, as it appeared on the neatly typed ship register, was passenger No.11821 aboard the Orcades, the pride of the Orient Line. The first purpose-built passenger vessel to enter the Australian migrant trade after World War II, she was different from the others, which were simply converted troop carriers from the war, sparse, with few facilities and packed to the gunwales with men, women and children looking for a new life.

The Orcades set a new standard in style and accommodation, more a cruise ship than a carrier, boasting bars, hair salons, a swimming pool and even little souvenir shops selling ash trays, spoons and postcards embossed with the ship's emblem, or brightly-coloured tea towels of exotic Middle Eastern scenes, sandy beaches or their ultimate destination, the Sydney Harbour Bridge. There were daily newsletters, port-of-call booklets and decorative menus. Balls, parties, even plays and sports events were organised. Free language classes were available for non-English-speaking migrants picked up in ports such a Naples where they stopped en route. It all smacked of an exciting new future, lives far away from the sadness of war and the struggle of poverty.

Maurice sailed B class, sharing a twin-bunk room with a drawstring wardrobe and a chest of drawers. The ticket would take him as far as Sydney but many got off well before, some as soon as they sighted land at Fremantle in Western Australia. Others disembarked as the boat made its way across the Great Australian Bight, perhaps in Adelaide or, as Maurice chose, the city of Melbourne, lured by news of bountiful job prospects in the southern states.

Like so many of his compatriots, Maurice had not returned to England. The financial rewards did not really match the struggle it took to establish the new life, and his plan was to use the profit from sale of the Sandy Bay farm to fund a trip back home. Instead, he met Carleen Cordwell and the money, what little there was, would be used to set up a new home with his new wife.

"Maurice was just a nice, ordinary man," his cousin Mavis Pyle, told the media after Port Arthur. "The family was very close. Maurice wrote often. He just decided to leave England to seek a better life, to start afresh."

Carleen, however, did not see Maurice as ordinary. Far from it. She doted on her new husband, seeing him as a victim of circumstance and opportunity, and always sure that he would make good. Conscious of her own academic difficulties, she interpreted her husband's interest and books on war and conflict as symbols of unfulfilled academic potential. This constant belief that Maurice was a stymied intellect, a thinker held down by fate, would be a hallmark of their relationship:

> *He was a real intellectual and could have gone on to achieve anything had he been given the opportunity. He really was a true academic, an avid reader, and was especially interested in history of the world, and the conflicts and development of nations. I'm sure he would have read every book published about wars.*

While Maurice's interest in armed conflict could have raised questions in light of what his only son would do later, the truth is that this was just one of his many interests. He had many over the years; they came and went in the same way his many jobs did, too.

Early on, Maurice and a mate, who had either travelled with him from Britain or whom he had met on board the boat, had taken jobs on the Melbourne docks while managing the boarding house where they ended up living. The partnership lasted a few years, good for both of them, but dissolved when his friend found a girl and decided it was time to settle down.

That spurred Maurice to move on; perhaps to explore more of Australia and her opportunities – perhaps even to find a wife of his own.

He was offered a transfer to Hobart, where he repeated the Victorian experiment and managed a nearby boarding house on the side, presumably in exchange for lodgings. The venture into the Sandy Bay farm seems to have been a short-lived attempt to expand his financial horizons. Then he met Carleen Cordwell, and his life changed.

The newlyweds did not look for their own home immediately but moved in with Carleen's mother, Freda, who was now living in the suburb of Claremont. There was very little consistent work on the wharf for Maurice other than during the apple-picking season in the autumn when the workforce often tripled in size for a few months when they spent days at a time stuffing crates into the bellies of refrigerated boats for 30 quid a week. For the rest of the year, wharf workers could only rely on what they called appearance money – turning up at the bottom of Argyle Street each morning to see if they might be needed for a shift – but eight bob or so a day was not enough to live on.

The mainland beckoned once more, and the new Mrs Carleen Bryant, nee Cordwell, was about to leave the shores of Tasmania for the first time in her life. It would be a short-lived adventure. Carleen was immediately homesick for her mother. Living in a rented flat in the inner-city Melbourne suburb of Prahran, she had no friends, and struggled to hold down a job, losing three in as many months, including a laboratory job at the Alfred Hospital. There, she recalled being sacked after telling a colleague that she had struggled with infected fingernails since she was 16, a condition she had been told was incurable. The hospital laboratory's response was swift although Carleen would dismiss it as concern for her own wellbeing rather than the hygiene problems her condition potentially created. The Melbourne experience was demoralising and made worse when, on his way to work one morning, Maurice was mistaken for an escaped prisoner from a detention centre, questioned and released.

The couple wanted to settle down and buy a house but prices on the mainland were far beyond their means. Within a few months Carleen and Maurice realised their mistake, packed up their belongings and headed back to Hobart where, even if financially difficult, life was more settled.

Work was picking up on the docks and life seemed to offer some opportunities. The couple moved back in with Carleen's mother in Claremont temporarily until they could find their own home.

Eventually, they bought in the same street – a Cape Cod-style house, as she would describe it, for which land titles records show they paid $7500, including a $3100 mortgage they took out with the Commonwealth Bank. If life was a financial struggle, Carleen and Maurice showed they could find the means to not only survive but to save and thrive.

Maurice's wharfie mates would recall in later years how "Morrie" was always looking for projects, whether it be buying and selling antiques or landscape gardening.

"He was like the rest of us," recalls Ron Harmon, a Waterside Workers Federation executive who worked beside Maurice for three decades, heaving bags of sugar and wheat and loading bales of wool and skins around the Princess Wharf and the Elizabeth Street Pier.

"He always seemed to be doing something. He was a generous bloke, too. If my wife and I went out to dinner with him and Carleen, which we did on several occasions, Morrie would always want to pay. He seemed to have money although he was very careful. I don't know where it came from but I assume it's from what he did on the side. He was always accumulating, cutting lawns, doing whatever."

Maurice and Carleen would also be lucky in the real estate market, at least for a time. Instead of moving into the Claremont house, they rented it to an English couple and continued to live with Freda. Again, it was typical of Maurice Bryant's careful management of money, and it would pay dividends. As well as helping to pay the mortgage, they were sitting on a tidy nest egg which would become the springboard to a frugal but comfortable existence.

Years later, they would make a critical error of judgment – one that would have tragic consequences. But for now, Carleen had also found work at the nearby Cadbury chocolate factory and life was looking up. She was back home in Hobart with her mother, she had found a good and seemingly reliable man – and she was pregnant with their first child.

CHAPTER 6
A Bouncing Boy

His entry into the world was as easy and manageable as his life would be fraught and uncontrollable. Martin John Bryant – weight six pounds even – was born on May 7, 1967, at the Queen Alexandra Hospital in Hobart after a labour lasting barely two hours. His father did not pace nervously outside the ward or wait down at the pub, as so many fathers of his era would have done, but was by his wife's side in the delivery room. Such was the ease not only of the birth but the entire pregnancy that Carleen, free of morning sickness and bloating – all baby and no fluid – had worked at the chocolate factory until she was within a few weeks of delivery. No one at work on the production line even seemed to notice her condition much less be concerned on her behalf that she hadn't abandoned work at an earlier stage. Not only would Maurice have been happy she was still earning but the apparent ease of motherhood was a fillip for a woman who questioned herself and suffered from poor self-esteem. Characteristically, Carleen would downplay the experience:

> It was all over so quickly. There were no marked signs leading up to the birth, so I was not that sure if he was going to arrive on time.

The birth notice in *The Mercury* was equally unadorned: *To Carleen and Maurice. A bouncing boy. Thanks to doctor and staff.*

In the hours after his arrival, the little boy was checked for signs of the congenital heart condition which had affected his mother throughout her life. All was well, there were no signs of abnormality, and while he was on the small side, he was perfectly healthy, at least physically. It would be some years before the family – and society – discovered that this little, blond boy with angelic blue eyes was born with the mysterious genetic map that, combined with experience, with events, with layers of childhood experience, adolescent disappointment and trauma – would lead him to action so brutal it would never be forgotten. A hole in the heart, like his mother's, would have been easily diagnosed, treatable, managed – the vacuum of compassion and empathy for the suffering of others that grows in the heart of alienated, furious young men is an entirely different condition, one which can be even more dangerous, both for them and wider society.

Indeed, little would be normal again for this kind, ordinary – and most deserving – of families. Their little boy was born, quietly and without fuss, and while the world would one day not only know, but fear, his name, baby Martin, at least for now, was Carleen's pride and joy, her greatest achievement so far in a life that had delivered much disappointment. A grainy black-and-white photograph taken shortly after mother and son's arrival home from hospital is a palpably happy snap, mother and son both looking straight into the camera, the baby alert and wide-eyed, his mum perfectly coiffed, their striking physical similarity visible even in the newborn.

A photo taken hastily 29 years later, just a few kilometres away across the Derwent – and three days before this very same child embarked on his killing spree – highlights the resemblances even more: mother and son were roughly the same age when each photo was taken, both with the same square jaws, clearly hewn cheekbones and lean faces framed by pale blond hair. The 1967 picture, presumably taken by Maurice, is a moment of joy, Carleen's hair smoothed into the fashionable beehive hairdo of the day, revealing a woman proud of her achievement.

Who could have known that she had just given life to one who would later take so many.

....

Maurice and Carleen finally moved into their first home at the beginning of the year, spared the ravages of the Black Tuesday fires that destroyed other houses in the heatwaves of February 1967. The deadly blazes had raced across the top of Mount Wellington, the dark hill that looms over the city, and back down through the suburbs, killing 52 people and razing 1300 homes. Ten more people died and hundreds more homes were destroyed as thousands of hectares of bush succumbed to the flames. The combination of dry summer heat, brisk winds and the hand of an arsonist had combined to produce a natural disaster of a magnitude rarely seen. It was an event that ended up shaping the community, galvanising the city and the entire island to rebuild together and overcome, as is hoped from the Victorian fires of 2009.

Maurice Bryant was among the thousands who gave their all in the united effort to beat back the monster. The family home, next door to a wood merchant's yard was particularly terrifying. Carleen, heavily pregnant, and her mother, Freda, chose to shelter indoors, with the river their refuge should the flames come too close.

The Bryants avoided the inferno. Now, three months later, Carleen was home with the baby. Life had changed inexorably but Maurice had not. While other men might have revelled in an opportunity to stay home and get to know the firstborn, Maurice was driven by the desire to explore new ways to earn a few extra dollars and make ends meet. There was no greed in his quest, more an entrepreneurial spirit keen to harness new opportunities. He began renovating the house, and even turned the attic into a flat which was then sublet. A local teacher and her jeweller boyfriend were tenants Carleen never forgot as they kept the Bryant family awake at night – not through noisy lovemaking but the dings and taps of a metal hammer as the young man created jewellery well into the early hours.

Down at the docks, work was still sporadic and, with a young family to feed, sacrifices had to be made. As the charred town mended itself, Maurice responded with characteristic resourcefulness, starting a business using a rotary hoe to re-lay scorched lawns around the neighbourhood. He also gradually turned the empty block next door into a farmyard. First it was a cow and calf then goats, which he also bred. By the time Martin was two years old, there was a greenhouse and chook yard next door, and Maurice had carved out a neat business supplying eggs and tomatoes to the local grocery store, which conveniently was also in the same street.

For Carleen, the first year or so as a mother passed relatively peacefully. She remembers her little boy as happy and contented and she appeared unfazed, even in hindsight, by a baby who rejected cuddles and any sign of physical affection. It says much about Carleen's own stoic nature that she also took his rejection of breastfeeding in her stride, explaining it away to his seemingly unquenchable appetite. By the time Martin was 16 months old, however, he was not only walking but running, climbing – and escaping – and his mother was starting to find it difficult to cope. If Carleen and Martin had difficulties bonding – and her recollections would clearly suggest this – she began to really struggle when he grew to a toddler. He would disappear regularly, his parents finding him in the strangest places, once on top of the chook pen next door or even further afield, playing quietly on a swing way across the other side of the railway line which ran along the foreshore and linked Hobart with the suburbs on its western shore.

Martin Bryant was not the first toddler to love wandering, to show a spirit for adventure or levels of energy that could try a saint and he too needed to be curbed for his own safety. But his mum's response was an unusual one:

> *I started to leave him on the house veranda, with a harness and lead to secure him, with plenty of toys all around him.*
>
> *Some person made a complaint about us tying him up like a dog. But of course as his mother, I knew he was happy and safe.*

For Carleen, Martin's energy appeared out of the norm and unmanageable. His father Maurice, however, saw nothing abnormal – a disagreement and pattern of response to their son that began early and was to colour the couple's parenting style throughout his life.

For Carleen, coping with Martin was a day-to-day reality, a problem of strategy, logistics and survival. Her own mother had parented in a similar mode, battling to feed, clothe and educate her children – but in the face of violence and alcoholism. There would be little time for physical affection or for day-to-day nurture in such dire circumstances.

It was perhaps her own childhood experience of mothering that shaped Carleen's response to her boy. She loved him but, like Martin, showing affection did not come naturally.

Maurice's fathering was different; hands-on, intense and as time went on, driven by the desire to normalise the boy. This split in approach and view never changed. In the weeks after his rampage, Melbourne forensic psychiatrist, Professor Paul Mullen, asked Bryant about his mother:

> Mr Bryant was not able to give a description of his mother other than as someone who washed his clothes and cooked him food. Despite this he considered himself to have a good relationship with her.

Bryant had a similar conversation with police as he lay in the prison hospital nursing burns:

"I'm missing my mum. I really miss her actually, what she cooks up for me, her rabbit stews and everything. She's not even allowed to bring a little bit of food in for me, that, that's a bit upsetting."

Decades later, Carleen would recall, without bitterness, her disappointment and frustrations with her son, such as the day he swallowed a nail, the lack of cuddles, his slow speech development. Other problems were appearing, too: while he ran and climbed and wandered the neighbourhood, his fine motor skills were impaired and he did not seem to be maturing. By the time Martin was three years old, it was clear something was seriously amiss.

••••••••••••••••••••••••••••

Three months after Martin's third birthday, in August 1970, Maurice Bryant decided it was time he went home to Britain. Almost two decades after striking out to build a new life on the other side of the world, he made plans to take Carleen back to the north of England to meet his family. Martin however, was to stay home with his grandmother. Finances for the long-awaited trip had received a boost thanks to the fortuitous sale in April of the house in Claremont. The buyer, a developer, had plans to bulldoze the neighbourhood to make way for a shopping centre, and while the timing would create problems of its own later, Maurice decided he wasn't keen on renting or waiting until they returned to find a new home. After scouring areas within comfortable reach of the docks, the couple found a place in the western suburb of New Town and moved in on August 20, just 48 hours before flying out for the six-week trip. Martin had a new backyard to explore.

In Britain, Maurice and Carleen used his family home in Dunston for a base but didn't stay too long. Maurice wanted to see his father again, for what he presumed would be the last time, but he and Carleen were far more comfortable on the road exploring the rest of England and Scotland. Typical of Maurice, rather than hiring a car, he found a good deal on a second-hand Mercedes, which he bought from a local doctor who was selling up hastily to move back to his native Egypt. The idea was to use the car carefully then sell again before flying back to Australia, recouping their costs or even making a small profit.

They drove 10,000 kilometres over the next five weeks, occasionally visiting family but mostly preferring their own company roaming the countryside. London was a fleeting visit; too big and confusing after living in Hobart. They preferred the regional areas, especially the walled city of York where the couple, full of ideas and hopes for the future, paused for a day and even wondered about buying a property; a three-storey house which had been recently used as a hairdressing salon. They imagined a commercial investment perhaps and wistfully even considered it as a place to start a new life in the old country. The idea passed quickly however. Carleen, who had found it difficult enough to relocate to Melbourne, couldn't countenance a move to the other side of the world with a young and difficult child to manage. Tasmania was her home and, besides, they had a new house in which to settle.

Back in No.65 Augusta Road, a few kilometres from Hobart's centre, the rambling red-brick and concrete structure awaited its new owners. Cut off from the road except for a flight of stairs built for pedestrians, the house was nestled out of sight behind the Calvary Hospital complex and on a block well below road level. Cars driving past would not notice or see past the white wooden fence that delineated the front yard.

Instead, access to the house was by a side avenue known as Raluana Lane, which separated the Bryant home from the hospital and which was used by locals, including the milkmen, as a short cut through the maze of large, at times strangely shaped blocks, as they made house deliveries through the area.

The house had been built in the early 1920s, with three bedrooms and two attached flats, positioned tight along the side and rear fence lines to maximise the use of the half-acre block. The garden, carefully planted with fruit trees, was full of mature plants. A huge fig dominated the front of the house, helping to conceal it even further from the road above. A largely disused tennis court owned by the hospital was on one side, and while no one quite knew why a hospital would build a court for sick or injured patients, it was happily adopted by the neighbourhood as a communal area. Local kids had cut their own entrance through the high wire fence to ride their bikes or play ball games and, in a way, it typified the sense of safety and solitude in an area where the gardens were overgrown but full of fun and mystery for children.

The land bought by Maurice and Carleen, in fact, had an interesting and distinguished history; it was once part of the special home and grounds of one of colonial Australia's most influential citizens, John Lee Archer. He was a Dublin-born architect who worked under the famous English civil engineer, John Rennie, and helped design London Bridge over the River Thames. Archer moved to Hobart in 1827 and was responsible for the design of most of Hobart's main public buildings, including Parliament House, the Treasury buildings and several in Salamanca Place. His home, Jutland House, remained but the grounds had long since been carved up and gradually sold off and redeveloped. The Bryant house was one of the last, and probably formed part of the lower garden and perhaps a carriageway – although it is unlikely they knew its pedigree.

Carleen was comfortable there. She had spent most of her life on the outskirts of the city and was now close to its heart. Maurice was nearer to his work at the docks, and he had a new project to work on, renovating the place so he could lease one of the flats to earn a few extra dollars.

But Carleen was also at home with Martin – and he was becoming more and more of a handful. She had quickly found that one way of corralling his frenetic energy was to take him for long walks on foot or in his stroller. There were shops nearby and the pair quickly became a common sight on the quiet streets, a pretty child with blond curls and bright, pale blue eyes like his mum. In the avalanche of press coverage that followed the Port Arthur massacre, one local recalled the duo strolling the streets: the boy was "a little slow, a little different", he said, but more endearing than a threat.

Maurice and Carleen, however, were starting to realise their boy had problems that could no longer be ignored. His energy, feverish and unstoppable, needed a proper outlet but when they enrolled him in a local preschool, it only highlighted his impaired development. Aged four, the staff could barely understand him. Speech therapy was quickly proposed and arranged at the Royal Hobart Hospital. Progress, however, was slow and again, the parents tried – this time at the suggestion of a teacher neighbour, Joan Pease, to enrol him at another nearby school. The Friends' School was the only Quaker school in the southern hemisphere, established in the late 19th century, ironically by Carleen's old employers, the Cadbury family. In reality, there was very little religious teaching, and very few of the staff or students were actually practising Quakers. However, the school had a reputation for academic excellence as well as a philosophical belief in taking in difficult children such as Martin Bryant. One of its least likely – but most famous alumni – was Errol Flynn.

Martin Bryant, however, would last less than a year at the school before its senior teachers wanted him out for causing disruption. It was the only time that Maurice and Carleen Bryant would be forced to respond to a call from a principal. The couple were given no choice: accept the decision and the accompanying advice to take their son to a child guidance service. After a visit to the Ellerslie Clinic, the drugs prescribed would provide brief respite, establishing another pattern, this time of rejection and failed medical intervention, which would be repeated throughout the boy's later life.

Martin's problems, however, were not viewed with the same urgency by everyone. Some, like Bryant's teacher and neighbour, Joan Pease, thought medicalising the young boy's problem was not the answer either: she saw him simply as "not the brightest".

"How could I forget him," she recalled after the murders. "He was a very nice boy, but he wasn't too bright up top … one of those little boys who you didn't know what he was going to do next. He wasn't completely backward; he could do some of the work but couldn't do other. He wasn't the brightest, but he was a nice boy. He behaved himself and was nice to the other children. He used to get excitable sometimes, he'd get fractious. But what boy doesn't?"

Mrs Pease, clearly mindful of Carleen Bryant's shame – and her honest efforts to do her best for the troubled boy through his childhood – may well have deliberately underplayed his problems in public because behind closed doors and in the classroom, his behaviour towards others was starting to cause profound anxieties.

Carleen, in her characteristically understated way, noticed too that her boy seemed to resent the other children:

> *Martin just could not settle to learn anything. This disturbed the class of other students whose parents were paying high fees for their education. After 12 months we were called to the headmistress' office. She suggested we take Martin to a child psychologist. It was also suggested that the New Town Primary School would be more suitable for Martin.*

The local primary school would not turn out to be the right option. If anything, it would highlight his inadequacies to a bigger group of children and spark a cycle of rejection, alienation and solitude that would dog Martin Bryant throughout his life.

CHAPTER 7
Early Signs

The year 1973 would be significant in Martin Bryant's life. Not only was he thrust into the public schoolyard but his life at home also changed dramatically when sister Lindy was born on July 24. If the challenges of being understood and accepted among the throng at New Town Primary weren't enough to cope with, he had now lost the undivided attention of his parents as they doted on the new addition. Rivalry and a craving for attention can be a common and normal response of older siblings but for a boy like Martin Bryant, it would herald the arrival of a comparative measure: his sister would become a beacon of what he could never be.

A simple family snapshot taken in the days following Lindy's arrival at home, similar to the one of Martin's homecoming six years earlier, seems to highlight the young boy's inadequacy. This time it was Carleen who was behind the lens and Maurice, for a rare moment, is in the frame. Six-year-old Martin, in dressing gown and pyjamas ready for bed on a cold Tasmanian winter's night, can be seen grinning ear to ear as if the camera – held by the doting new mother – is focused on him rather than the newborn in his father's careful hands. Maurice, 44 years old with a receding hairline and greying temples, is gazing in wonder at his baby daughter but has a hand wrapped in an iron grip around his son's waist. It is a hold he would not relax for the next two decades until, weary with the never-ending struggle and desperate at his failure to find a solution and peace, he simply gave up on life.

Martin's existence at school was already on a downhill path, his problems almost immediate from his baby-like speech and the sight of him wandering the playground on the fringes of the other kids.

"He used to walk around with his face all squinted up, as if the sun was too bright," one former classmate recalled, the imprint of Bryant's oddness already heavy long before his unfathomable deeds at Port Arthur.

He stood out as a loner at New Town Primary in Forster Street, not by choice but simply because he was so different that it would drive the others away. Efforts to make friends were misinterpreted as aggravating, such as his "silly games" of creeping up and leaping on other kids as they walked home after school. Instead of welcoming friendship, it would be a reason to gang up and chase him away. Not only was he rejected but isolated, the message clear that he did not belong. If he was caught in the chase through the laneways, Martin would cry and squeal as if he was being hurt: "We'd always let him go because we felt sorry for him," one would recall.

Carleen's memories of her son's primary school days – few, short and spare – portray him as a normal child, one admittedly prone to accidents and high-jinks, embarrassing at times but nothing out of the ordinary. Even the more serious childhood incidents are downplayed, concurrent events taking precedence over the primary event at play: on one day, for example, she remembers Martin and an unnamed friend setting fire to a large pile of wooden crates, creating a hazard for the Calvary Hospital next door. Rather than a sign that the boy might need watching, the event was presented more as an embarrassment for the other boy's father who worked at the hospital.

Another is her recollection of the day she went to her half-sister Joyce's house for a perm. While her hair was being done, Martin slipped off a balcony, fell onto concrete and cut open his head, needing stitches in hospital after a traumatic fight against sedation.

Some children need stronger sedatives than others. Martin needed a stronger dose, and it was at least an hour before it took sufficient effect for the medical staff to stitch his wound.

> *For this emergency trip to hospital, a scarf was placed over my half-permed hair, and as the solution in perms is very strong, it felt right to*

> *apologise to the staff for the smell. There were also some moments of concern that my hair would fall out from the chemicals used. It didn't. Later that evening we started work on the hair again and it was a success.*

The problem wasn't glaring, and the complexity of reading Martin Bryant was evident too in his local neighbourhood. There were those such as Andrew Cox, who saw a normal, albeit quiet family whose son was a little different. Cox recalled the Bryants as a private family with a couple of "noisy, yappy" sheltie dogs. The son may have appeared simple-minded but there were no alarm bells. Another, Stella Sampson, recalled how she once caught young Martin smoking behind a fence: "There was a cloud of smoke coming up from behind the fence. I put my head over and the poor kid nearly went to Heaven. He said: 'Don't tell my mum.'"

It would be this way as Martin grew; an obnoxious nuisance or even menace to some, and a smiling, perhaps slow and overly polite young man to others.

School reports tell another story, not only about Martin but the difficulties his family were having reconciling his problems. By 1975, when he had turned eight, Martin's behaviour had returned him to the diagnostic centre where an assessment of his problems concluded that he simply wasn't very smart: "fair low intelligence", as they described it.

But his parents, it was noted under "parental mismanagement", either could not accept or were unable to respond to the problem:

> *Father has high ambitions for him. Mother finds a consistent calm approach very difficult. If his real problems can be uncovered and defined so that we know how to deal with him we are willing that he return to Class 2 in Term 3.*

The bigger warnings came under the heading "Additional information":

> *His aggressive, often physical wounding actions can no longer be tolerated, but we would welcome any assistance which professionals could give class teachers as to how to deal with the many problems Martin seems to have. Our concerted efforts over the past two years have met with little success unfortunately.*

Two years later, there was another grim assessment of his intellectual capacities. His written expression, for example:

> *Writing a mixture. Uses capitals anywhere. Enjoys writing stories about other children (in a nasty way). Difficult to read. No idea of a sentence.*

Mathematics was no better. Martin was already at least a year behind his classmates, while his speech was at times unintelligible and at other times babyish: "Can I go toilet?" he would ask.

His motor co-ordination was normal but his behaviour inside school was not, described variously as easily distracted and attention-seeking, rarely conforming and most often, simply unco-operative. The range of observations made by the teachers reveal how confusing it was for them, too:

> *I used to think Martin was hyperactive but now I'm not so sure ... No tolerance when others speaking.*

There were more hints under a section dealing with all-important relationships with other children:

> *Has no special friends, join in group games. Children just tolerate him. In class Martin bothers children trying to work, calls out, trips, hits when they go past him or leaves his seat and goes over to them.*

Another teacher painted a much darker picture:

> *Aggressive, destructive, kicks, spits and has been known to urinate over other children. Over two years has acquired a bad reputation with other children.*

His impression on adults was vastly different, perhaps underlining his lack of development, or even a level of duplicity or manipulation within his character. Under strengths and assets, the teacher noted:

> *Affectionate to teachers and seems genuinely upset he causes so much bother.*

There was the odd friend but they never lasted long. In grade four, he struck up a friendship with a boy named Nigel Hickman. The friendship, as fleeting as it was, began one afternoon after school when Nigel invited Martin around to his house even though they weren't in the same class at school. It continued because Martin kept turning up at his front gate every week.

Sometimes they walked home from school together and dropped into his house for a few hours where, "We played just normal games: Americans and Russians, things like that," Nigel recalled. He never knew exactly where Martin lived, much less met his parents or stayed over. The friendship never developed beyond school.

More than a decade later, Hickman still ponders. He is wary about the issue and stands uncomfortably on the street outside his workplace in the suburb of Howrah. The subject of Bryant clearly irritates him, mainly because of what he calls the paranoia surrounding the case. He was a freak of circumstances and of nature, he argues, the like of which will probably never be seen again: "We were kids. Nothing seemed wrong at the time. He might go and do something stupid but so would I. We never hung out in a group but he didn't have any friends that I was aware of."

The pair drifted apart in late primary school and then reunited at high school briefly before the relationship ended suddenly one day in a fight in the street on the way home. They parted company, both with bloodied noses, a friendship never to be rekindled.

Hickman didn't even recognise the name when television and radio reports began naming Bryant on the morning after the massacre: "I realised when I saw the photos in the papers. The name didn't mean anything to me because it was so long ago and I only knew him a short time. But I recognised the eyes."

Did he notice anything abnormal when they were kids?

The only abnormality, as such, was Martin's speech difficulty: "He had trouble getting words out. I thought he was partly deaf because my sister was deaf and had the same sort of problem."

Nigel never saw the bad behaviour inside the classroom because they always had different teachers. But even as the two boys shared spy games, unbeknown to Nigel, the behaviour of his playmate was getting worse. A report in August 1977 noted:

> He's a very disturbing influence in other teachers' classes. He is not interested in participating in class activities, excursions. He prefers to slide on floors, chase other children and often ruins an otherwise excellent outing. The most disturbing and worrying aspect of Martin's behaviour is his violent nature. He kicks and torments [another child] in particular, often reducing him to tears. He often hurls objects around the room which continually necessitates his expulsion from the room which only puts him further behind in his work.
>
> It is regrettable that Martin has to be continually sent out of the room. However, experience has told me that this procedure is the only satisfactory method when one has to consider the other children. A direct reprimand only results in blatant laughing and an obvious hope that other children will be impressed at his behaviour.

....

It was June 1976 and Maurice and Carleen had just returned from their second holiday to Britain. This time they had taken the children as well as his mother-in-law, Freda, on what had been a bittersweet journey for Maurice. It was the last time he would see his father, who had fallen ill and would soon pass away, but he was also able to rekindle relationships, if only fleetingly, with his sisters and cousins and even the farming family who took him in when they were evacuated during the war. Despite the wartime backdrop, the farm held treasured memories in an otherwise dark childhood. He regarded the farmer's son as a brother in many respects. This time, the journey home to England seemed like he was able to find a peaceful resolution to his departure more than a quarter of a century before.

Martin had made the holiday very difficult. He was impossible for much of the time – restless, testing and oblivious to his impact on others – and not just on the aircraft for the 36-hour flight but each day as they visited family or roamed across England in a borrowed car, sometimes staying with friends and family, at other times camping in a tent or caravan. Keeping him occupied was exhausting, particularly with another young child to care for. Lindy was now five, and her "normalness" merely highlighted the strange behaviour of her elder brother. Even he recognised the difference, which only added to his frustration.

The boy was now aged nine and needed space to roam beyond the Augusta Road backyard and streets of New Town, which were familiar and safe but too restrictive, and his attempts to make friends had continued to backfire. Even children who once played with him had become wary of his strange behaviour. What could be embraced as endearing in a young boy was now a point of distinction. As a teenager, these traits would become alarming and something to be sneered at among his peers.

It was a mystery to Carleen, who acknowledged her son's problems, but railed against the seemingly cold attitude of others. Tiny incidents prickled and obsessed her, such as the time he tried tenpin bowling and came home carrying a bowling bag and pair of socks he'd won, apparently by beating the other kids at a game he'd only just started.

It seems improbable but Carleen preferred to believe Martin's story, even when he never went back and refused to explain the reasons. His mother, in her haze of love, frustration and loyalty, could only surmise that it was because he was self-conscious and shy, something she understood given her own childhood clouded by meek self-doubt. She was projecting her own experiences and doubts. As she lamented:

> *If only he had been with a friend or had known somebody that would have encouraged him to continue playing. It was a bit too much to be in the limelight alone.*

Maurice, too, struggled to cope with his son. He had not shied from medical intervention, but embraced it only to be disappointed that, unlike the flu or a broken leg, there seemed no definitive diagnosis, let alone management. Patience and a hope it would pass in time, as he would tell the doctors, counsellors and psychiatrists, expecting Martin "to grow like an oak" even though he must have known in his heart it was not to be.

He had even tried a diet created for hyperactive children after reading about the theories of Californian pediatrician Dr Benjamin Feingold, an early exponent of the theory that there is a link between behaviour and diet, and that artificial colours and flavours, even naturally occurring salicylic acid, used in preservatives, could cause hyperactivity in children. But it too ended in disappointment, doing little to quell Martin's elevated moods. They refused a local doctor's suggestion that they experiment using aspirin tablets on Martin to see if there was any discernible change. He was not a guinea pig, Maurice insisted, and besides, the doctor didn't have to live with the consequences of giving him a drug, however innocent, that could make his moods even worse.

Instead, Maurice had resorted to long walks in a bid to calm Martin down and give him an outlet for his almost ferocious energy. The pair would frequently stroll to the Royal Botanical Gardens a kilometre from their home, but when that wasn't enough they headed into the foothills of Mount Wellington towering behind and over the city. Father and son would set off in the morning, following the Lenah Valley Road until it petered out into a series of fire trails that criss-crossed through the thick forest which had regenerated after the devastating fires of 1967. The best known of these trails is the Pipeline Track, built by convict labour in the early 19th century to provide the fledgling settlement with fresh water, but Maurice and Martin tended to follow other tracks with names such as Old Farm, Rivulet, Myrtle Gully, O'Grady's Falls and Fingerpost, virtually skirting the back of the city as they climbed, passed only by a handful of other walkers.

Some days they would make it as far as the village of Fern Tree, a climb of 450 metres and 13 kilometres by road up the mountain, before heading back. Maurice would arrive home hours later tired and sore while Martin was still bounding as if he had just walked around the corner. It was like having an exuberant dog in a suburban backyard. As Carleen would recall, her husband never once complained but it was clear something had to give.

Outside his work at the wharves and family life, Maurice fed three main interests: a fascination with military history that prompted him to buy an old left-hand drive US Army jeep; a desire to work at the Hobart Maritime Museum when he retired from the docks; and an avid, at times over-zealous, interest in buying and selling second-hand furniture. He frequented weekend auctions around the town and country areas, at one stage managing to squeeze three antique dining settings into the Augusta Road house. Carleen would stumble over new objects every week as she cleaned the house.

Even though Maurice, who had begun to excel as a specialist forklift driver, was always circumspect with workmates about Martin and his problems, those close to him could not help but be aware there were some difficulties at home. It would emerge mostly with a shrug of the shoulders or the shake of his head when the men got together to have a beer, mostly at Howard's

Hotel opposite "The Pickup", as they called the gate where the men gathered in the hope of getting a shift, at the bottom of Argyle Street, or Customs House Hotel further down in Murray Street. There wasn't much drinking in a time where work remained uncertain and money short. Most drank at home and many brewed their own beer.

Ron Harmon worked alongside Maurice for almost 30 years. They were also trade union delegates for the Waterside Workers' Federation where Maurice at one time held down the post of Hobart branch vice-president. The pair mixed socially, sometimes "getting silly" at a pub, and on the odd occasion travelled together on union business, even a couple of overnight trips to Melbourne: "He was a quiet bloke except on occasions when we'd had a few drinks. I never knew him to let his guard down but I had the sense that something was wrong. Morrie never really gave away anything specific," Harmon recalled.

Terry Weeding was another workmate on the dock. His family owned a property down near Port Arthur. There was a bay behind the main settlement – Opossum Bay as it was recorded in early maps but Carnarvon Bay as it later became known – where the shoreline was a cluster of shacks mainly used by fishermen and basic weekend accommodation for families from the city. It was a close-knit community and might be perfect for young kids with too much energy. Terry had noticed that one of the shacks was up for sale. Why didn't they come down for a weekend and see what they thought of the area. His kids loved the place, and it could give Martin some room to move. They might consider putting in an offer.

CHAPTER 8
The Arsenal

'How many guns do you own?" Inspector Ross Paine looks across the table at the man he is questioning: Martin Bryant is trussed up as if he were the fictional serial killer Hannibal Lecter rather than the dishevelled, real-life mass murderer he is. As harmless as he appears, no one is taking any chances with this guy. He smells, too, probably from the burns which are still heavily bandaged more than two months after he staggered out of the Seascape guest house, tearing off the clothes that were melting into his back and legs. Most of the officers trying to clean up his mess were hoping they still hurt like hell.

Bryant looks blankly, as if struggling to concentrate, his hair falling over his eyes in a wash of lank blond curls: "I own, um, a shotgun and a semi-automatic and another semi-automatic – three altogether."

The conversation had begun half an hour earlier inside the bare interview room at Risdon Prison. It had been niceties mainly, or wooden politeness might be a better expression. Whatever they feel personally, there is no sense in putting the guy off. Paine and his investigation partner, John Warren, don't want to blow their chance. There is too much at stake. It seems the whole world is watching Tasmania – the biggest massacre by a lone gunman in history.

It is July 4 – 10 weeks since the massacre – and Bryant has finally agreed to a formal interview after refusing Warren during a visit to the hospital the morning after he was arrested. They'd decided to wait until after he was out of hospital and in Risdon, away from the hordes of media who have descended on the city. In the meantime, the pair have headed a taskforce investigation involving two dozen officers and support staff. More than 600 people have been interviewed. If a trial is required there would be more than 200 witnesses. It all depends on the bastard sitting in front of them.

Bryant's burns, although still raw, are healing, unlike the wounds he has inflicted on an entire community. These will never close completely.

"Where'd you get those guns?" Paine's delivery indicates he doesn't want any nonsense but Bryant, in his high, sing-song voice, ignores the authority: "Oh, um, I can't really say. I haven't got my lawyer here so …"

Paine hesitates. No matter what he has done Bryant is entitled to proper representation, and even though his lawyer, David Gunson, has approved the interview, he has to be careful. "Well, we have spoken to your lawyer, and he knows that we're talking to you … and has no problem with that …"

Bryant seems satisfied: "OK. Yeah, I got um, one off a gun dealer and also I got two of 'em off …" His answer was lost in a mumble.

Paine continues: "We have got some of your guns here. Mr Warren might hold them up and we'll talk about each one individually. That might be the best way …"

Bryant looks in wonder at the shotgun Warren is holding, as if he hasn't seen it before: "It's big, isn't it. Is it loaded?"

Warren scoffs at the suggestion: "Definitely not loaded, Martin, I can tell you."

Paine continues: "This is a Daewoo 12-gauge shotgun."

"Oh sorry, yeah, I bought that one off, um, Hill. Do you know Terry Hill?"

"You bought that one off Terry Hill?"

"Yeah, yeah. I paid three thousand for it."

"What's his business name?"

"Guns and Ammo. But, I mean, it's a rare bird isn't it, really."

It is as if they are admiring a museum piece rather than one of the guns used to murder more than 30 people.

"Yeah, very," Paine concedes. "How long ago did you buy it?"

Bryant isn't listening: "The funny thing is, I never got round to using it. It scared me; the thought of it not working and probably ricocheting out."

Paine tries again: "Martin, how long ago did you get that one, can you remember?"

"Um, that one? I bought that one about four months ago."

"Now this is a .223 Remington, or Colt AR-15. Do you remember where you bought that one?"

"Yeah Terry Hill, Terry Hill."

"At Guns and Ammo?"

"Mmm."

"How long ago?"

"Month after, ah, before that one. Five months ago."

"Five months ago. And you can remember how much you paid for that one?"

"Ah, five grand with the scope. It was gunna be four-and-a-half thousand without the scope but it was five thousand with the scope and strap. Also got some ammunition thrown in."

"So that scope that's on it now was on it when you purchased it?"

"Can I just look through it? Am I allowed to have a look through the scope? Yeah. That's a special one for the gun itself."

"Right. Did you have it especially made for the gun or was it in stock and just came with the gun?"

"Terry Hill said, 'There's extras with that AR-15,' and I said, 'Well, I'd be interested in some extras,' but he said, 'It'll cost you more.' He said there's a scope, little Colt scope that goes with it, and he said a strap and some ammo, and he said it'll cost you $500 more."

"All right. How many rounds of ammunition did you get with that, can you remember?"

"Oh, about 80 to 100 rounds."

"Eighty to 100 rounds. Have you purchased any more rounds, um, since, you know, you've bought the firearm itself?"

"Um, yeah, I've probably purchased eight packets of 20 rounds in each."

"From Terry?" Paine checks.

"Terry, yeah. Still in business is he?"

"Yes, he's still in business. Now the next one ..." Paine stops himself and looks at Bryant: "Why do you ask if Terry's still in business?"

"Ah, 'cos I didn't have a licence."

"Sorry I didn't hear you."

"I had no gun licence, and I thought …"

Paine interrupts him. This is important: "So, just let me get this straight. You didn't have a gun licence?"

"No."

"Did you make out you had a gun licence when you purchased them?"

"No, I never discussed it. I just said I had the cash on me, and he said that's all right."

"Did he ever ask to see if you had a gun licence?"

"No, never."

"Do you know Terry Hill like as a friend?"

"No, not really." Bryant thought for a moment before correcting himself: "I can still remember when I was young, and he said to come in here and just look around after I'd finished school, so I knew him."

"So Guns and Ammo's been in New Town Road for quite a long time?"

"Yeah."

"When you got the guns, did you always deal with Terry?"

"Oh yes. But I bought some out of the paper."

"Have you ever had a .308?"

"Yes. I bought the .308 … out of a paper; out of *The Mercury*."

"Right. And where did you buy .308 ammunition?"

Bryant thinks for a moment. "Um, I managed to get a load of it; about six, seven boxes with 20 in each box. That was about four or five years ago but I had it stored away. It's only recently that I got to use it but they were the wrong bullets, so I went over to Terry Hill for the first time for years, and he said, 'You're using the wrong bullets, Martin. You should be using the military hard, hard-top bullets.' He said, 'The only ones I've got in stock is a case of 3000 rounds,' and he said, 'It'll cost you,' think it was $930. And I said, 'I'll think about it. I'll get back to you on Monday.' So it was on the Friday. I phoned him up a few hours later. I said, 'I've got the money. I'll come over and buy the rounds.'"

"So you bought 3000?"

"I couldn't buy anything smaller off him because that's all he had at the time …"

"And when was that?"

"That's going back five months."

Bryant seems to be taking everything back to a point four or five months ago. Even though he has owned one of the rifles for six or seven years, he has never fired the weapon. It was only in the weeks leading up to the massacre when he realised he had the wrong ammunition and went to this dealer Terry Hill. Then he started buying guns again, although Hill has always denied selling Bryant any weapons.

"All right," Paine continues. "We'll have a look at the last gun, which is on the floor. This is a .223 calibre self-loading rifle."

Bryant shakes his head: "I've never seen that one before. Mmm."

"Well, we recovered that one from being repaired. Does that ring any bells?"

"That one was repaired for me, that other one, the AR10," Bryant says, pointing to the previous gun shown to him. "That, I took over to Terry Hill."

"Oh, so I've got them confused." Paine accepts his error but the point is that Bryant has identified the gun as his own. It is time to change tack: "All right. Where did you develop your love of using firearms?"

"Um, oh I just, just loved the thought of owning them. I wish I had that AR-15 in here, then I could probably get out. Jump part of the window, I could probably jump through the window and escape because of this. I don't like being locked up, it's not very nice."

"How long have you owned firearms for, Martin?"

"Um, going back six, seven years. This was the first one I bought, the one out of the paper. I owned air rifles when I was younger."

"Did your dad sort of encourage you to use firearms?"

"No, no, definitely not."

"He was against it, was he?"

"Mmm."

"Did mum know you had those guns?"

"Yeah my, ah, mum never knew, no. But the funny thing is my dad said if, when we used to go over to Richmond, he used to point it out. He said, 'If you ever go over there, Martin, to that prison any time, I'm not gunna ever come and visit you,' he said. 'So stay away, stay out of trouble.' This, I mean, it's wrong isn't it. I shouldn't be in here."

CHAPTER 9
The Convict

How far back into the tangle of genetics, chance and opportunity does one delve to find causes or clues for a crime such as the Port Arthur massacre? Are Martin Bryant's forefathers and mothers, their personal flaws and deeds relevant in the search for answers? Was it nature or nurture or, as neuroscience increasingly shows, a random cocktail of DNA and experience, a series of events, which, layered one upon the other – or interacting with each other – can lead one man to express himself in greatness and another in destruction.

In the case of Martin Bryant, nothing is irrelevant; every experience, every encounter, every relationship – from birth to the terrible moment when he set out on that drive to Port Arthur – could potentially shed light on what changed him from a seemingly harmless, intellectually impaired young man with a love of animals and scuba diving into an unflinching, emotionless mass murderer. The Tasmanian Government has sealed access to most of the Martin Bryant story and to evidence collected against him. In a bid to shield the community from more anguish, it has also stymied discussion and further study of a phenomenon that tragically, has now manifested in western nations the world over, including the two high-profile massacres in the United States, at Columbine High School in April 1999 when 14 people, including the two gunmen, Eric Harris and Dylan Klebold, were killed, and most recently at Virginia Tech in April 2007 when 33, including the gunman, Seung-Hui Cho, died.

Tasmania's very essence is shaped and defined by its dark, penal past. Visitors are attracted to its rugged natural beauty and the remnants and stories of its prisons and pioneers. And yet the story of a young man who left an indelible bloodstain on the modern island, a tragedy that reverberated throughout the world – and was copied, emulated and repeated with equally terrible consequences in other cities – has remained shrouded in secrecy. Tasmania has refused to look back into the recent past – even if it might have helped the system avoid a similar future.

In fact, the Martin Bryant story probably began 172 years ago, when another young man responded violently and impulsively to an innocent set of circumstances, placing the first footstep on the long path to tragedy.

It was about 10pm on Monday April 13, 1824, and the sun had only just set over London, the long twilight of the northern hemisphere a welcome respite after the dark, freezing winter. Chelsea, still a little village, barely three kilometres from the city centre, was, connected mainly by the Kings Road, a dirt track used by royalty to travel between Hampton Court Palace and the rural hunting grounds and mansions. Progress was just starting to change the city; gas street lighting was on its way.

That night, a hairdresser named Richard Wright was standing at the half-hatch front door of his home at No.10 Royal Hospital Row, enjoying the warm mid-spring night and watching closing time at the Duke of York public house next door. Like many small businessmen of the day, he ran his salon from the ground floor and lived above. He'd just shut up shop and, as was his wont, he spent a few contemplative minutes watching the passing trade before retiring for the night.

It was a busy part of town, near the banks of the Thames, and the Duke of York was one of several public houses in the neighbourhood, serving watery pots of beer or gin as well as providing cheap overnight accommodation. Wright considered himself something of a neighbourhood watchdog – an old-fashioned busybody – and would appear in the Old Bailey a number of times as a willing witness to local crime, much of it fuelled by too much alcohol or poverty and not enough food.

Among the drinkers who tumbled into the street that night were 19-year-old Richard John Cordwell and his young companion, Sarah Wilkins. The young man, a gardener from nearby Fulham, as he would describe himself, stood out in the crowd. At 173 centimetres he was quite tall for a man of his time, with "pock pitted" skin, light brown hair and piercing grey eyes. It is a reasonable assumption that Miss Wilkins was his girlfriend, given the rough tattoo of a ring pricked onto the knuckles of a finger of his left hand and the script *S.W 4 R.C.* on the back of the same hand. The young man also sported a pair of tattoos on the inside of his arm – a strange peace and war combination of a soldier and a flower pot. Tattoos were a storybook for the hard men and women who etched them into their skin with a combination of soot and black sediment from lamps. They recorded the hopes, loves and disappointments of 19th century life and, in Cordwell's case, told of his devotion to Sarah Wilkins, and the flowerpot was probably a symbol of his livelihood. The soldier might have been an unfulfilled desire or perhaps a sign of his provenance, given the local area's military hospital and its close connection with returning soldiers.

The scene outside the pub that night is easily imagined because it was captured just two years earlier by the Scottish artist Sir Douglas Wilkie in his painting *Chelsea Pensioners Reading the Gazette after the Battle of Waterloo*. The canvas, commissioned by the Duke of Wellington to celebrate his victory in 1815 over Napoleon, depicts a street scene outside the walls of the famous Royal Hospital for war veterans (hence the term Chelsea pensioner) where a crowd of soldiers representing various regiments and drinkers are reading about, and celebrating, the victory.

Behind them is a lovely old stone wall, and beyond that is the hospital graveyard, already full just a century after its design and construction by Sir Christopher Wren. It still stands today, although the wall has been replaced by an iron fence, and the jumble of tired headstones is now a visible reminder of its age. The line of buildings on the opposite side of the dirt track – then known as Royal Hospital Row – has changed dramatically in the two centuries that have passed, and is now lined with multimillion-dollar apartments.

In Wilkie's scene, a group of drinkers lean from the windows of the public house as if to see for themselves what the ruckus is all about. The name of the pub is impossible to discern but its insignia is a man on a horse – the Duke of York. The road leads on towards Sloane Square and the Duke's headquarters, which today has been converted to the fashionable shopping precinct known as Duke of York Square. Records from that period show that the Duke of York public house was originally at No.9 Royal Hospital Row and its landlord, a Mr M'Pherson, was probably the man who ushered Cordwell and his mates back into the street on that spring night.

Across the way – and also depicted in the painting – is the newly built St Luke's Anglican Church which was about to be consecrated. A few years later it would host the marriage of a struggling author named Charles Dickens, a union that would coincide with the publication of his first novel, *The Pickwick Papers*.

The painting was, of course, a fictional scene, but not for Richard Cordwell, whose life would change irrevocably on this very spot. He was already known to the police after his arrest the year earlier for punching a man named Robert Buckle and stealing his hat. The incident had happened in the very same street and at the same time of day but in a different month – October – on the cusp of winter. Buckle, who lived two doors from the Duke of York, was returning home about 10.30pm, gave this account to police:

"I saw the prisoner coming along with a gang of six or seven; he separated from them, and knocked me down with his fist. My hat was then taken off, and he ran off. I called out when I recovered myself. I ran home, and applied at Queen Square next morning, and told the officer the prisoner's name. I had known him well for upwards of two years, and have not the least doubt of him – there was a lamp about forty yards off. He was taken that morning; I have seen him loitering about the streets, and heard him called by his name."

There was only one witness. Isaac Dutton, another Hospital Row resident, who was also returning home when he saw the attack. But it was late and he couldn't be sure of the assailant in the encroaching darkness.

Cordwell was obviously confident. When he heard the next day that policeman John Weale was searching for him, he came forward:"Do you want me?" he challenged as he walked into the station at nearby Queens Square.

His presumption was correct. The jury before magistrate Baron William Garrow, a famous defence lawyer, Member of Parliament and Attorney-General, let him off.

There was much more light that night six months later when Richard Wright watched Cordwell, Wilkins and their noisy companions begin walking down the road after leaving the Duke of York. As they passed by, they crossed paths with a woman named Elizabeth Arms who was walking towards Wright on the other side of the road. She was trying to find her husband, a Chelsea pensioner named William Arms, before visiting her parents.

Without warning, one of the women in Cordwell's group rushed across the road towards Mrs Arms, shoved her against the hospital's boundary wall and punched her in the eye. Wright was shocked by the sudden attack then watched, horrified, as Cordwell responded, not to break up the fight and protect the stricken woman who was now lying on the ground but to join the attack. He would tell Magistrate Baron John Hullock at the Old Bailey in late June, when the pair appeared on charges of "theft with violence; highway robbery", exactly what he saw: "The male prisoner ran over directly and caught her by the shoulder, dragged her on the ground, kicked her, and gave the shawl to the female prisoner. The prosecutrix had fallen into the road. He kicked her while she was down, and when he had got the shawl, he wrapped it up and brought it to the female prisoner, who put it under her apron."

The account of Mrs Arms about the unprovoked attack was even more dramatic: "I was going down the road, and the prisoners met me; another woman was with them, whom I had seen before, but never spoke to her; she (the one not present) gave me a blow with her fist, and gave me a black eye, cut my eyebrow, and knocked me down; Cordwell then came and took my shawl off my shoulders, and kicked me in the breast while I was down. I am certain that he is the man. He took my shawl and gave it to Wilkins. They left me laying on the ground ... I was half an hour on the ground, laying to recover myself, as my eye bled."

Cordwell could not contain himself: "Were you not fighting on that night?" he yelled across the court, challenging her story. "No. I was perfectly sober," she replied.

John Dance, a Bow Street constable, was also called to give evidence. He'd been on patrol nearby, overseeing pension handouts at the hospital, as he told the court:

"I came out of the Duke of York public house, and heard Wright: 'It is a great shame that a poor woman should be knocked down and robbed.' I went to him. He pointed out the female prisoner. I took her, and took the shawl from her hand. She had it behind her. Cordwell ran away. I left the female in custody – pursued, and found him in a house in Castle Yard, Jew's Row [renamed Hospital Row]. I had seen him before; Wright told me that it was Cordwell. I knew his name before ..."

In her defence, Sarah Wilkins claimed she had been an innocent bystander: "I was coming out of the public house and saw this woman on the other side of the way – several women and girls were round her, beating her. I saw the shawl on the ground, picked it up, and crossed over, and Wright said he saw this young man cross and give it to me. I had it in my hand intending to give it to her, when I got her from the crowd."

Cordwell remained belligerent, declaring: "The woman was beastly drunk, and I never had the shawl."

The record does not indicate how long the jury deliberated over the charge of highway robbery. Given the enormous caseload of a court which only sat eight times a year, it would not have taken more than a few minutes.

It is also doubtful that Sir John – Baron of the Exchequer and, according to an 1833 text, "a judge for integrity, sagacity and knowledge" – would have made any comments before passing sentence which read, simply:

Wilkins: Not Guilty. Cordwell: Guilty. Death.

Richard Cordwell's life was not about to end, however. Quite the contrary. His death sentence, for which he would have been hanged publicly at Tyburn where Marble Arch stands today, was commuted to a life of servitude. This was not unusual. The death sentence, handed out liberally, was often commuted and replaced by military or naval service or, in Cordwell's case, transportation to the other side of the world. On April 26, 1825, after 10 months in the squalor of the notorious Newgate Prison, Cordwell and 177 fellow prisoners were loaded into the convict ship Medina at the Sheerness Dockyard for the long journey to Van Diemen's Land.

Martin Bryant's great-great-grandfather was on his way to Tasmania.

....

Richard Cordwell was a lucky man although it would be many years before he would feel fortunate. His crime was vicious and opportunistic but the punishment meted out to him by the Old Bailey jury would be seen as harsh by modern standards. He had also lost his love, Sarah Wilkins, and probably never saw her again, as well as his family – his father Henry and mother Martha, brother George and sisters Amey, May and Martha. Another brother, Thomas, would get into trouble a couple of years later when he appeared in the same court after being charged with stealing a watch from a sleeping man. He suffered the same fate – transportation for life. Unlike his brother, his records provide no detail of where he went or what befell him.

Richard's sea journey to Australia took 141 days, according to log records kept by the ship's master, John Briggs. The convicts were housed below decks, often behind bars and even in chains, allowed on deck only occasionally. There is little information about the layout of the convict ships, although artist impressions typically show hellish, cramped quarters in which scurvy, dysentery and typhoid thrived and death was a frequent visitor. Cordwell, clearly a strapping young man, escaped illness and the ship's sick list kept by the onboard surgeon, William Gregor.

He arrived in Hobart on September 14, 1825, and was assigned to a wealthy landowner, William Kimberley, who had come from convict stock himself. Kimberley had been granted land at Pontville, 25 kilometres north of Hobart on the Midland Highway, an area which supplied much of the building stone for southern Tasmania.

The area had been explored in the early 1800s when food supplies in Hobart were critical, and soldiers were sent out in a desperate search for food. It is said that it was during one of these expeditions a Private Hugh Germain, an apparently well-educated member of the Royal Marines, began to give exotic names to places, among them Jerusalem, Jericho, Lake Tiberius, the river Jordan and even Bagdad, as he rode through the countryside with a copy of The Bible and *The Arabian Nights*.

The Cordwell family would remain in the area for the next two centuries.

Richard would end up having three masters over the next 13 years, and records show that, by and large, convict No.596 stayed out of trouble. There were three occasions however, when he strayed. On August 3, 1826, Cordwell got 50 lashes for refusing to work. On May 7, 1833, he received another 50 lashes for being absent without leave at midnight from his second master's residence, ironically, a Mr Bryant. He was noticed missing at midnight.

Cordwell appears to have mended his ways after that. Nothing appears on his record for the next three years until May 1836 when he went missing once more but escaped with an admonishment from the local magistrate, a Mr T. Roper.

This particular night would have a lasting impact on his life for another reason: he had met his future wife.

CHAPTER 10
Eliza

The careful script of early convict records, as fascinating as they are, can be notoriously inaccurate. Take the case of Eliza Bridget Fitzgerald. All available records show the farm servant was born in Limerick, Ireland, but the year varies wildly, depending on the source. Some say she was born in 1814 while another nominated 1823. The Old Bailey transcripts of her court case of October 16, 1834, record her age as 27, which means she would have been born in 1807, and yet the register at Newgate Prison where she'd already languished for several weeks before the trial said she was 23, which means she was born in 1811. Irish birth records suggest she was probably born on April 4, 1814, in the parish of Bruff to James Fitzgerald and his wife Ellen O'Shea. When or why she came to London has been lost in history but prison records provide a meticulous physical description. Eliza was tiny, barely 152 centimetres (five feet) tall, with medium-length dark brown hair and blue eyes. Her face is described as oval, her nose long with a medium-wide mouth and small chin. Her most prominent feature was her "fresh, freckled" complexion.

The young woman, lately from Middlesex, was facing two charges of pickpocketing, both of which occurred on September 28. Her first victim was James Knowles, a gardener of Paddington, who had just delivered some linen for his wife, who was working as a laundress. It was after 2am but there were still people on the street as he went to get a cup of coffee, carrying a pocket book containing three shillings.

He told the court: "I felt some woman's hand in my pocket – I cannot tell who. I spoke to her rather roughly, and away she went. I then went to a public house, and received information. I felt in my pocket, and my pocketbook was gone. I saw the prisoner in the station house, and my book was found in her bosom."

Henry Lovett, a police constable, was called to arrest the young woman: "I took the prisoner on another charge – I found this book and 26s. on her," he said.

Fitzgerald's defence was simple, and effective: "I picked it up."

The second incident happened three hours later after Fitzgerald "fell in" with a labourer named Thomas Hopkins in Paddington.

Hopkins testified: "She asked me to go with her, which I did. I gave her a shilling, and she pointed out the place where we were to go, about forty yards out of the road, into a field. While we were there, I found her hand in my pocket, and told her to take it away, as there was nothing for her there. She took her hand away, and we were together about a minute, when she turned her head, and said, 'There stands a man.' I turned, and saw a man, she gave me a push, and made away towards him. I then missed six half-crowns, one half-sovereign, a shilling and a duplicate, which were wrapped up in a rag. She went off as quick as she could, but I pursued her, and caught hold of her just as she was getting through the fence. The officer came and took her to the station house. The pocket book, these six half-crowns, the half-sovereign, and the shilling, fell on the ground. The duplicate and the rag were not found on her."

Constable Lovett had been quietly watching Fitzgerald's movements since her earlier arrest: "I was going along by the fence, which concealed me, 'til I got within five or six yards of the prisoner. I said to the prosecutor, 'Have you been with this woman?' He said she had done the trick, she had robbed him of six half-crowns, a half-sovereign, and a shilling. I seized her two hands, and took her to the station. I went up to the table with her, and this money dropped from her – she then pulled out 12s. 10d., which she said belonged to her. I found the pocket book on her. I then went back to where they had been, and found this rag and the duplicate. It was a very foggy morning, and I could trace them by the marks on the dew."

This time there was no room for explanation – none is even recorded – and the decision was swift: *Guilty. Transported for life.*

So, too, Martin Bryant's great-great-grandmother was on her way to Van Diemen's Land.

There were 165 women convicts, including Eliza Fitzgerald, aboard the New Grove when it left the Isles of Scilly, off the south-west tip of England, on November 25, 1834. The voyage, under Master Robert Brown, would take 122 days, stopping on the way for repairs and supplies at Gibraltar, then at ports in the West Indies, South America and the Cape of Good Hope. There were two surgeons aboard, George Rowe and Dave Thomson, not only because of concern about maintaining the health of convicts but the cargo was female and considered more problematic. Fitzgerald's condition when she arrived in Hobart on March 27, 1835, was described simply as "single" and "indifferent".

Unlike the men, most of whom were now being incarcerated in the new prison at Port Arthur, which had opened five years earlier, she went into service with a settler as a farm servant. But like Richard Cordwell before her, Eliza would find it impossible to completely shake her ways, and in a raw, rural settlement such as Hobart there was little else to dream of but the dull sanctuary of alcohol and the attentions of one or several men, who outnumbered the women by seven to one.

Within a few weeks she was thrown into the washhouse and given hard labour for one month after being found drunk. In November the same year, now with a new master named Mortimer, she repeated the crime, this time "absenting herself from charge and being found drunk at 11 o'clock at night". A new accusation was added the next day – soliciting – and she was sentenced to three months in the cells and placed on probation. The charge had been implicit in the description of her activities back in London on the night she was caught stealing. The prison documents also mentioned "two years on the town", which was a common euphemism for prostitution, and probably explained how she supplemented her meagre wages as a housemaid after arriving in London from Ireland.

It was something her new master regarded as "gross misconduct" despite it being commonplace among the thousands who were taken from the streets of London and Ireland and dumped on the other side of the world.

Each time she transgressed and was punished she would be handed to a new master upon her release. Convicts were exchangeable, particularly the troublesome ones like Eliza Fitzgerald.

On April 26, 1836, with a master named Hutton, she got drunk again, then again a month later when a magistrate named Roper returned her to the washhouse for a month to dry out. It didn't solve the problem. She rebelled again on June 14, within days of being released to a new master, a Mr Dixon, and was reprimanded for being "grossly disorderly" towards police constables. On August 11, she was in the lock-up again, but this time her conduct was placed in the category "extreme violence" and she was given six months. On March 25, 1837, just a month after being released, she was at it again. Working at the orphan school now, she had returned one night drunk and swearing in front of the children. It led to another three months in the cells. The pattern was repeated on July 11 when, after being hauled into the lock-up, she became disorderly and was given another month in the washhouse. In the three years she had been in Hobart, Eliza Fitzgerald had spent one third of the time in police cells or the washhouse.

The Cascades Female Factory in Hobart was a rum distillery yard converted into a complex to house the growing numbers of women convicts as they arrived in the colony – the female equivalent to Port Arthur. More than 3700 women spent time here in appalling conditions, serving sentences or waiting to be put into service in a household, or serving time for minor transgressions. Many also met husbands in the most perfunctory of fashions, paraded to allow the men to choose a wife by dropping a kerchief in front of his chosen bride. It epitomised the role and value of women in a brutal society. Meals consisted of bread and gruel or a meat and vegetable soup, regularly made with offcuts, the head of a sheep or ox.

How and where Eliza met Richard Cordwell is not recorded but when is obvious, and their union spelled trouble from the first night. Their respective records show both absconded from their masters on the night of May 9, 1836. Eliza was given one month at the "wash tub" but Cordwell was let off with a warning.

The relationship endured, however, and on October 2, 1837, Cordwell and Fitzgerald sought permission to marry, as convicts were required to do. The application was approved 10 days later and they were wed on November 12.

The service, like their trials years earlier, was swift and without emotion, conducted by the Chaplain William Hutchins and witnessed by two men who almost certainly were strangers and paid for their attendance. James Undy and J.H. Smales could sign their own names, unlike the newlyweds who, like most convicts, could not read or write. Instead they signed with an X.

Life, however, was definitely improving for Richard Cordwell. Not only did he have a wife but six months later, in July 1838, he was granted a conditional pardon, which made him an emancipated man. He was free for the first time in 15 years, a 34-year-old man whose only condition of freedom was that he could never return to England. Eliza Fitzgerald, as his wife, was effectively freed as well. Technically, she was assigned to her husband but it was as good as being pardoned. In 1841, her sentence would be over.

Their problems nevertheless were not over. In October of that year, just 10 months after their marriage, Eliza was thrown back into the female factory after appearing before the police magistrate, charged yet again with being drunk and disorderly. Cordwell, presumably through an intermediary, given that he was illiterate, penned a flowery but well-argued letter to Sir John Franklin, the colony's Lieutenant-Governor, pleading for the return of his wife: she was needed to guard his home from intruders during the day while he worked. The three-page letter, which still exists, reads:

> *The humble petition of Richard Cordwell most specifically herewith. That petitioner carried here in 1825 on Medina and is now free of service tide (emancipated) that about 12 months ago he married Eliza Fitzgerald, a prisoner of the Crown, and is residing ... in the district of Brighton. That petitioner's wife, the said Eliza Fitzgerald, was some time back brought before the Police Magistrate at Brighton charged with irregular conduct and with being under the influence of liquor, and sent by the magistrate to the female factory. That no man can deplore more than [the] Petitioner any irregularity in the behaviour of his wife but hopes your Excellency will consider her punishment sufficiently served having now been nearly two months confined in the female factory. That Petitioner is put to very great inconvenience in consequence of not having a person to live in his dwelling during the day time when from the nature of his avocations he is obliged to be from home and trusts therefore your Excellency will be pleased to take his case into consideration and restore to him his wife once more.*
>
> *Said Petitioner prayed.*

It was attached to a note written by a factory official seeking official permission to free Eliza:

> *This person called on me two days ago. He wanted me to return his wife to him but I informed him that she had been returned to the factory by the police magistrate at Brighton. I could not do so without reference to that official and I have written to inquire if there is any police objection to his again receiving her and if there is not of course he will obtain her.*

It was dated December 20 and received by the Colonial Secretary's Office the following day. There is no indication of Franklin's decision although she was eventually released and the couple moved to Lachlan, 20 kilometres west of Hobart. On April 12, 1841, the first of their eight children, Richard, was born – Martin Bryant's great-grandfather. The rest followed at regular intervals – Martha in 1843, Catherine 1844, Henry 1846, Mary 1848, Emma and Hannah both in 1850 and finally John in 1853.

The final document which mentions Richard Cordwell is an 1866 census, which contains a list of New Norfolk residents in which, now aged 62, the former teenage London street thug is listed simply as a "householder". There is no mention of Eliza, nor of their children, several of whom would have been young adults, and all lived their lives in the same area. He died in Hobart on January 6, 1875, aged 71, but his wife would live for another 26 years with a second husband – another "New Norfolk householder" named James Beasley, whom she married six months after Cordwell's death. Both were in their 60s. She died on August 12, 1901, at the age of 87 and is buried in the Catholic section of the Cornelian Bay Cemetery under the name Bridget Cordwell.

•••••••••••••••••••••••••••

Richard Cordwell junior, like his father, could not read or write. It was a luxury for a poor family, and a skill not required to be a farmer. On September 14, 1909, the New Norfolk farmer made out his will and signed it with an X, assuring the witnesses around his bedside – farmer Thos Gleeson and labourer William Graham as well as his executor, storekeeper Julian Brown – that he knew what he was doing. The next day he died and left his estate – worth a tidy £416 – to his wife of 47 years, Martha Wilton.

Richard had married the local girl on May 8, 1862, a month after his 21st birthday and a month before her 16th. Over the next 25 years, they had 12 children, living in the Lachlan district where 1890-91 Post Office director records mention him as a hop grower.

Their first child, William, arrived in 1864 and the last, Norman, in 1889. Some died young, including the ninth child, Albert, who died in October 1883 at just 20 months. His mother was already six months pregnant with her 10th, who when born on January 9, 1884, was promptly given his late brother's first name. Albert Arthur Cordwell, maternal grandfather of Martin John Bryant, Carleen's dad, had entered the world.

CHAPTER 11
Carnarvon Bay

Nineteenth-century convict ships arriving in Van Diemen's Land from London after four months at sea would negotiate their way to safe harbour through the last heaving swell of the Southern Ocean and into the calm of Port Arthur. They would anchor not off the main bustling settlement set against the towering, tree-lined hills but in a peaceful bay behind, the buildings hidden from view and noisy thrum muffled behind a wall of pine. The first land seen by the bedraggled survivors of those long voyages must have seemed a paradise as they stepped ashore, only to find that behind its raw natural beauty was a man-made hellhole of trepidation and misery.

Port Arthur, named after Van Diemen's Land Lieutenant-Governor Sir George Arthur, might have been a mighty industrial town. Indeed its beginnings were such, as a timber station hacked from the bush in 1830. Instead, it was transformed over the next three decades into one of the most infamous of colonial prisons, where the physical demands of servitude and brutal lashings were supplemented by the psychological torture of silence. Historians have yet to finalise the list of men and boys who came here between 1833 and 1855. Many did not survive their sentence, as the 1646 graves on the Isle of the Dead attest, while others found their way back into society to make some sort of a life and raise a family. The only proviso for them all was that none were permitted to go back to England, unlike the tens of thousands, who, in the following century, would choose to sail across the world to seek out a better way of life. These men and women – pioneers in one century, the immigrant backbone of postwar Australia in the next – would become intrinsic parts of the Australian story.

After it closed in 1877, the Port Arthur settlement was renamed Carnarvon, the land parcelled up and put to auction. It became a legitimate town, at one stage during the 1920s and '30s boasting three hotels and two museums as the tourism potential began to be recognised. And so it remained, a small, but sweet outpost within striking distance of Hobart, even before the dirt track became a sealed road and cars replaced horses. There was a series of devastating fires which reduced its buildings, in large part, to rubble before a 20th-century restoration gave them a ghostly quality and the name changed back to its original – Port Arthur – to reclaim its dark heritage. The name Carnarvon was reduced to the hidden bay where the convict ships once moored, itself a jumble of shacks and huts for fishermen until the 1960s when a proposed hotel development was shelved and the land subdivided. The middle classes jumped at the chance to buy up the blocks relatively cheaply for weekend escapes. What had been a place of misery in its European infancy was now a place of great joy.

For Maurice and Carleen, it offered hope. The properties were basic but affordable. In October 1975, he and Carleen made the 90-minute drive one Sunday, past the entrance to the historic penal settlement and down a steep, rutted track which threatened to disembowel their ageing Mercedes sedan. The vista at the base of the hill seemed beyond belief, even in this part of the world. A fine-grained, white beach stretched before them in an almost perfect half moon, broken only by a couple of timber jetties jutting out into clear, flat water. Behind them tree-lined hills rose sharply to a peak known locally as Palmers Lookout from which you could see out across the south-westernmost tip of Tasmania and into the dark and dangerous Southern Ocean beyond.

The cottage they sought was one of the first as they drove into the bay, at the corner of McCormick's Drive and Tasman Street. It was nothing to look at from the road – plain and fibro with two bedrooms, a kitchen, bathroom, living room and little else. The garden was spare, typical of a property not regularly tended, but the house was set well back on a big block, which gave it a sense of space with only one line of houses, the quiet road and a brace of tea trees separating the front fence from the beach. It was, literally, a stone's throw to the water. At $6000, it seemed a bargain, particularly as the Augusta Road house was now paid off and Carleen was back working, cleaning at the ANZ bank and even doing a few waitressing shifts in a local cafe. It served the dual purpose of a little extra money and getting her out of the house for some respite. Freda, now in one of the renovated flats at the house, would look after Martin and Lindy while she worked. Maurice and Carleen had decided to buy the place before getting out of the car. They signed in late October and settled in early November in time for the summer school holidays. Martin was eight years old and Lindy just two. Both would remember their childhoods in paradise but for very different reasons.

Most weekends and holidays were now spent down at the shack. If Maurice was working on the docks or on union business, Carleen would make the trip alone with the two children in tow. Martin seemed to respond immediately to the change of environment. He had been suspended from school the previous year but appeared to have calmed when he returned. Maybe they had found the solution. He was in a new place where there was much more freedom, where he could be a bit wilder without anyone noticing. Carleen's recollections paint a sanitised picture:

> Both Lindy and Martin would invite friends to the Port Arthur cottage for weekends and holidays. I also bred little Sheltie Collie dogs. We kept three and Martin would take them for long walks. Some evenings there would be a fire on the beach and the young ones would sit around and enjoy themselves. Maurice and I soon realised that this place was the best purchase we had made, especially for Martin to burn up some of that excess energy and give him satisfying interests to occupy him and give him health and happiness. There were always others to socialize with, most of whom owned a bicycle and a surfboard so they could surf or cycle together. They could also go rowing in the boat in calm conditions. They would walk or ride into the jetty at Port Arthur and come home with a small bucket full of mackerel fish. And later, there were many very good tracks on which to ride the horses. For many years we would take the horses in the float and take part in the Gymkhanas, which were held in Taranna on the Tasman Peninsula. We also played badminton in the Taranna Hall.

It would not last long. As they settled into the easy routine of weekend life, Martin's strange habits were quickly noticed and assessed. There were times he would be like any of the youngsters who ran wild with freedom at their doorstep, except there was always an edge to his behaviour.

The "shackies", as they called themselves, at first accepted and then at best tolerated the blond kid who looked and acted as if he would never slow down. But there was something odd about him, nothing specific but a feeling that he should be avoided. Sometimes it was the blank stares when he was challenged, as if he didn't get it and had no idea how to respond. Others read his glaring as silent threats.

It only heightened their reaction when Martin's mother kept trying to intervene and force the kids together. She couldn't understand why no one wanted to play with her son, or that was the way it appeared, as he stood behind her grinning in triumph, even laughing maniacally. Carleen wasn't blind to the problems. She simply had no answers.

Despite the frustrations over their son, the Bryants were happy at Carnarvon Bay. In June 1978, Maurice and Carleen snapped up another block of land, immediately across the road from their shack with its front fence barely 20 metres from the beach. The price of $4500 seemed reasonable even though there was no structure. They might consider building a bigger and better house in years to come.

Although they were looking to the future, Carleen and Maurice could not avoid the present. Their frustrations over Martin were echoed by the school, and yet the teaching staff had no answers either. In May 1979, Martin's last primary year, the Education Department's specialist centre in Albuera Street sent an assessor to observe him in the classroom.

The scene inside the classroom was relatively normal when the assessor arrived except that Martin was sitting alone next to the teacher, away from the other students. He was quiet and appeared interested in the lesson but the seating was a visible distinction between him and the others. It was necessary, argued the teacher, who insisted there had been little change in his behaviour during the year. The boy remained difficult to motivate, and his academic performance had fallen further behind. He was limited to using simple maths sheets rather than textbooks, and a program for problem readers because the language being studied by classmates was too complex. Despite his own difficulties, Martin would invariably taunt other children when they made mistakes or fell behind. It was as if it somehow took the attention away from him or lessened his own sense of failure. The assessor concluded:

> I suggested various behavioral modification techniques to [the teacher] who showed interest but said he would prefer to continue with a more informal approach to the problem. He does have some difficult children in the class and doesn't see Martin as his main problem. I spoke to Martin and he told me he liked [the teacher] and the school. However, he did admit that he didn't like maths or spelling. He seemed worried and asked me if he was coming back to the assessment centre. He seemed very relieved when I said no.

A few weeks after the classroom assessment, Martin was on the television evening news. He'd had an accident while playing with some fireworks found from a stock his father kept and burned himself badly, ending up in hospital. Somehow the incident came to the attention of a commercial television channel, which decided it was a timely story as a warning to others. The news crew found the boy sitting up in bed, bright and cheerful, with the inevitable sloppy grin.

"Will you be playing with fire crackers any more?" the reporter asked.

"Yes," Martin replied brightly.

"And have you learned a lesson from this?"

"Yes, but I'm still playing with them."

It was not exactly the response a mother might have hoped her son would deliver on television – no contrition, not even a hint that he understood the dangers of fire and explosives, more that it was exciting enough to ignore the dangers again if he ever had the chance – and yet Carleen still dismissed the incident. The fireworks had been the remnants kept from a Guy Fawkes Day celebration the previous November. Maurice had thought they were in a safe place but Martin had found them. He was simply being inquisitive, she insisted in the memoir:

> Typical of some young boys, unbeknown to Maurice and myself, Martin was in possession of a skyrocket in the attic where he slept. Martin decided to experiment. He lit the rocket. But once it was alight, he panicked, and

tried to extinguish it by pushing it into his clothes, which burnt a hole in his jeans. It was a relief to me that it was strong material. If he had had his pyjamas on, the burn would have been much more serious.

Once in hospital, the burn was serious enough for him to be admitted for several days.

If anything she was proud, perhaps relieved that he was doing something relatively normal – "typical" as she wrote. The burns, which required skin grafts, were secondary almost. They would heal.

The six-week stint away from school had quietened Martin but test results taken in mid-July after he returned confirmed his difficulties. There was little that could be done, the assessor wrote:

I was shown standardised test results and these showed Martin to be three years below his chronological age in spelling and word knowledge and two years below his mathematical understanding. I saw some of his work – it was remarkably neat – and the spelling was phonetically correct. Martin was quiet, embarrassed by my visit and told me everything was fine.

But everything was not fine.

CHAPTER 12
High School

The face peering out of the black-and-white photo clipped to the admission form was of a happy, carefree boy within a few months of the challenges of becoming a teenager. But Martin Bryant's strange, sandy-haired grin belied not only his own challenges but the conundrum his future presented for others. Of all the new students to be enrolled at the beginning of February 1980 at New Town High School, an all-boys school of 800 students in Midwood Street a couple of kilometres west of Augusta Road, his were by far the most difficult. The form, filled out in his father's basic, printed handwriting told why. Hobart was a small town wrapped up as a capital city. Telephone numbers had five digits (the Bryants' home number was noted on the form as 28270) and everybody knew everybody, their problems especially.

In the last months of Martin's primary school days, an assessment had been conducted behind closed doors. One of the documents they considered was the last of the "follow-up" visits conducted by the Education Department assessor in mid-November. The teacher noted there had not been any improvement in Martin's behaviour or class work, other than spelling, which seemed some minor consolation, since the middle of the year when he had returned to school after his fireworks accident.

The assessment went on:

> *He seemed to have lost interest in school work in general. He was still having reading problems, being in the bottom reading group in the class and seemed unable to retain many maths concepts. I spoke to Martin who had a noticeable intermittent head shake. I asked Mr [name removed] about this and he said it was a recent development and he felt that Martin should control it as he had threatened him with a visit to the principal if it continued, and Martin stopped the head shaking. I looked at Martin's folder, which was extremely untidy and disorganized. There was a great deal of unfinished work in the folder and it was obvious that Martin was finding the general level of work set very difficult. Martin told me he was looking forward to going to New Town High School next year.*

It was the last sentence which presented the problem. Martin Bryant, as difficult as he could be, was entitled to continue into high school and finish his education. Besides, there was a legal and moral obligation to accommodate him. There had to be a way of dealing with the problem of his impact on a class of 30-odd male peers, who were inevitably drawn into the fray either directly or simply because it interrupted the normal functions of a classroom.

The answer, it seemed, was a new special unit created to harvest students with difficulties from many classes and place them in a single, "junior opportunity group". The idea, new to the school but not to state education systems around Australia, had two goals: it would remove a single problem for the greater good but also allow a more focused attention on the children involved, among them problem students like Martin, as well as others with physical problems such as blindness or deafness. Some had simply slipped behind their peers. But it had its drawbacks. It set him apart from the others, highlighting the problems they sought to overcome. For Martin, being singled out had a profound psychological effect: he wanted to be included, not set apart and corralled away from the pack. Just as his victims felt harassed by this strange boy, he too felt picked on, bullied and intimidated by their responses to him, unable to understand that his actions were inappropriate and self-defeating.

Now he had been made an exhibit, he responded by withdrawing further. The theatrical high-voltage child of primary school quickly became reclusive. Contemporaries reflecting on the boy they knew at school would struggle to recall anything specific about him other than his blond hair, ice-blue eyes and isolated nature. He did not participate in school activities or sports. There would be no team photographs of him. At the school camp – if he went at all – Martin would sleep in his own tent.

"I knew the face as soon as I saw it, but I honestly can't remember anything he did at school," one former student would say in the rush of media interviews following the massacre. "The kids in the special class more or less stuck to themselves, and that was their whack, and no one in the mainstream of the school had anything to do with them. Kids can be the biggest bastards in the world, and if you're not in with them, they'll make your life a misery. So they kept to themselves."

While others in the special class responded positively to the extra attention, some returning to the mainstream school body and a few going on to some form of tertiary education, Martin Bryant made little or no progress. He wasn't the only one, according to teachers who dealt with him and spoke out in bewilderment after the killings. Even in a class of 15 teenagers who remained in the "senior special unit", Martin kept his own company, often sitting by himself in a corner for hours at a time, reading magazines or drawing. Art and woodwork seemed his only joy although he would dismiss any interest when questioned by police and lawyers after the killings.

The level of his intellect was bewildering to those with whom he dealt. He clearly had learning difficulties but he was also manipulative, at times able to discern that doing just enough prevented repercussions in class. He was also impeccably polite most of the time to adults, which, when coupled with his raw good looks and athletic build, often gave the initial impression of a young man who was comfortable with himself and the world when the opposite was true.

"He was a kid I would never call retarded, but he was slow," one teacher told the media. "He was definitely slow. He was slower to conceptualise. He showed no initiative. He didn't have strong retention of information, but he was not thick. He should have been able to get along; except he was the most isolated person I ever worked with. It was partly his personality; he was inward-looking and reserved. He was not disruptive or naughty ... just dreadfully reserved. He was very bland. He did not do things that would draw attention to himself."

Bryant presented with other tendencies often seen in the autism spectrum: he had difficulty meeting or retaining eye contact and was obsessively neat and compulsive about cleanliness, a trait his mother had noticed even before he started school when the little boy insisted she wash her hands before handling his food. But it was Martin's social dislocation that bothered most of his teachers, who found even deaf students in the class had better communication skills:

"I would say he was socially disabled, not intellectually disabled, and of his own choice. He had a good facility of language, a good vocabulary, yet he spoke very slowly and deliberately," one said. "He had no soul mate ... no one to whom he was close. I turned myself inside-out but I never really reached him."

Another teacher would remember a child who could be obstinate, refusing to accept reality or believing something deemed implausible no matter what evidence was put before him.

"I had never come across a kid like that. Mostly they were open and inquiring. He would shut off. I thought when he pleaded not guilty he could be saying; 'No, that did not happen.' He doesn't stand out as a kid with a behaviour problem. The main reason I can remember him is the striking physical appearance. I daresay if I had a classroom of kids only with fair hair and blue eyes I would not have remembered him so well."

Pressed later by forensic psychiatrist Professor Paul Mullen about his memories of school, Bryant talked about fear and loneliness. Classmates regarded his actions as provocative and his laugh silly and inappropriate but Bryant felt he was the one being bullied, as Mullen's report to the court concluded:

> Mr Bryant's memories of school are that he found it an unpleasant and distressing experience for virtually the whole of his attendance. He recalls frequently being bullied. He said "I was hazed and knocked around all the time, no-one wanted to be my friend". He only recalls one companion at school and this for a relatively brief period during his childhood. The predominant memory is of being by himself, ignored by the other children, or attended to in a bullying and frightening manner. Mr Bryant remembers both refusing to go to school because he was afraid and pretending to have various minor maladies to persuade his mother to keep him away from school. He described himself as having been "terrified" of going to school and of facing his tormentors.

These are not the memories of Carleen Bryant, however. Although freely acknowledging her son's learning difficulties, she insists that few complaints ever reached home, and that her son always went to school. Even when confronted with the school reports which talk of him urinating on other children, she writes simply: *Be fair!*

Whether this is a plea to be fair to her son or considerate of her own sense of failure is unclear although the latter is most likely. Her recollections read:

> *I'm sure that there would have been some unpleasant incidents during his school years, however Martin did not mention any to us, nor did we receive any telephone calls from teachers concerning any fights or bad behaviour. There were only two calls from high school. One was from Mr Featherstone, the music teacher who Martin admired, to say that Martin was not interested and would slide and shuffle his music book back and forth on the floor from boredom. It was decided he would not attend music class from then on. The other call was from Mr Coomb who was Martin's teacher for children with learning difficulties. He simply asked if I could make sure that Martin took his PE clothes to school each Monday. Martin didn't like competitive sports except tennis, badminton and table tennis. But he did enjoy any board games, like draughts.*

One incident did disturb her, however. One night, at the age of 14, he did not come home after school. After searching for several hours, she and Maurice raised the alarm with police, who dismissed the concern and would not list him as missing until the following morning. He arrived home at seven o'clock the next morning, his crumpled school uniform covered in pieces of foam, apparently from sleeping in an old railway carriage at the Hobart railway station. Carleen's comments best summed up her naivety or ignorance:

> *After questioning as to why he had not come home, there was no real reason given. Maurice and I could only assume there had been some unpleasant incident at school which caused him enough stress to leave. This was the only time that had caused us concern during Martin's high school years.*

By this stage, the reports on the young boy had dried up. It appeared that the school authorities felt that little more could be done. A physical education report ranked him poor in attitude and social adjustment, satisfactory at fitness and good at skill development. However, no further comments were attached.

Another from an art teacher gave him a lower pass even though his effort and conduct were marked at the lowest rung of "poor". The comments beneath read:

> *Martin has had a negative attitude towards this subject and has at times totally lost his temper and self control. It is a shame because he has ability.*

It was one of the few times in his school years that anyone had recognised a potential but by then it was too late. Martin was simply waiting to turn 16 so he could leave for good – just like his mother years before.

CHAPTER 13
Silly Marty

If there was a single incident in Martin Bryant's troubled childhood that sends shivers down the spine it is his mother's description of the day her teenage son was chased out of Port Arthur and the Broad Arrow Cafe.

The incident unfolded in 1980, during the summer holidays between primary and high school. Martin was approaching his 13th birthday and the dramatic physical and emotional changes that puberty and adolescence bring. He and two brothers who lived next door at Carnarvon Bay – or perhaps their respective dads – came up with the idea of the boys earning a little holiday pocket money by collecting sea shells and creating ornaments to sell to visitors and tourists to Port Arthur. The seven-year government restoration project of the old convict settlement had finished, and its importance – and beauty – was starting to become known through word of mouth.

As usual, Maurice played a significant role in Martin's activities, driving the boys around to nearby beaches to collect the right-shaped shells and help them soak and clean them to ensure the molluscs did not leave their distinctive smell. The simplest project was to make an ashtray with a cute shell mouse glued to the top. The ashtray base was made out of scallop shell bought in their dozens from a local fish factory. They sold their souvenirs for $1 each, as Carleen wrote excitedly:

They sold hundreds. I'm sure half the households of New Town had one.

Buoyed by their success, the boys began experimenting with more ambitious creations and came up with a combination of shells which, when glued together, resembled a bullfrog smoking a cigar. After making a few dozen they put the collection in a shoebox and walked up to the settlement with plans to sell them for 60c each.

But they struck trouble. Carleen remembers the moment vividly:

> *A local man was selling similar items in the souvenir shop, called The Broad Arrow, and this meant he was in competition with three boys trying to make a little pocket money. They were so proud of their achievement. Then some big-head official told them to leave the park. Can you imagine how disheartened they felt after spending so many hours making them.*

Ordered away, Martin Bryant never forgot the encounter, only confirming that even in this seaside paradise every joy seemed to attract a matching complication or rejection. Not long after, he angered a group of local kids so much that they chased him through the bush but instead of running away, Martin stalked them as they searched for him. Bored after an hour or so, the kids returned to whatever they were doing before – when Martin would appear suddenly from the trees, grinning inanely as he recounted in detail their every previous move.

In the weeks after the killings, some looked back and reminisced to journalists who flocked to the area about the kid they knew who tried at first to fit in but then withdrew, as he had done in the classroom:

"We were happy-go-lucky sort of fellas and he always seemed to be down in the dumps," said one. "He kept to himself. He'd be off in the bush or just looking out of his window. He kept his distance."

They called him "Silly Marty", often to his face: "One day someone said, 'Here comes that bloody simple Martin,' and it just stuck," one recalled. Others associated it with an incident one night at one of the beach parties that dotted the bay during the summer months. Martin turned up carrying a can of petrol and promptly set fire to himself. It was the firecracker incident all over again although he escaped serious injury – this time by the quick action of others who rolled the burning boy in sand. He seemed impervious to emotion, physical discomfort – or pain – often swimming in the dead of winter with snow on the ground.

While Martin remained an outsider, his sister was embraced. Unlike her brother, whom she resembled physically, Lindy had little trouble finding friends and fitting in with the local kids. By the early 1980s, she was developing an interest in horse riding and starting to invite school friends for weekend sleepovers. Her brother reacted angrily.

Martin found it increasingly difficult to find anyone to play with and only ever had one friend come to stay. His father even resorted to playing cricket on the beach opposite the house with his son day after day because no one else would. The games never lasted long because Martin would lose interest and wander off: "He was more of a worry to his father than anything else," one local said. "His father would go fishing, play cricket on the beach. He tried to be more of a kid himself to compensate for Martin not having anyone else. His father was a real nice bloke. He never treated any of us different from the way he treated his own kids."

It seemed that Maurice's only option was to shepherd his son every step of the way. They only had to walk 100 metres from their front gate to the water's edge, dragging a four-metre fibreglass dinghy with a 10-horsepower engine which they used to putter around the bay, fishing, snorkelling and, when Martin got older, diving for crayfish. As Carleen recalled:

> When Martin went fishing he always came back with a feast of seafood. I'm sure he would have liked to be a fish. We were surprised at how much calmer and relaxed he was after a dive. Dear patient Maurice would sit in that little dingy for hours, almost frozen at times, but he never complained. He would also panic if he lost the sight of Martin's air bubbles. So it was arranged that Martin came to the surface every ten minutes, to let Maurice know he was all right.

This brief exchange between Bryant and police during his official interview six weeks after the massacre captures his own feelings about the place:

Police: "Did Lindy like ... used to like going down there?"
Bryant: "Yeah Lindy loved it. Lindy had a lot of friends."
"Did you have many friends down there when you were a young fella?"
"I had friends under the water."

"On the water?"

"Sea. They were my friends, mmm, weekend used to scuba dive. Maybe once, maybe twice a day. Dad used to take me out a lot, over."

"Did Dad do any diving when you were diving or ...?"

"No."

"He'd just sort of take you out?"

"Mmm. Start the little Seagull engine up."

"Your father always encouraged you though to sort of get into the diving?"

"Yeah always."

Maurice and Jillian Williams built the first house in Carnarvon Bay, back in the 1960s. Others followed over the years, and by the time Maurice and Carleen Bryant bought the house at the end of Tasman Street in 1975, there were almost 100 houses in the bay, some weekenders and other permanent homes like the Williams's family home, where they raised their family and live in retirement.

Their eldest son Paul was a dominant figure among the local kids, including Martin Bryant, who was around the same age. Williams regrets it now but accepts that during their teenage years, he was a protagonist in the story of Martin's isolation: "I probably contributed to sending him off the rails," Paul says, afraid that his jest might somehow be at least partly true.

"There'd be 30 kids hanging around on weekends and holidays and maybe a dozen fulltime," he recalls. "There was one other kid who we didn't like but he matured. Martin never did. I tried when he first got there but ..." His answer trails off.

Paul Williams's tales of weekends and holidays at Carnarvon Bay clearly show that Bryant was spurned within a few months of his family buying the property. For the rest of his childhood, the setting remained a place of rejection, one in which his mother was remembered too, seated in the front room at her spinning wheel – or perched on the balcony with a pair of binoculars – watching her son's alienation. "She was always watching us, bitter I suppose that we wouldn't play with Martin and looking for some reason to complain about our behaviour. We called her the old possum."

Williams recalls the Bryants' outhouse as being the only one in the street in which the door opened outwards rather than inwards: "Whenever Martin went inside we'd tie it shut and rock the thing," he laughs – hesitantly – the notion not so amusing in light of the young man's actions later.

The Port Arthur settlement was a place where the local kids not only could enjoy freedom and a pristine natural environment but often got their first holiday jobs: "We all worked up there at the Port Arthur settlement at some stage, peeling potatoes or making chips; everyone but Martin. Even Lindy. She was a normal kid and hung around with the rest of us."

Then there was the ghost tour incident. Local kids would hide in the solitary confinement cells of the old jail – "It was pitch black there even in the day" – and wait for the tour guide shepherding a group of apprehensive tourists through the forbidding structure to finish his speech: "They knew at least one of us and probably several were hiding inside, and at some stage would come out and scare the shit out of them. But Martin, as usual, didn't get it. One night he started pelting apples and rocks, and they banned the lot of us. Said it was too much of a risk. They didn't know who it was but we all did."

Not all the stories are funny. Williams frowns as he relates the day Martin poked him with a speargun while the pair were diving for crays off the bay. "He could swim like a fish and scuba dive like no one else. We were down there one day and he just attacked me. I have no idea why he did it but I was bloody angry. I ripped off his mask and pulled out his mouthpiece so he had to come to the surface. If it had happened on the surface I would have smacked his head in."

Williams pauses for a moment, shakes his head and grins sideways towards his wife Susan, another Port Arthur local.

"Bet you haven't heard this one," he says mysteriously. "It didn't come out at the time but we're lucky to be alive."

Williams then relates the tale of their escape from a man he believes would have gleefully added him to his list of victims. The couple had booked the old church at Port Arthur on Saturday April 27 for their wedding. David and Sally Martin – "my second mum and dad" – had given them two nights accommodation at Seascape but they didn't take a honeymoon gift, which would have placed them at the cottage when Bryant arrived to kill the Martins.

Susan chips in: "We had a barney six months before and I cancelled the wedding on him. Can't remember what it was about but thank God it happened."

The reason Williams is so sure about his fate lies in the slash marks still visible on the front door of his parents' house at Carnarvon Bay. They were made by Bryant in the hour or so between murdering the Martins and the mayhem at Port Arthur.

"It seems Bryant had made a list. The Martins were on top and I was next. He was looking for me when he went to my parents' house."

Were there others on the list?

"They wouldn't say, so that means yes. Marion Larner was supposedly on it. She was saved by [her husband] Roger, who met Bryant at the gate and told him she wasn't home."

••••••••••••••••••••••••••

Greg is another who looks back with regret, perhaps the only person whom Martin Bryant could regard as a friend during high school and early adulthood. He will talk, but only on the proviso that we don't use his surname. Even now the spectre of Bryant's deeds hangs heavily on those who knew him, even if only briefly and in childhood.

Greg and Bryant spent days together in the special class at New Town High School, occasional nights at the Augusta Road house and even some weekends down at Carnarvon Bay between the ages of 14 and 18. It ended suddenly one afternoon when Martin stuck a spear gun tip into the top of Greg's head as he surfaced while fishing for crayfish off the rocks opposite the Bryant shack.

"I felt this sharp stab in the top of my head as I came up to the surface. I looked up and Martin was there grinning at me. I said, 'That was you, wasn't it Martin?' He laughed, and I asked why he did it. He said, 'Because I felt like it.' That was it. I punched him in the face and left. I'd had enough. I hope he rots in hell for what he did. He doesn't deserve to be alive. He was always cruel. I don't know what I saw in him; I suppose I was just sorry for him."

Greg gave a statement to police and even provided a class photo of the 18 members of the special class, including himself and Martin Bryant. The photo was never returned, and he is angry his statement was leaked to a reporter and published in part.

He is hesitant, at first, to speak about the man he befriended because he was sorry for him. Bryant was singled out, even in the special class because he was different; a loner who, just as he had in his primary school days, somehow found ways to annoy the others.

"He used to purse his lips together all the time. It was a strange expression as if he was trying to think of something he couldn't quite grasp. That's how he got his nickname."

Nickname?

"They called him 'Rubber Lips'."

"There was a big fight in the room one day," Greg recalls. "Wayne had Martin up against the wall and punched the absolute shit out of him. The bastard deserved it but the teacher broke it up before things got too bad."

Why did Bryant deserve a beating?

"Because he found ways constantly to annoy the others. He was irritating."

Greg tells stories about Bryant's cruelty to animals. In his police statement, he told of an incident on the way home to the Bryant house one afternoon when Martin spotted a cat, caught the animal and tried to pull it apart with his hands. He didn't like cats, he told Greg, who stopped him and forced him to let the terrified animal go.

Another time Martin rode on the back of a goat in a neighbourhood property. "I thought it was pretty funny at the time but I realise looking back that he was just being cruel. He tried it a second time and got his balls hooked up on the goat's horns."

Greg watched Martin's parents try in their own ways to deal with their troubled son. Maurice, he said, was "a good man", patient although he sometimes lost his cool, particularly when Martin acted the fool in the family car.

"He tried to grab the wheel a few times, once when his mum was driving. Maurice lost his temper and told him to stop being a fucking clown. But mostly he was patient. His mum was the same. She was nice. So was Lindy."

"I suppose you don't notice things when you're a teenager. I was there to be with Martin."

The biggest impression at the Augusta Road house was the cleanliness. It was a picture of domestic order, always neat as if nothing should be touched. Martin's bedroom was at the back of the house in an upstairs attic where he could see out over the neighbourhood. On occasions, he slept in a downstairs room also at the rear of the house.

Guns were the other aspect that scared Greg. They both had air rifles. One day Martin pointed his gun at Greg, pulled the trigger and laughed. It wasn't loaded.

At night during weekends at Carnarvon Bay, Greg watched with horror as Martin stood on the beach in the pitch dark and fired at yachts moored in the bay. "He'd just fire out into the dark, out into the water. He didn't care."

So why were they friends for so long? Greg thinks for a time then says quietly: "I didn't have many friends myself."

Life was clearly difficult for teenage boys placed in a special class, isolated and yet clearly marked as difficult or inadequate. He still feels the sting: "It wasn't easy. Other kids can be cruel in their own way. I wasn't there all the time. I went and did tech drawing and social sciences in other classes, things like that. I don't think Martin did.

"And then I got out," he adds. "I made something of myself. I'm a surveyor's assistant."

There's something else that bothers Greg; his nine-year-old daughter: "She has Asperger's syndrome," he offers. "She's a very affectionate kid; she'll hug anybody. But she finds it difficult to socialise."

He doesn't mention Bryant but it's clear that he is aware – and naturally sensitive – about the aspects of Bryant's behaviour that fall within the Asperger's spectrum.

"Lots of people have Asperger's, don't they," he says in more of a statement than a question. "And people with Asperger's are supposed to be really clever at other things."

Greg's poignant anxieties reflect those of so many parents: many children have difficulties – some with potentially greater handicaps than those exhibited by Martin Bryant – and will mature to live fruitful and fulfilling lives.

Is it a lottery, and there but for the grace of God go I?

CHAPTER 14
A Family Myth

Maurice Bryant had always made sound and fortuitous financial decisions when it came to real estate. His first house bought with Carleen, at Claremont, had doubled in value and helped them buy into a bigger, family home in New Town, and their hard-working and frugal lifestyle combined with increasing city prices had given them the freedom to buy at Carnarvon Bay when the opportunity arose. But in March 1982, after six memorable years of summer holidays and weekends at Port Arthur, he would make a miscalculation – and in doing so create a family myth that would figure large in his son's rampage 14 years later.

Frank Heron was a Hobart truck driver in his mid 40s, working 18-hour days and not seeing much of his family. Port Arthur seemed to offer a solution to his attempts to recast his life before it was too late. He already owned a plot of land at Carnarvon Bay but the Bryant's block was a much better option for what he was trying to achieve. It was higher ground, relatively flat and directly across the road from the water, which meant he could get easy access to his intended new professional pursuit – fishing. The Bryant family didn't seem to be using their land other than their letting their young boy Martin sleep in the tiny timber humpy, which was on the property when they bought it.

He approached Maurice and asked if he would sell. It seemed another fortuitous opportunity. Martin and Lindy had both indicated an interest in horse riding but the front block was not suitable to run animals. They still had the cottage on the back plot and, cashed up, they could begin searching for a block back in the hills to run a couple of horses. Maurice agreed to sell for $7000, which although not a bonanza was a tidy profit on his $4500 purchase four years before. And they still had the house on the block behind, which, based on the sale price of the front block, would have doubled in value.

A month earlier another property had come on the market several kilometres the other side of the Port Arthur township. The place was huge – almost 4.5 hectares – and ideally wedged between the Arthur Highway and the foreshore of Long Bay, a rundown but tranquil setting perfect for a small farmhouse and paddock to keep horses. It was owned by an old wharfie named Cornelius Walsh, who was selling up to move back to town as his health failed, something he had made known around the district. He raised it one day in idle conversation with nearby general store manager Glenn Martin, who then told his parents. His father, David Martin, was a former colleague of Walsh, having worked on the apple boats back in Hobart before he and his wife Noelene, better known as Sally, had opened a small business in Hobart. In 1979, they moved again, this time to Port Arthur where they bought a farm just above the historic settlement on the road leading to the main tourist lookout. They were now looking for a tourist-style business, like a guest house, to take advantage of the trade, which was starting to grow as the restoration of the Port Arthur site as a historical tourist attraction progressed. The Walsh place sounded perfect, and a deal was struck on November 30, when the documents were signed to sell the property, Seascape, for $44,000.

Maurice Bryant was also aware the property was on the market but was finding difficulty raising the money to meet the asking price. When he missed out, Maurice, still searching for a property for horses, offered to buy part of the Martins' farm at the top of the hill before the road descended into the bay, but the family wasn't interested, given that their own son, Daren, was working the property.

Maurice had missed out and spent the summer of 1983 fuming at his bad luck. Martin, it seems, misunderstood the disappointment. During his police interview, he was asked about the sequence of events. Although he denied the family wanted to buy Seascape, he recalled his own desire to negotiate buying part of the Martins' farm off Safety Cove Road. This is a condensed version of what he told them:

"I would've loved to have bought the Martins' farm next door to the Larsons'. It's beautiful. I asked them a few times but Mrs Martin didn't want to sell. She said, 'No I'm not interested in helping out. That upset me that did."

The Martins' eldest son, Glenn, confirmed that the teenager came knocking once and asked to buy the property but had been turned away by Mrs Martin, who, understandably, didn't take his request seriously.

Frank Heron meanwhile had finished his home – double brick with three bedrooms and a view over the peaceful bay – and had spent the year not only overseeing the construction but observing the previous owners. "Queer," he responds when asked to recall Martin. It is meant in the traditional form. The boy was strange, rarely responding when spoken to other than with a sloppy grin, shuffling his feet and looking at the ground. Frank caught him a few times hiding in a dry creek bed across the road from where he would take pot shots at passing cars with an air rifle. The younger sister was a sweet thing, he recalls, sometimes playing with his daughter who was roughly the same age.

What struck Frank were the parents. Both were clearly affected by their troubled son. The mother, Carleen, would sit in the front window of their cottage, spinning wool, as if waiting expectantly for something to happen that she needed to either witness or respond quickly to. The father was entirely different. Frank didn't see the man who sat fishing all day with his son. Time had wearied Maurice Bryant by then. Instead he saw the man who hid his troubles behind the "happy go lucky" screen of alcohol.

"You'd hear him singing as he came through the trees from the pub," he says, hesitating to describe the man as having an alcohol problem. "One day a couple of the local boys found him face up in a blackberry bush. He was sound asleep, and they had to carry him home to the cottage."

Frank saw Maurice in the local pub occasionally where the subject of Martin was inevitably raised: "He seemed to speak about him as if he was someone else's kid; Carleen's boy rather than his own. He'd say something like, 'What's that bastard done now?' but that was about it. It wore him out, and the alcohol was a way to escape for a while."

Frank Heron's own plans were also falling apart. The house was finished and the kids seemed to enjoy the place but his marriage was under pressure and he decided to sell. "I stuck a peg in the ground, and the Bryants couldn't get there quick enough. They got a fair deal. I sold it for what the place cost me."

Less than a year after selling out, Maurice repurchased the block complete with a new house he had never intended building. It cost him $37,500 for a place he had sold for $7000 the previous year, and forced the sale of the family's original house (for $12,800) to ensure it did not put them back in too much debt.

Instead, the horses they had bought were agisted to a property just up the hill owned by Roger Larner and his wife Marion which happened to be next door to the Martins' place, a constant reminder of the deal that never occurred. To make matters worse, Maurice's troubled son quickly lost interest in riding.

During Bryant's brief appearance at the trial after the murders, his lawyer John Avery confirmed there had been an ongoing bitterness by Bryant, fed by his father. He told the court:

"It appears that this was indeed a family myth about their misfortunes, and according to Mrs Bryant, her late husband would often complain to Martin Bryant of the damage to the family inflicted by what was viewed as the double dealing of the Martin family."

The terrible irony was that when Maurice and Carleen finally sold out of Carnarvon Bay in February 1993, after it was clear the children had moved on and they needed cash for retirement, the couple got $81,500 for the place by the water. Far from a financial disaster, the family had yet again doubled its money on a property deal. But money was not the problem.

CHAPTER 15
The Story Changes

"Do you know David and Sally Martin?" The question seems to come out of the blue to Bryant, who has been telling the two police inspectors, Paine and Warren, about what he did on Sunday, April 28, the day of the fire at Seascape. He has told them he'd woken up at the Clare Street house with Petra before sending her home to her family and then driving to Roaring Beach in the yellow Volvo to go surfing. They seem to accept his story, or at least haven't challenged the details as he tells of stopping on the way down towards Port Arthur to buy petrol, a cup of coffee and tomato sauce before turning off the highway at Taranna and taking the snaking road to the isolated surf beach which looks back across the bay towards Bruny Island. Nor do they question his incongruous revelation that he has not taken a wetsuit or a towel or even waxed his board, let alone attempted to go surfing in the benign ocean conditions that day without a wave in sight. The only people he says he saw were two other surfers but they never spoke because he chose to go to the other end of the beach.

Now they want to know about the Martins, the focus of his frustration all these years. Still, it is a question Bryant knows is coming, and there is no harm in admitting the obvious, is there?

"Oh yeah, I knew them well."

"When did you last see them?" John Warren isn't mincing words now. He and Ross Paine have suffered the surfing story in silence. The surfboard had probably been strapped to the top of his yellow Volvo for months, and yet he expects them to believe he had stripped off, gone surfing on a board with no grip before standing shivering for 20 minutes on the beach to dry off because he had no towel. It is as if he has made it up on the spot, rather than planned it, so ridiculous it can hardly be called an alibi.

"I saw them I reckon back in 1991 when I saw them in town. They were going to Calvary Hospital to visit some friends."

"I don't believe that," Warren retorts. It is time to get serious with the bloke. He is full of bullshit.

Bryant recognises the change in tone. They know he'd been at the Seascape. He backtracks: "I went down, I went to their, their house on the Sunday but they weren't home. You said, 'last time you saw them'. You didn't say, 'Did you go and see them?' I went down to see them but they weren't there. I knocked on the door, and there was no one at the guest house."

"And that's on the Sunday you went surfing?"

"Yes. I stopped, ah, at Nubeena and got a coffee and I think I got a toasted sandwich, too. Then I left and drove around past Port Arthur and went and, went in to see the Martins. I thought I'll call in and see them and have a chat to them."

Ross Paine takes over.

"So what you're saying is you wouldn't have ever spoken to them for some years?"

"Yeah, that's right. Would've been good to have seen them but there was no answer at the door."

"What about the Martin boys, have you seen them recently?"

Bryant had mixed with Glenn and his younger brother, Daren, since they were kids, well sometimes. Like everything else in his childhood, it was a troubled relationship. He knew they'd barely tolerated him down at Port Arthur but he hung around, sometimes up at the Martin place up the road, sometimes diving for crays. He doesn't have any particular feelings about them, just their parents:

"Yes, I was with me girlfriend, must've been, ah, eight months ago. We were over at Eastlands doing a bit of shopping, and Glenn, Glenn Martin, that's one of the sons, we went back and had, I think it was a cappuccino, ice coffee that day at the cafeteria."

"Did you know that he had a shop there?"

"I'd known for quite a while, yeah. Me and me Mum, we used to go up to the shop and just look in, 'Oh, he must own the shop.' See him working in there, 'cos his daughter's got a shop, too, at Sandy Bay. A milk bar."

"His daughter?"

"Mmm."

"Can you remember what you said to Glenn that day or at the shop?"

"I asked for a cappuccino. 'How are you, Glenn, and how is your brother? How's your mum and dad?'"

Paine shifts the timeframe. He wants to explore the past to see if there are links to the murders.

"Did your mum and dad ever want to buy Seascape?"

"No, no."

"Did you ever want to buy it?"

"No, umm, I would've loved to have bought the Martins' farm, that other one. That's just beautiful. I asked them a few times but Mrs Martin didn't want to sell."

"When did she tell you that?"

"When I was smaller, when I was about 16, 17. I talked to my mother that night, and she said, 'No, I'm not interested in helping out.'"

"Is that when the Martins bought it?"

"Yes … That upset me that did. Mmm."

Warren fills the silence as Bryant seems lost in his thoughts:

"Can you remember when the Martins bought Seascape?"

Bryant looks up: "Back in the '80s … I think they bought it."

"Did you go down there at all any time after they'd bought it?"

"Ah, this is the first time in my life that I've been down there to see them."

"What did you think about it?"

"I thought it was great, having a host farm. Worked hard all their lives, renovating, took them years to build it, renovate it and to start it all up, and it's just so sad to see. Apparently, it's burnt down. It's so sad to see it burnt down."

"So you know Seascape's burnt down?"

"Yeah. Been informed."

"Who told you that?"

"A doctor and security guards."

"What else have they told you?"

"They said that people had been burnt inside there. Mmm. So I don't know how many people were burnt inside the Seascape guest house."

Warren pauses. For a man who wants to appear so innocent, he certainly seems to know a lot. It is time to call his bluff:

"I'm just a little bit confused here, Martin, because you seem to know a little bit about, or a fair bit about, what's happened and what they've done to that place. How did you know that happened?"

"'Cos when you used to drive past you could see, you, every few weeks, while my parents had a shack, you could see them working on the place, renovating the homestead. Took 'em five or six years to build it up."

Paine moves the conversation back to the present: "Was there anyone else there at Seascape when you called in?"

The question is innocent enough but Bryant's answer changes the entire complexion of the interview:

"No, I, umm, unfortunately, I held up a car. I saw this car, I liked it and got, umm, held up the person in the car and kidnapped him."

Where did this come from? One minute Bryant is innocent of anything other than going surfing without a wetsuit and suddenly he's admitted taking a hostage. It has come from nowhere. It changes everything.

"When you say 'held up'..."

"I didn't really, didn't know whether I'd let you know," Bryant stammers, perhaps realising he's made a mistake. There is no turning back. "You're not gunna let anyone else know. You're not gunna let anyone else know?"

When Paine and Warren don't say anything, he continues: "Yeah, no, I stopped the car. I was in the Volvo. I stopped the car on the corner. There was a nice looking BMW, and I asked them to get out of the car but the ..."

Paine cut in: "How many people were in it?"

"There was a child in there, in the back, and a lady and the man. The man, I got him out the car. I had my gun with me, and I said, 'I want to take your car.' So I took his car. I got, then his wife or girlfriend got into the Volvo with the child and I left, I drove off."

"So you drove away in the BMW?"

"Yes."

"With another male person?"

"Yeah, he was in the boot. I put him in the boot of the car."

"How did he get into the boot?"

"I put him in the boot because I had a gun."

"Which gun did you have?"

"I had the, um ... that AR-15. You see, if people didn't do these unfortunate things, you guys wouldn't have a job."

"Well there's a lot of truth in that Martin, let me tell you."

"And where did this take place Martin, sorry?"

"At the Fortescue Bay turnoff, just, oh about three or four minutes away from the Martins' farm."

"Why did you put the man in the boot?"

"Oh, because to take him hostage. I thought I'd get in less trouble if I got caught having him in the boot, but I don't know, I just thought, I was a bit worried that if he didn't go, he'd go off in my car."

"And why'd you think you'd be in less trouble?"

"I didn't, I didn't want to shoo...". Bryant stopped himself short of admitting using his gun. "'Cos I wouldn't have got caught, you see. He would've gone off in my car, rang the police straight away. I thought I'd take him hostage and let him go later after taking the car for a spin but, and when I drove along, I thought I'd go down and see the Martins."

"What trouble did you think you were in?"

"Oh, it just came to me to take, take this car, get hold of this car and take it for a drive, and it just felt good."

"Right. And where did you drive then?"

"I drove full speed. It was about, I was going about 140ks up the road and went into Seascape. Just drove down there in the BMW. I remember skidding on some grass, and I had a heap of petrol, had some petrol with me. I put some petrol in the BMW."

"And what happened then?"

"Well, what happened then, I knocked on the door to see the Martins but there was no answer. And what happened is I remember the explosion."

"Sorry?"

"I don't know whether I lit the car up or not but there was an explosion."

"Where was the man that was?"

"He must've been trapped in the boot, the hostage."

"How do you feel about that, Martin?"

"Pretty awful. Mmm."

CHAPTER 16
Lawn Mower Man

It came as no surprise to the staff at New Town High School when Martin Bryant left for good on Friday May 6, 1983. The next day was his 16th birthday, and there was no sense in continuing the frustration of his teachers, the naive despair of his parents or his own despondency and silent anger. He and his family faced a bleak future, and there was no more the education system could do.

Even the weekends down at Carnarvon Bay had become intolerable as Martin reacted more frequently and more violently to his frustrations, although he was happy when his father took him out on the water. Sometimes they would go out twice a day, and he was now old enough to scuba dive alone. He surprised himself and his parents when he passed the diving theory exam. But there was little joy back on land where his run-ins with other shack kids were becoming more frequent, epitomised by the way he ruined their fun during the tourist season.

Maurice had given his son an air rifle for his 14th birthday. It was the worst decision he ever made because it introduced Martin to the power of firearms, however harmlessly. It coincided with a marked change in behaviour, from an annoying young but ultimately harmless boy to a potentially destructive teenager. Martin took to hiding in a creek bed alongside the house and firing at passing traffic or wildly out into the bay at night. There were also shooting incidents back at Augusta Road, where Martin now occupied an upstairs bedroom at the back of the house where he could look out over the neighbourhood. There is a chilling story of the day he shot a parrot out of a tree then walked up to the dead bird and fired several more slugs into its head. He was also blamed for untying boats from moorings. It was around this time that his school mate Greg ended their friendship after Martin stuck the point of a spear gun into the top of his head.

The Larner farm is at the crest of the Sandy Cove Road hill before it tilts down into the bay. The property occupied one corner of the turnoff to Palmers Lookout, a peak several hundred metres above the bay, and across the road from the Martin property, coveted by the Bryants. When their dreams of a property died, Maurice and Carleen had agisted their two horses, Tambora and Delta, at the Larner place where Marion Larner also taught the Bryant kids to ride. But only Carleen, and occasionally Lindy, would retain an interest in horses. Martin couldn't even fit a bridle and found it difficult to stay on the horse. He preferred the solitary nature of the ocean where his mistakes were not seen.

Aged 16, he felled dozens of plantation trees on the Larner property but instead of confronting the boy, Roger offered him a job mowing lawns. It lasted a few months before Bryant shredded a lemon tree and ripped up a crop of carrots.

The decision to take Martin out of school was vindicated in February 1984 when Maurice and Carleen took him to a clinical psychiatrist, ostensibly to assess him for a pension. Dr Eric Cunningham Dax was an esteemed psychiatrist who had helped establish community mental health awareness services in Tasmania as well as a research unit. His long career, which had begun in England in the 1930s, included the use of art as a treatment component in mainstream psychiatry and a collection of artworks by people who had experienced mental illness or psychological trauma. The collection now numbers more than 12,000 pieces. Even though he had retired and lived in Melbourne, Cunningham Dax, now in his late 70s, continued to travel to Tasmania to see patients, among them a teenage Martin Bryant. He had no hesitation in supporting the application for a pension.

Carleen says the pension was only part of the reason for the assessment. She and Maurice were desperate to find a solution to the growing problem which was placing their marriage under pressure. Martin's jealousy of his sister had reached new heights, particularly when they were at Carnarvon Bay, where he began fielding telephone calls seemingly to prevent her bringing friends.

> *Martin had been very nasty and aggressive to his sister Lindy's friends. This had been going on for years. He would even hang up the phone if anyone called to speak with Lindy. Maurice and I knew the reason. Martin had no close friends of his own and he was hurting and very jealous. In desperation we took Martin to see Dr Cunningham Dax. It didn't take him long to see that Martin had a problem. Martin was not able to concentrate on what Dr Dax was saying and interrupted him to talk about the age of the house and the fireplace in the room. After a few more consultations Dr Dax said Martin would be unemployable as he would upset and annoy people to the extent he would always be in trouble. He would have to be put on a disability pension.*

Cunningham Dax, who died in 2008, made an even more profound assessment and warning. His surviving case notes state:

> *Cannot read or write. Does a bit of gardening and watches TV ... Only his parents' efforts that prevent further deterioration. Could be schizophrenic and parents face a bleak future with him.*

Carleen didn't mention this in her account although it was clearly on her mind over the years. As Professor Mullen, the defence forensic psychiatrist who assessed Bryant after the massacre and found him to be sane, pointed out she misinterpreted Cunningham Dax's warning as a pronouncement that he was schizophrenic, which clouded later assessments:

> *There are subsequent references to Mr Bryant having a schizophrenic illness and of being a paranoid schizophrenic in the records of Dr Mather (1991) and Dr PM McCartney (1991). These diagnostic formulations, it transpired, were not the results of the doctors own conclusions, but based on the report of Mr Bryant's mother that he had been diagnosed by Dr Cunningham Dax as suffering from this illness. This was a misunderstanding on Mrs Bryant's part and it is this misunderstanding*

which led to an opinion by Dr Cunningham Dax that Mr Bryant might develop schizophrenia being transmuted into a diagnosis of this severe mental illness.

Maurice Bryant again resorted to his own experiences to find a solution for his troubled son. He was still working at the docks but was senior enough to organise roster changes so he could work late into the night or in the early hours of the morning to spend the days with Martin. Together they built up a small business selling door-to-door vegetables grown at Augusta Road and cream provided by a dairy farm at Port Arthur where Martin would fill a five-litre bucket and transfer it into small plastic containers, which were then sold back in Hobart. They also set up a lawn mowing round and quickly gathered a dozen or so regular customers, mainly elderly pensioners who were glad of the cheap help. Maurice was doing what he knew, crafting an existence by supplying small needs, only this time it was for his son. It wasn't the money so much as a means to keep Martin in check. It was clear their son would have to be managed all his life.

The neighbours could see what was going on and sympathised, at least to a degree. Despite his oddities, Martin wasn't regarded as a threat even if he was inappropriate from time to time. Stella Sampson was one: "I think, because it was fairly obvious to him that Martin would have been limited in his choice of work, that that is why Maurice bought the little place. He used to take him down at weekends, just the two of them, and they used to grow vegetables. He'd front up on our doorstep about 6 o'clock every Sunday evening with an overnight bag full of vegies. Occasionally, he'd also have some home-made butter or lovely thick cream that I think he'd got from the locals."

Restaurant owners also remember father and son fronting up with ducks for sale. George Haddad ran Capers Restaurant in the Cat and Fiddle Arcade in Hobart where a number of hawkers plied their wares, including herbs, eggs, vegetables: "He appeared to be slow-witted, but you really don't make a study of a young fellow who's coming along with his dad to exchange a few ducks for a few bucks," he recalled of Bryant to the media in the days following the killings.

The Heidenreich family was another who knew the Bryants and regarded Martin with a level of sympathy. John Heidenreich was a Lutheran pastor who often bought vegetables from Bryant, joking that his wife's young boyfriend was at the door: "He would go bright red. He was such a nice fellow," Heidenreich told one newspaper. His daughter Heidi was friends with Lindy, and regarded her brother as quiet and shy. She would cry at the revelation that he was responsible for the massacre.

There was a visual conflict with Bryant. He was tall, slim and good looking with longish curly hair, high cheekbones and a broad smile – the classic Aussie surfie. But his good looks were in some ways a bane because, to those who met him, when he opened his mouth, the reality did not meet the expectation. He read the disappointment as rejection, even revulsion.

CHAPTER 17
The Man in the Hat

Fortune doesn't only favour the brave. It can also, by chance, fall at the feet of the incapable, the damaged and the undeserving. Likewise, opportunity is not always embraced for good or to enhance a life but can also be harnessed to aid retribution and cause ill. Let's call it misfortune.

Such is the case in the Martin Bryant saga. If fate dealt its hand through the crimes and transportation to Van Diemen's Land of Richard Cordwell and Eliza Fitzgerald then chance – a roll of the dice – came in the form of a man named George Adams.

The iconic figure of Australian gambling, the "man in the hat" who created the Tattersall's gambling empire, played a pivotal role in the events long after his death simply because he had spent his life making money, playing politics and spreading bonhomie and financial aid for the needy in equal measure but, either through choice or inability – almost certainly the latter – had no children to whom he could leave his empire. Instead it was distributed, firstly to his closest advisers and friends but ultimately to thousands as two or three generations passed. Its effect spread beyond familial surety and the safety of gratitude to the vagaries of luck. There, the treasure now measured in its millions found a man who would use the legacy to destroy.

The day after his death on September 23, 1904, the four men anointed by Adams to be the trustees of his estate met in the company's offices at

77 Collins Street, Hobart, to discuss the future of the operation and the need to keep the business flourishing rather than prepare for a sell-off. Their own futures depended on it as much as anything else. They were Adams's nephew, William James Adams, his general manager David Harvey, and two solicitors, William Findlay of Hobart and Gerald Barry of Sydney. The will, read out a week later in front of relatives at Adams's grand home, Highfield Hall, in Murray Street, was clear enough although over the next century there would be numerous legal challenges and family spats over its carve-up, such is the debilitation of wealth on the human spirit.

Each of the men in the room was a beneficiary of the document; not a cash handout accumulated from the profits of what many regarded (and still do) as the ruin of others, but an ongoing share of the business devised to ensure the company's operations continued, their fortunes linked to the prosperity of the business and the legend of the Australian thirst for gambling.

Adams and Harvey were given one-tenth of the annual net profits, and Findlay and Barry one-twentieth. The rest was distributed to men who had helped Adams carve his name into the history books, such as the company sweeps manager Elliot Edward Grant, who got one-tenth, as did a business associate Thomas Lyons. Another series of other men, most notably the then Tasmanian premier Sir Edward Braddon, the chief secretary and Braddon's predecessor Sir Philip Fysh, the former chief secretary Henry Rooke and Upper House backbencher Alfred Page got one-twentieth as did Sydney businessmen Henry Thorpe and John Curran. The rest was divided between the staff, and a sum was kept to pour back into the business and donate to charities.

It was neat and effective, as seen a century later when the company was floated on the stock exchange for what had become a list of almost 2500 beneficiaries, each with a share in the Australian passion for gambling and hope that their numbers would one day come up. None of the descendants of the original beneficiaries objected to the float because each would benefit greatly by doing as George Adams had done years before – give the public a piece of the pie. Many, however, reacted bitterly to having their identities revealed publicly after so many years, their shares now worth, in some cases, tens of millions. To understand the handout by Adams and its subsequent, unforeseen impact, it is necessary to know the basics of his classic rags to riches story.

George Adams was born on March 14, 1839 in Redhill, a village in Hertfordshire north of London, barely 50 kilometres from Richard Cordwell's birthplace. There were other similarities between the two men although they would lead greatly different lives. Both were born into poor working-class families (Adams was the fourth son of a farm labourer William Adams and his wife Martha Gilbey) and both were teenagers when they emigrated to Australia. But this is where their life stories diverge – one to fame and wealth but no heirs; the other to infamy and poverty but a large familial legacy.

Cordwell came alone in chains aboard a convict ship. Adams came with his parents and three brothers, Charles, William and John, virtually penniless but free. Farm life had been difficult for the family of six, particularly since the year George was born when crops across England failed. Then, in 1846, came the repeal of the Corn Laws – tariff legislation which protected English farmers from cheaper imported corn and grain from North America – and farms began either closing or turning their land from crops to grazing. Hundreds of labourers lost their jobs.

William Adams stuck it out for another nine years until 1855 when, faced with an uncertain future, his family boarded the ship Constitution packed with 370 emigrants, mostly labourers and mechanics looking for a new life in the colonies. It was a journey made almost a century later by another young Englishman seeking a new and better life – Maurice Bryant.

That chance never came for 25, who died of smallpox, typhus, pneumonia, whooping cough, dysentery and erysipilis (a deadly form of cellulitis) onboard or during the two months the passengers and crew spent in quarantine after arriving in Sydney Harbour on May 26. A monument, crafted by four immigrant stonemasons, still stands at North Head as a memorial to those who died, their bodies sewn into bags and buried in bush graves by survivors.

William Adams and his family escaped the disease and settled quickly in a city still captured by the romance and expectation of the Victorian gold rush. They resisted following other families to the fields of Bendigo and Ballarat, instead sticking to the small-scale farming they knew best. Adams was still a market gardener in the inner west of Sydney when he died at the age of 91, as was at least one of his sons.

Not young George, who, after a time driving stagecoaches for Cobb & Co, joined the gold rush throng and headed for Queensland to try his luck – a notion that would become the hallmark of his business career. His early adult years were unspectacular and gave no indication of the mark Adams would leave on society, other than a man who was unfazed by hard work and acquiring new skills. Although he made some money, by all accounts it was far from the fortune he was seeking. He returned to NSW and laboured on sheep farms, part-owning a property near Crookwell, but also trying his hand at jobs such as stock dealer, saddler, baker and even confectioner before turning his hand to being a butcher and setting up shop in Goulburn. He had also found a wife, marrying a Sydney lacemaker named Fanny Franklin in June 1858.

Adams's life changed in 1875 when he bought the Steam Packet Inn, at Kiama on the southern coast of NSW, a ramshackle weatherboard building overlooking the main bay whose customers consisted mainly of cattlemen – hardly the basis to build a fortune. Adams's real interest lay in nearby Sydney, and he would regularly hire a coach to take him to the city where he became a frequent and popular figure during race meetings, particularly at O'Brien's Hotel in Pitt Street where the Hilton Hotel now stands.

The hotel hosted a private club called Tattersall's, which had taken its name from the English bloodstock agents and met in rooms behind the main "Tin Bar" that fronted Pitt Street. As well as the normal functions of a club, members would conduct sweepstakes among themselves during major race meetings – a tradition now played out in almost every office building in Australia each November for the Melbourne Cup.

An advertisement in *The Sydney Morning Herald* on May 13, 1858, is regarded as the beginnings of the club, which is now based in ornate rooms above Elizabeth Street overlooking Hyde Park, where Australia's first horseracing meetings took place. It read:

> **TATTERSALLS, late of Mayor's Inn, Pitt Street**
> *A meeting of subscribers to the above rooms will be held on May 14 at 8pm to appoint a committee of management for the current year.*

The club was well established by the time Adams came on the scene. He was a large, square man with red hair and an equally big personality – "chunky, chesty, fiery-whiskered", as he was described. Adams quickly became a welcome addition to the club; a larger than life figure who often remarked how he dreamed of owning the place. It happened in the most unusual fashion when he was presented with the hotel a few years later by three friends – George Hill, Bill Archer and George Loseby – who had bought the lease on his behalf and simply told him to pay them back when he could afford to do so. Adams accepted the unexplained largesse and got his break. He renamed the watering hole Adam's Tattersall's Hotel (later Tattersall's Family Hotel) and began building the lottery business by opening it to the public, manoeuvring around a long-established ban on lotteries because it didn't depend on the luck of a draw but the performance of a horse.

The first public sweepstake was in 1881; 25,000 tickets sold at five shillings each with a prize of £900 on the Sydney Cup won, prophetically, that year by a horse named Progress. The business boomed, as did Adams, who not only repaid his backers but later acquired the freehold and refurbished the hotel, installing the famous Marble Bar (recently dismantled and rebuilt in the new Hilton). He also invested widely in real estate and industry, including two collieries and several electricity plants, and built the now-demolished Palace Theatre next to his hotel.

In 1892, his fortunes changed again when sustained opposition by church groups persuaded the NSW Government to pass laws banning the postal delivery of letters containing sweep investments. It was the beginning of a roller-coaster ride for the operation, which would walk the line between generous contributor to charities and the accusations, particularly among church groups, that it traded on the misfortune and moral frailties of others. Adams moved to Queensland the following year but the church opposition followed, and the state government there used the Post and Telegraph Act to block Tattersall's from using the mail to take wagers. Victoria followed and there seemed nowhere to go. By now there were other sweepstakes businesses, which all gradually crumbled under the legislative onslaught. But not Adams and Tattersall's.

The white knight came from the far south in the form of Hobart businessman Thomas Lyons, a director of the struggling Bank of Van Diemen's Land, which had crashed amid the international financial crisis in 1892-93. The bank owned a large amount of property, which, if sold off in a fire sale, would be disastrous. Instead, Lyons suggested a public lottery, run by Adams, with 100,000 tickets. First prize was an office building known as Miller's Corner, second prize the Orient Hotel and third and fourth bank premises. There were 221 prizes in all.

The one-off event was so successful that Adams moved his operation from Queensland and began running sweepstakes on races being held along the east coast of the mainland. The number of tickets varied between 10,000 and 25,000.

The landscape changed again in 1897 when legislation was created for a more permanent licence for Adams alone that would ensure the lotteries were overseen by the government in return for a payment to treasury. Churches again raised a protest, which almost succeeded. The legislation survived a tight vote in Parliament with the aid of four MPs – Braddon, Fysh, Rooke and Page – whose support collectively would earn them 20 per cent of Adams' posthumous generosity. Legend has it that Adams paid £10,000 into the Treasury a few days later, counting out the contribution in cash.

It was a great economic decision for Adams and Tasmania, with his business accounting, at times, for almost half the state's revenue. For the next seven years, George Adams was king of Hobart, although controversy would erupt again in 1902 following Federation when the combined opposition to Adams from the mainland states and churches attempted to thwart his operation by banning any mail addressed specifically to him or addressed to the offices in Collins Street, which was the only way people could buy tickets. He got around the problem by getting mainland newsagents prepared to take the lucrative risk of being ticketing agents to have signs in their windows mentioning relatives in Tasmania looking for correspondence, hence the phrase "all my aunt". In one week there were 6000 letters delivered to Tattersall's in Hobart, only 47 of which were posted from within Tasmania. None after 1902 were addressed to Adams himself, and many were delivered to the homes of his managers. Nowadays the remaining few envelopes, crossed with red ink and punctured from being spiked, are collector's items on eBay.

Adams had become a rich and powerful man far beyond the boundaries of Hobart, but for all his success he had one, personal significant failing in life – the lack of an heir. In 1883, just as Adams's fortune had begun to boom, Fanny, his wife of 25 years, died "without issue", as the terminology of the day referred to children. Three years later, at the height of his fame in Sydney, Adams married Norah Louie Malone at Randwick. She was still with him in 1903 when his lifestyle and genetics finally caught up with him in the form of a massive stroke that left him bed-ridden and almost incapable of speech. History would have been very different if his will had not been finalised two years beforehand when he decided that there were two phases of his life which required acknowledgment – his Sydney beginnings and his Hobart crowning glory.

In 1901, perhaps aware his health was failing, Adams –"of Bulli and of the Marble Bar Pitt Street, both in the state of NSW, and of Collins Street in the state of Tasmania"– sat down and tried to dissect his empire. For a man who famously described spending £32,000 building the famous bar in his Sydney hotel "a mere bagatelle", the estimated gross value of his estate at death might have been slightly disappointing. The will states that he was worth £180,000, which, even though it is the equivalent of $37 million in 2008 (using RPI comparison), was still a ludicrously low figure but a necessary understatement to avoid tax implications.

First Adams allotted £1000 each to his four trustees – nephew William Adams, manager David Harvey and lawyers Gerard Barry and William Findlay – for their troubles in agreeing to oversee a document that made them rich men. Then he dealt with those on the periphery of his generosity, prescribing a series of annual payments ranging from £100 to £500 a year for life to family and friends, including his wife Louie, his widowed stepmother, brothers Charles, William and John and their children, friends and their wives, even his bookie, Phil Glenister. Among these handouts was a bonus which perhaps showed most clearly his angst at not having children, and particularly a son. He offered an extra annuity of £500 a year to Rita, the wife of his nephew, if she bore a son and then named the boy George after his great uncle. Even if William Adams, for some reason, had a son with another woman, his great uncle was willing to pay £100 a year to the mother.

In a document that runs for 10 pages and thousands of careful descriptions and flowery caveats, the bulk of the estate was then divided into two geographic locations. The NSW legacy, businesses and real estate holdings mostly in the city block bounded by Pitt, Market, George and Park streets as well as the Bulli electricity plant and even a share in a steamboat, were largely left to his nephew and to a lesser degree his four trustees.

The carve-up in Tasmania was different. The real estate holdings, including an interest in a brewery, were left to the five men: David Harvey got half, emphasising his importance in Adams's success; sweeps manager Elliott Grant got 30 per cent; Thomas Lyons 15 per cent; and Barry and Findlay split the remaining five per cent. Adams would use a similar formula to bequeath the vast and ongoing profits of the sweepstakes business.

Finally, and significantly, Adams gave his trustees a free rein and encouragement to set aside money to contribute to charitable institutions of their choice but made it clear his intention was "for the good of any cause which has for its object the amelioration of the lot of the unfortunate, risk affected, wounded or suffering".

Adams died an admired figure, the iconic rags to riches story of a man respected for his business acumen, trusted for managing his lotteries honestly and loved for his philanthropy. His prominent grave at Cornelian Bay Cemetery bears this epitaph:

Beloved by all who knew him,
The poor, the needy and the suffering
ever found in him a true friend.

More fitting, perhaps, was a quote attributed to him: "If I had come into this world better equipped, I would have done nothing." It was a prophetic statement given what happened to his money over the next 92 years.

CHAPTER 18
The Fortune

If George Adams was the visible, boisterous pin-up boy of Australian gambling then David Hastie Harvey was its inventive, enigmatic guide, a man whose only flamboyance was his habit of breaking Cuban cigars in half before smoking them. His role in the chain of events that led to the Port Arthur massacre was, like Adams, as an innocent conduit – one that inadvertently presented Martin Bryant with the means to create a life he would otherwise have been incapable of conceiving, let alone achieving and, when that fell apart, the money to buy the weapons that would ultimately destroy the lives of those he believed represented his own failings.

David Harvey was in many ways a miniature version of his benefactor, in physical stature as well as business sense and willingness to take a calculated risk. He was a short, stout man, who, like his boss had been born and raised around London, in his case the son of a Congregational minister, born on June 3, 1855, from the northern suburb of Islington.

Harvey's journey to the colonies was very different and circuitous, as the 1980 book, *The Luck of the Draw* by Trevor Wilson, traces. After leaving school with barely an education, he took a job as a clerk in the offices of transport company Pickfords but quickly became dispirited by what he regarded as a dull future. Despite his limited schooling, Harvey had a head for figures and an ambition for something greater than a desk job.

Instead of accepting his fate, the young man took a chance and a job as a purser aboard a ship bound not for Australia but New Zealand. Like Maurice Bryant many years later, David Harvey was alone and intent on establishing his new home by acquiring land. He spent the next few years working several jobs at a time – overnight in an ironmongers and daytime in the front office of a newspaper, as well as stints as a painter and handyman – to save enough money to buy a farming property where, despite his city background, he saw his future. Harvey achieved his goal and bought a selection at Blueskin Bay, near the city of Dunedin at the bottom of the south island, but soon realised that New Zealand did not provide the excitement and adventure he was seeking. He packed his bags and, still not quite 20 years old, bought a ticket across the Tasman to NSW to start yet again.

Harvey took a job on a farm at Kiama and, according to previous books on the Tattersall's history, may have met George Adams, who owned the Steam Packet Inn, around this time. If they met, which seems probable, it did not result immediately in a professional relationship because Harvey, realising he needed to be in the city to succeed, made his way to Sydney and worked firstly for a property developer, selling land in the southern suburbs of the expanding city, and then for another stint in an ironmongers.

Then he met Adams, either by chance or because of their previous social association, in Kiama, and this time the two men joined forces. Adams had just acquired O'Brien's, changed its name and was looking to expand the sweepstakes business. David Harvey was his man. Sharp in matters arithmetic and a no-nonsense manager, he ran the back of the house while Adams lorded over the front. A partnership was forged that would create the financial empire both were craving.

In 1883, now aged 28 and firmly established in the city, Harvey married Elizabeth Caroline Packman (the same year George Adams lost his first wife, Fanny Franklin).

Elizabeth, like her husband, was born in England. Her death at the age of 92 in 1957 – three decades after her husband – indicates she was born in 1865. It matches the record of an Elizabeth Caroline who was born around August 1865 in Bromley, a south-east borough of London, not far from her husband's birthplace.

It is easy to track the ups and downs of their married life through the births of their children. Unlike his boss and benefactor, Harvey had a large family. There were eight children in all, born over a span of 22 years in a number of different locations and amid great fluctuations in fortunes. Daisy Minnie was the eldest, born in 1885 and registered in the Sydney district. Horace A. followed in 1886 (the same year Adams married Norah Malone). His birth was registered in St Peters – indicating the family had moved house in the meantime – but he died the next year, an event which would have been more traumatic than usual given that Elizabeth was heavily pregnant with daughter, Violet Florence, and gave birth in the same year, this time at a new house in Kogarah, suggesting that Harvey had kept his hand in the real estate business. The last of the initial cluster of children came in 1890 when Horace Lyonal was born, again in a new residence in nearby Rockdale. All of this occurred during the height of George Adams's early fame and prosperity in Sydney. The unchallenged clerk from Islington had found his niche.

There were no more children for six years though, the barren period coinciding with the years in which the Tattersall's business faltered because of the church protest across NSW and Queensland. Harvey had followed Adams to Brisbane but quit in 1895 when the gambling businessman decided, after Victoria too passed anti-gambling laws, to shift the operation south to Hobart. Instead, the Harveys and their three surviving children moved to Bega on the south coast of NSW where he returned to the land, at least for a time, and helped to build a home. The following year, they had their fifth child, David Hova, followed two years later by daughter Lucy.

By this time Adams had managed to re-establish himself in Hobart and, with the aid of Lyons and the four MPs, had won a permanent licence to operate from the colonial city seemingly at the bottom of the world. But he was unhappy with the business and decided he needed Harvey so he made the long journey back to NSW to personally appeal to his former manager. Harvey accepted and moved his family of five children to Hobart where he bought a rambling home at the top end of Davey Street, in the shadow of Mount Wellington, which he called Islington after his birthplace. The purchase was secured by a loan of £1820 from his boss – clearly part of the lure to come south, and one he would never have to repay.

Harvey's arrival had an immediate impact, not only in regenerating the sweepstakes but expanding the game to New Zealand even though it was illegal to buy overseas lottery tickets. Harvey helped to create a clandestine system of agents, usually tobacconists or newsagents, who sold the tickets from their shops. The tickets would then be collected by middlemen and posted to Tasmania where the lottery draw would take place, like the Australian version of the game, inside the Collins Street headquarters. The winning numbers were circulated by the same men who distributed the prizemoney, all under the guise of the euphemistic phrase, *"We Post to Hobart"*, which appeared on billboards, pamphlets and shop windows across the country. It was simply a play of the scheme which had worked so well in Australia.

In 1904, the same year George Adams died and the famous will was dispensed, David Harvey's seventh child, Harold Hastie, was born, followed three years later by the last of his children, Lorimer Escott.

In between the last two children, David Harvey decided to go home to Europe. It would be a triumphant homecoming in many regards – not unlike the journey made years later by Maurice Bryant – to return and show to themselves and their families that they had made a fist of things. In Harvey's case, his new life was a flipside of the one he left behind more than three decades before. In that time, he had turned from a poor but determined son of a church minister into a wealthy but determined man who ran a gambling empire. He would have been a wealthy man even if he had not benefited so greatly from the business success and personal failings of George Adams, although not to the same degree. His homecoming turned into a grand tour of Europe, through the galleries of Paris and Rome where he bought lavish works – if mainly copies of masterpieces – to fill his home back in Hobart.

He had now bought a new home, Manresa on Sandy Bay Road not far from where the Wrest Point Casino now stands, with a commanding position almost on the banks of the Derwent. Harvey was king in this truly Victorian family, a dour and traditional household served by an army of staff and divided by customs such as his male-only private study with its stack of newspapers posted from London, which he read meticulously from front to back, and the journey each morning into the office in his dark green Daimler driven by a chauffeur named Forsyth. His children referred to him as "the Pater", and each helped him with the family bookkeeping on Sunday mornings, often accompanying him or "the Mater" on weekly rounds to collect rent from a dozen properties scattered through the city centre. Family outings required accompanying staff lugging tables to be laden with food, and photographers hired to organise grand photos.

For a man who required such formality in his private life, Harvey was much more liberal in his business, hailed as a financial genius not only in finding ways around mainland attempts to thwart the lottery but in taxation matters. He had a hail-fellow, well-met attitude in personal dealings, trading on his London accent and habit of addressing anyone under the age of 18 as "Johnny" and anyone older as "old man".

It was his business acumen which left the biggest impression. It prompted one newspaper in 1920 to estimate his worth at £500,000 – the equivalent to $38 million in 2008 – and went on to suggest:

> *Demolish Tatts and commandeer David Hastie Harvey as Treasurer and premier and the island would be the most prosperous state in the Commonwealth.*

Of course, not everything Harvey touched turned to gold, but unlike the thousands of punters he depended on to run his thriving gambling operation, he was generally careful with his investments, preferring government loans such as war bonds as well as stock in the Tattersall's company and real estate. He insisted on keeping assets long-term once bought and living from the income they derived. Such was his meticulous nature that he carried an accounting book with him at all times, carefully noting financial moments in his business and private life, even down to the cost of shoelaces and lamp oil.

And like his benefactor, Harvey devised his own scheme designed to minimise tax – in life and after death – by splitting his empire into roughly equal portions among his wife and children. The scheme, which would become the focus of a bitter court dispute years later, hinged on the children accepting the benefit on the condition they allow their father to collect and maintain control of the income, which was then distributed to them as he saw fit.

He announced the idea in the sitting room at Manresa one evening in early 1916 to a brood ranging in age from Daisy, who was by then 31 years old, to Lorimer, who had just turned nine. Harold, who was 12 at the time, would later say: "He wanted to control it so he could guide us and we would not be spendthrifts. He would often speak to us when looking through the papers and see how some people had squandered their estates. He used to say he didn't want anything like that to happen to any member of his family." It was a sadly prophetic statement because despite his best efforts, it is exactly what would occur.

Over the next eight years, David Harvey rolled out his grand plan, first dividing ownership of the family home into equal parts, complete with a clause that they provide money "toward the upkeep of Manresa grounds, cars and servants", then his real estate legacy left by George Adams and, finally, the share in Tattersall's. The income went into a family fund and, as they grew older, into bank accounts set up for each of his children. Such was the flood of money that he bought them more properties and stock portfolios worth at least $17 million in today's values. Without touching the assets, he estimated their mini empires would guarantee each an annual income the equivalent to $600,000.

The financial superstructure did not shelter the Harveys from the harsher aspects of life in the fledgling Federation of Australia. Two of his children, Violet and David junior, both went to war in 1917. Despite the family's great wealth and influence, both held down regular jobs at the time. Violet was a nurse in Melbourne, and David jnr an apprentice electrical engineer with the Hydro Electric Corporation. Eldest daughter Daisy would train in massage and live in India for three years. Most likely it was their father's insistence on personal achievement. He had come from nothing so they should also make their own way in the world.

Unlike many families, both the Harvey children came home from the muddy battlefields of Europe. The relief appears to have softened their father's tough attitude somewhat as he began lavishing his wealth more liberally on family members. Grandchildren recalled a benevolent figure in his later years, and the two youngest children, Harold and Lorimer, were sent away to boarding school at Melbourne Grammar. Their appearance at the school in the 1920s immediately created attention, a former school friend of Lorimer's would later recount, because of the amount of pocket money they were sent each week. Most of the 100 or so boys received two shillings and sixpence (roughly $10) but 17-year-old Harold and his 15-year-old brother were getting the astonishing amount of two pounds each, equivalent to about $150 a week.

Such wealth, or at least the showmanship of it, was unheard of even within the bluestone walls of what had already become in its first 70 years one of the country's best schools. It would have presented something of a conundrum to their father. It was, above all to a man who treasured his birthplace, the best of British public education and therefore the only place to send his youngest two sons now that he had the financial means to do so. But it also represented the Anglican Church, one of the bodies which had so vigorously and unfairly pursued George Adams and himself for all those years, disapproving of his business activities. And the school was in Victoria which, like NSW and Queensland, had conspired to stop their flourishing empire by blocking delivery of the sweepstakes tickets. They had failed ultimately, defeated by determined and resourceful businessmen, so in many respects this was a way for Harvey to thumb his nose at the establishment. And why not rub it in by showering his sons with a little extra cash?

Harold was enrolled in 1920 and went on to complete a tertiary course from the Dookie Agricultural College, near Shepparton, in 1924 before returning to Tasmania to become a pastoralist and run Fonthill, a 250-hectare sheep farming property near Oatlands, a historic town on the Midland Highway a little under halfway between Hobart and Launceston. It was bought with his father's help and the pool of cash earned on his behalf through the fund. He retired aged just 42 and lived out his days in Hobart in a house not far from the parents' mansion in Sandy Bay. In fact, none of David Harvey's children followed him into the business (although David jnr would later become a trustee of the estate) but at least three pursued his other passion for farming. Lorimer was another, leaving Melbourne Grammar in 1925 to become an orchardist at Margate, a small seaside town south of Hobart. In the early 1930s, he met and married Hilza Kalbfell, whose family owned one of Hobart's better-known shoe stores in Elizabeth Street.

Lorimer's portfolio of property and stock bought by his father on his behalf included shares in office buildings in Liverpool Street, Montpelier Retreat as well as Commonwealth loans and shares in the Bulli Coal Company, the Rosny Ferry Company and the Tasmanian Cider Company. His piece of the Tattersall's pie was in addition.

Despite their burgeoning wealth, the Harvey clan was not immune from family problems although the patriarch would not live to see either of the embarrassing feuds reach the High Court. The first was in 1932-33 when the husband of Lucy May, who died suddenly a few months after her father in 1927, challenged the legitimacy of the Harvey family fund. The case was eventually settled on appeal.

The second case came in 1969. *Harvey v Harvey*, as it became known, involved the ownership of Fonthill. Harold had farmed there until 1946 when, probably brought on by the economic hardships of the war years, he suffered a nervous breakdown and contemplated selling the property. His elder brother Horace, a successful grazier himself, suggested instead that they enter an agreement under which Horace's three sons would run the place and split the profits with Harold, until Harold's son Robin, who was six at the time, was old enough to take over. The agreement ran for two decades until Robin decided he wanted the farm back. It resulted in a three-year battle that split the family, as fights over money often do. In April 1970, High Court judges Barwick, Menzies and Walsh decided in favour of Robin Harvey, who promptly sold the property and evicted his cousins. It would take more than 30 years before the daughters of those cousins, who had grown up on the property, bought back what they regarded as the family farm. Yet, a far worse family tragedy loomed.

David Hastie Harvey's final will, in which he modestly described himself as an accountant rather than the entrepreneur he clearly had become, was signed less than a month before his death on June 29, 1927. It is flowery but, in essence at least, far less complicated than the one prepared by his benefactor, mainly because the bulk of his fortune was already tied up in trusts shared among his surviving seven children. Given the earlier estimate of his worth, the declared gross value of his estate at just £23,867 ($2.7 million in 2008) is an indication of how little he kept in his own name. It allotted annual payments of the equivalent today of $5000 to the two sisters of his wife Elizabeth and a similar amount for herself. He ordered his "tree" not to sell the residual estate, including a share of the George Adams estate and its Tattersall's treasure trove but to invest it in Commonwealth loans and inscribed stock then divide the annual income from the pool equally between his living and future grandchildren. The youngest grandchild would arrive only six years later, born into a family divided by its own wealth and privilege and a legacy that for her, at least, had lost its foundation. The consequences would be far-reaching and destructive.

CHAPTER 19
You're Looking for Me

The three men know where the interview is heading. The two cops and their prey have been circling each other for more than two hours now, and the polite, almost jovial banter has all but disappeared. The confrontation, the accusation has to come soon, but when?

It is starting to bug Bryant. He wants it out in the open where he can see it, the extent of what he's done, so he can deny everything; make them work to prove it.

He might have been dead and then it wouldn't have mattered but he isn't. Probably would rather be, actually. Thought he'd be shot but he is still alive. The burns still hurt and the bandages smell like rotting flesh. The chair is uncomfortable, and he can't move his legs. There is no one to talk to, not even mum. She isn't allowed in, they say. There are just the guards and the doctors, but they don't say much either.

His lawyer, David Gunson, isn't even in the room to tell him if he is saying the right things. It is hard to keep track because the cops keep changing the subject; first the guns, then surfing, the Martins. Now they are asking about Seascape and burning the car with the hostage in the back. He has admitted to taking the bloke and the gold BMW but nothing else. He knows they want to ask about the shootings. He'll help them out and get to the point.

"Is there other things that you reckon I've done down there?"

Ross Paine sits back and looked at the strange, trussed figure on the other side of the table. "Yes, there are."

Bryant has his opening: "What like?" he challenges defiantly.

John Warren chips in: "You've already said that you remembered me going to see you at the hospital. I told you that you were being charged with …"

"A murder count." Of course he remembers. That day he could hardly move from the pain and the bandages and the drugs.

Warren persists: "What recollection have you got of that?"

"Must've been the hostage, the bloke in the BMW must've died."

Warren scoffs: "That's what you think it is? Do you remember me mentioning a name?"

"I remember you mentioning a name but …"

"Right, well I told you that you were being charged with the murder of a woman called Kate Scott. Does that register with you?"

"No. I mean, I let the lady go … I didn't hurt her or anything. No, I don't register, it doesn't register."

"What happened at Port Arthur?"

"I didn't go, definitely didn't go to Port Arthur."

"Well, what would you say if I told you that you were seen going into Port Arthur and in fact you were at the toll gate?"

"I couldn't have been."

"We have lots of people who are telling us that they saw you at Port Arthur and your car."

"Well, it must've been another, there's other Volvos …"

"With surfboards on the top and someone with long, blond hair driving them?"

"There's not many with surfboards on top," he agrees, reluctantly.

"Martin, what if I said to you that neither Inspector Paine nor myself believe what you're saying to us?"

"You don't believe one little thing?" He sounds deflated.

"Martin, I want you to have a look at this photo. In it is a car I believe to be yours, and it's depicted adjacent to the toll booth."

"Couldn't be mine. Where'd you get that?"

"Do you agree that that could be a surfboard on the top?"

"Yes I think it probably is."

"The registration number is CG 2835. That's your car."

"How could the car be there when I didn't go there in the first place?"

Paine has had enough: "Did you go to the Broad Arrow Cafe?"

"The last time I've been into the Broad Arrow Cafe was about, I can't recall, must've been two or three years ago."

"Once again, lots of people are saying they saw you in the Broad Arrow Cafe on Sunday the 28th of April."

"Mmm, that's untrue."

"So how do you account for the car being there?"

"That lady could've driven it down there. That one, the wife or girlfriend of the chap I took hostage 'cos I said to get into my, the Volvo."

"Martin. I believe that you took the BMW near the toll booth, not on the highway. We have spoken to the people that say the car was taken from the toll booth area."

"It's not true."

"Not true?"

"Must've been someone else ..."

"Martin, I believe you went to the Broad Arrow Cafe at Port Arthur on Sunday the 28th."

"That's nonsense. Like I said. I didn't go to Port Arthur."

"What would you say if I said that someone's identified you having a meal at the Broad Arrow Cafe?"

"Having a meal? I had a toasted sandwich at Nubeena and that was it."

They were getting nowhere. Paine tried another tack:

"Do you know what's happened on that day?"

"No."

"Are you sure about that?"

"Positive."

"Well, I'll tell you what's happened. There have been 20 people in that Broad Arrow Cafe who were shot and killed, and there were a lot of others injured. There were also a number of people in the car park were killed ... there were four people taken out of that BMW shot and killed ... and two children and their mother on the way to the toll booth."

Bryant chips in: "Oh God, it's awful isn't it."

Paine ignores the comment: "And we believe you're responsible."

Martin Bryant has his answer. An innocent man might have expressed his outrage at such an emphatic accusation but he only wants the details: "How many people died altogether?"

The question catches the detective off-guard: "Including the people at Seascape?"

"Mmm."

"Thirty-five."

"How many other people injured?"

"Approximately 20."

"What, seriously or not?"

"Some more serious than others but they're all OK. Martin, we have spoken to over 600 people …"

Paine is trying to get the interview back on track but Bryant seems lost in his own thoughts:

"I, I had two guns with me, I took them for target practising. I took the shotgun and the little other gun, the Colt. And I, I must've got that burnt that little, little one in the middle," he says pointing to the AR-15.

"How do you reckon that got burnt?"

"Striking a match, a match. Why did I stop?"

"Where was the petrol?"

"Would've saved you a lot of time if I'd been blown up with the hostage."

He's done it again, another half-confession leaking out amid the denials.

"We've got, we've got all the time in the world, Martin."

"Obviously I have too, so what does it matter?"

"What matters is we'd like to know why you've done what you've done mate. It's simple."

"What have I done? I mean, I know I've done the wrong."

"I've just told you what you've done." The time for games is over.

"I've done, I've done the wrong thing by stealing the car."

"Are you understanding what I just said to you?"

"What have I done?"

"You've killed 35 people."

"Oh."

They are going around in circles. One moment Bryant seems to be admitting the crimes; the next he is unable to understand the extent of the allegations. Paine tries again:

"We believe you went into Port Arthur and had a slight argument with the toll gate person about the price on entry ... We believe you went to the Broad Arrow Cafe with that bag over there, containing some guns and your video camera. You purchased a meal, you went outside, sat down, and then went back into the cafe. Took one ..."

Bryant interrupts: "But ... that's like me saying to you, that you were down there."

"But the difference is Martin, my car wasn't down there and I haven't been identified as being down there." He tries to continue: "And then you took one of the guns out of your bag and opened fire in the cafe ..."

"Why would I do that?" Bryant stops him again.

"I don't know, you tell me."

"Why, why would anyone do a thing like that?"

"That's what we want to know, Martin, why?"

"What, what, would, I wouldn't hurt a person in my life."

"Well you've already said you'd put the man in your boot of the car."

"Only, yes, yes ..."

"Then you've set fire to the car, and you thought that he was in the boot. So how do you explain that?"

"It was a bad thing. But I got burnt too. That doesn't worry you, I suppose."

Suddenly he wants sympathy for being burned by his own fire. Paine resists the temptation to point it out: "Well, it does. Of course it worries us."

Bryant is defiant. "Well, that's all I can recall. That's all I know. I've got a pretty clear mind. I definitely wasn't there at Port Arthur that Sunday."

Paine ignores him and presses on: "After opening fire in the cafe and walking through the cafe, you left the cafe and went down near the bus park, shooting, shooting several people. Then you got in your car and drove back towards the toll booth. Before reaching the toll booth, you stopped and shot dead a lady and two small children ..."

"Go on."

"Then you got to the toll booth, took the BMW, shooting the occupants ..."

"Must've been [another car] ... The BMW was back there at the Fortescue Bay turnoff."

"No, the BMW wasn't there."

"Was it the same colour BMW?"

"Yes," Paine continues. Bryant's interruptions are not going to stop him from finishing. "Shooting the four occupants. Then driving to the service

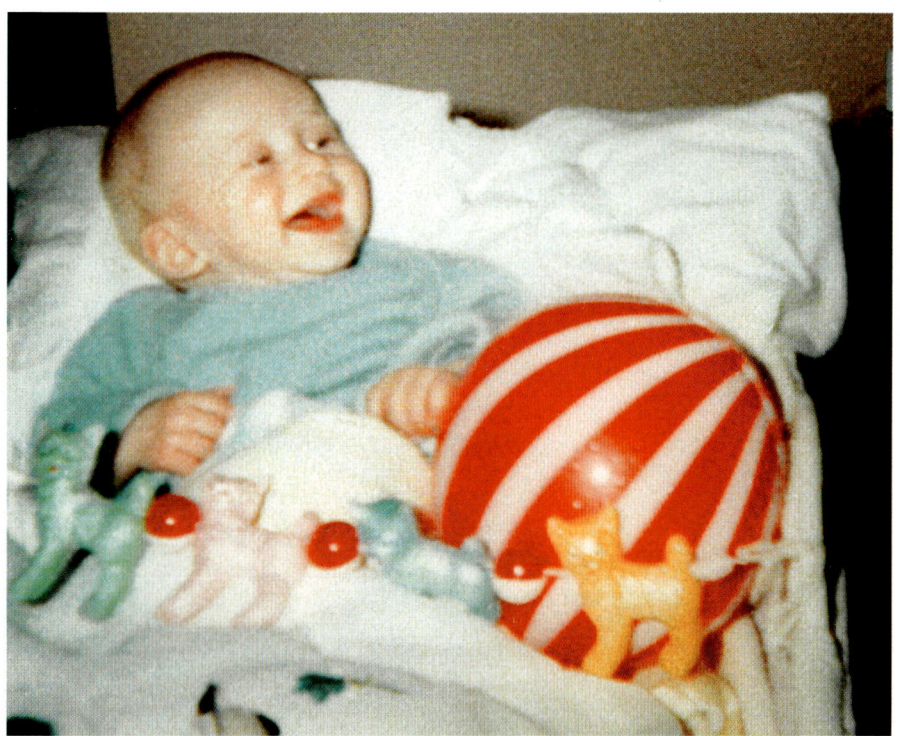

↑ Bouncing baby: At five months, Martin Bryant was like any other baby, before his antisocial behaviour became apparent.

← Blue-eyed boy: Bryant plays happily at 18 months, his distinctive blond hair and blue eyes already apparent. Years of torment, rejection and ostracisation lay ahead.

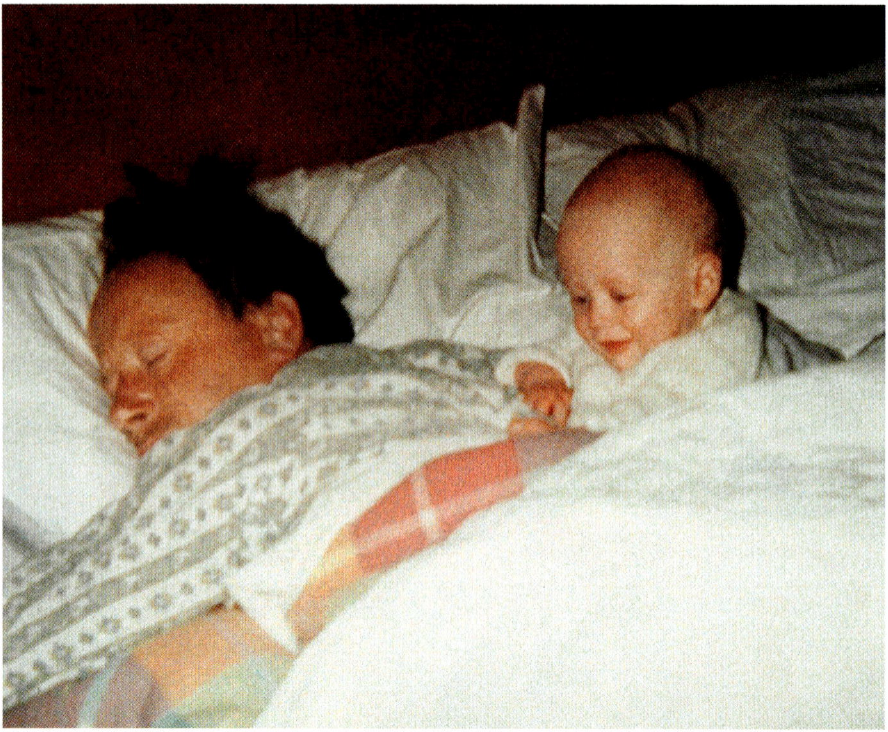

↑ Father and son: Martin, aged six months, with his beloved dad Maurice, who would dedicate his life to trying to support, guide and control his increasingly erratic son, ultimately to his own detriment.

→ Happy day: Maurice Bryant and new bride Carleen (nee Cordwell) at their wedding reception on September 4, 1965. The resemblance between Carleen, then in her late 20s, and her son Martin at the same age is striking.

⬆ Look at me: Maurice holds his newborn baby daughter Lindy while Martin mugs for the camera. He would grow to deeply resent his little sister's normality.

⬆ What a catch: A skilled diver Martin, aged 16, proudly displays a lobster caught off Carnarvon Bay, where he would spend long days fishing with his father.

⬆ Watchful eye: Maurice keeps an eye on Martin, aged 26 months, as he plays in the Augusta Road house.

⬆ Happy snap: A teenage Martin shows off his trademark "silly grin" as he poses for Carleen with a worn-looking Maurice and Lindy in Hobart.

⬅ Giddy-up: Martin finds a saddle cloth is not quite enough at Port Arthur in 1984. Lindy took to horse riding but Martin's interest was short-lived.

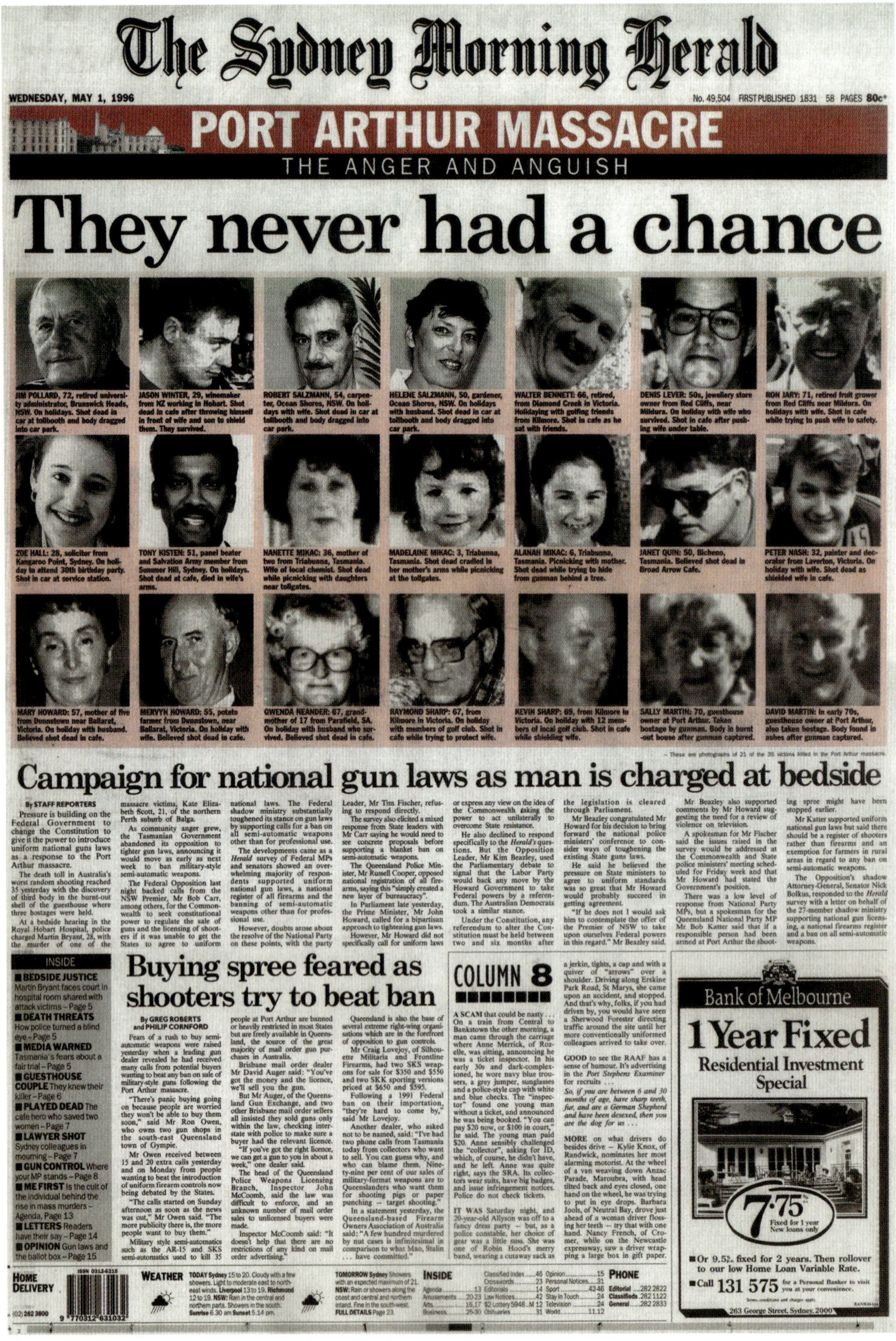

The Sydney Morning Herald

WEDNESDAY, MAY 1, 1996 — No. 49,504 FIRST PUBLISHED 1831 58 PAGES 80c*

PORT ARTHUR MASSACRE

THE ANGER AND ANGUISH

They never had a chance

JIM POLLARD, 72, retired university administrator, Brunswick Heads, NSW. On holidays. Shot dead in car at tollbooth and body dragged into car park.

JASON WINTER, 29, winemaker from NZ working in Hobart. Shot dead in cafe after throwing himself in front of wife and son to shield them. They survived.

ROBERT SALZMANN, 54, carpenter, Ocean Shores, NSW. On holidays with wife. Shot dead in car at tollbooth and body dragged into car park.

HELENE SALZMANN, 50, gardener, Ocean Shores, NSW. On holidays with husband. Shot dead in car at tollbooth and body dragged into car park.

WALTER BENNETT: 66, retired, from Diamond Creek in Victoria. Holidaying with golfing friends from Kilmore. Shot in cafe as he sat with friends.

DENIS LEVER: 50s, jewellery store owner from Red Cliffs, near Mildura. On holiday with wife who survived. Shot in cafe after pushing wife under table.

RON JARY: 71, retired fruit grower from Red Cliffs near Mildura. On holidays with wife. Shot in cafe while trying to push wife to safety.

ZOE HALL: 28, solicitor from Kangaroo Point, Sydney. On holiday to attend 30th birthday party. Shot in car at service station.

TONY KISTEN: 51, panel beater and Salvation Army member from Summer Hill, Sydney. On holidays. Shot dead at cafe, died in wife's arms.

NANETTE MIKAC: 36, mother of two from Triabunna, Tasmania. Wife of local chemist. Shot dead while picnicking with daughters near tollgates.

MADELAINE MIKAC: 3, Triabunna, Tasmania. Shot dead cradled in her mother's arms while picnicking at the tollgates.

ALANAH MIKAC: 6, Triabunna, Tasmania. Picnicking with mother. Shot dead while trying to hide from gunman behind a tree.

JANET QUIN: 50, Bicheno, Tasmania. Believed shot dead in Broad Arrow Cafe.

PETER NASH: 32, painter and decorator from Laverton, Victoria. On holiday with wife. Shot dead as shielded wife in cafe.

MARY HOWARD: 57, mother of five from Dunnstown near Ballarat, Victoria. On holiday with husband. Believed shot dead in cafe.

MERVYN HOWARD: 55, potato farmer from Dunnstown, near Ballarat, Victoria. On holiday with wife. Believed shot dead in cafe.

GWENDA NEANDER: 67, grandmother of 17 from Parafield, SA. On holiday with husband who survived. Believed shot dead in cafe.

RAYMOND SHARP: 67, from Kilmore in Victoria. On holiday with members of golf club. Shot in cafe while trying to protect wife.

KEVIN SHARP: 69, from Kilmore in Victoria. On holiday with 12 members of local golf club. Shot in cafe while shielding wife.

SALLY MARTIN: 70, guesthouse owner at Port Arthur. Taken hostage by gunman. Body in burnt-out house after gunman captured.

DAVID MARTIN: In early 70s, guesthouse owner at Port Arthur, also taken hostage. Body found in ashes after gunman captured.

– These are photographs of 21 of the 35 victims killed in the Port Arthur massacre.

Campaign for national gun laws as man is charged at bedside

By STAFF REPORTERS

Pressure is building on the Federal Government to change the Constitution to give it the power to introduce uniform national guns laws as a response to the Port Arthur massacre.

The death toll in Australia's worst random shooting reached 35 yesterday with the discovery of third body in the burnt-out shell of the guesthouse where three hostages were held.

At a bedside hearing in the Royal Hobart Hospital, police charged Martin Bryant, 28, with the murder of one of the massacre victims, Kate Elizabeth Scott, 21, of the northern Perth suburb of Balga.

As community anger grew, the Tasmanian Government abandoned its opposition to tighter gun laws, announcing it would move as early as next week to ban military-style semi-automatic weapons.

The Federal Opposition last night backed calls from the NSW Premier, Mr Bob Carr, among others, for the Commonwealth to seek constitutional power to regulate the sale of guns and the licensing of shooters if it was unable to get the States to agree to uniform national laws. The Federal shadow ministry substantially toughened its stance on gun laws by supporting calls for a ban on all semi-automatic weapons other than for professional use.

The developments came as a *Herald* survey of Federal MPs and senators showed an overwhelming majority of respondents supported uniform national gun laws, a national register of all firearms and the banning of semi-automatic weapons other than for professional use.

However, doubts arose about the resolve of the National Party on these points, with the party Leader, Mr Tim Fischer, refusing to respond directly.

The survey also elicited a mixed response from State leaders with Mr Carr saying he would need to see concrete proposals before supporting a blanket ban on semi-automatic weapons.

The Queensland Police Minister, Mr Russell Cooper, opposed national registration of all firearms, saying this "simply created a new layer of bureaucracy".

In Parliament late yesterday, the Prime Minister, Mr John Howard, called for a bipartisan approach to tightening gun laws.

However, Mr Howard did not specifically call for uniform laws or express any view on the idea of the Commonwealth taking the power to act unilaterally to overcome State resistance.

He also declined to respond specifically to the *Herald's* questions. But the Opposition Leader, Mr Kim Beazley, used the Parliamentary debate to signal that the Labor Party would back any move by the Howard Government to take Federal powers by a referendum. The Australian Democrats took a similar stance.

Under the Constitution, any referendum to alter the Constitution must be held between two and six months after the legislation is cleared through Parliament.

Mr Beazley congratulated Mr Howard for his decision to bring forward the national police ministers' conference to consider ways of toughening the existing State guns laws.

He said he believed the pressure on State ministers to agree to uniform standards was so great that Mr Howard would probably succeed in getting agreement.

"If he does not I would ask him to contemplate the offer of the Premier of NSW to take upon ourselves Federal powers in this regard," Mr Beazley said.

Mr Beazley also supported comments by Mr Howard suggesting the need for a review of violence on television.

A spokesman for Mr Fischer said the issues raised in the survey would be addressed at the Commonwealth and State police ministers' meeting scheduled for Friday week and that Mr Howard had stated the Government's position.

There was a low level of response from National Party MPs, but a spokesman for the Queensland National Party MP Mr Bob Katter said that if a responsible person had been armed at Port Arthur the shooting spree might have been stopped earlier.

Mr Katter supported uniform national gun laws but said there should be a register of shooters rather than firearms and an exemption for farmers in rural areas in regard to any ban on semi-automatic weapons.

The Opposition's shadow Attorney-General, Senator Nick Bolkus, responded to the *Herald* survey with a letter on behalf of the 27-member shadow ministry supporting national gun licensing, a national firearms register and a ban on all semi-automatic weapons.

INSIDE

BEDSIDE JUSTICE Martin Bryant faces court in hospital room shared with attack victims – Page 5
DEATH THREATS How police turned a blind eye – Page 5
MEDIA WARNED Tasmania's fears about a fair trial – Page 5
GUESTHOUSE COUPLE They knew their killer – Page 6
PLAYED DEAD The cafe hero who saved two women – Page 7
LAWYER SHOT Sydney colleagues in mourning – Page 7
GUN CONTROL Where your MP stands – Page 8
ME FIRST Is the cult of the individual behind the rise in mass murders – Agenda, Page 13
LETTERS Readers have their say – Page 14
OPINION Gun laws and the ballot box – Page 15

Buying spree feared as shooters try to beat ban

By GREG ROBERTS and PHILIP CORNFORD

Fears of a rush to buy semi-automatic weapons were raised yesterday when a leading gun dealer revealed he had received many calls from potential buyers wanting to beat any ban on sale of military-style guns following the Port Arthur massacre.

"There's panic buying going on because people are worried they won't be able to buy them soon," said Mr Ron Owen, who owns two gun shops in the south-east Queensland town of Gympie.

Mr Owen received between 15 and 20 extra calls yesterday and on Monday from people wanting to beat the introduction of uniform firearm controls now being debated by the States.

"The calls started on Sunday afternoon as soon as the news was out," Mr Owen said. "The more publicity there is, the more people want to buy them."

Military style semi-automatics such as the AR-15 and SKS semi-automatics used to kill 35 people at Port Arthur are banned or heavily restricted in most States but are freely available in Queensland, the source of the great majority of mail order gun purchases in Australia.

Brisbane mail order dealer Mr David Auger said: "You've got the money and the licence, we'll sell you the gun.

But Mr Auger, of the Queensland Gun Exchange, and two other Brisbane mail order sellers all insisted they sold guns only within the law, checking interstate with police to make sure a buyer had the relevant licence.

"If you've got the right licence, we can get a gun to you in about a week," one dealer said.

The head of the Queensland Police Weapons Licensing Branch, Inspector John McCoomb, said the law was difficult to enforce, and an unknown number of mail order sales to unlicensed buyers were made.

Inspector McCoomb said: "It doesn't help that there are no restrictions of any kind on mail order advertising."

Queensland is also the base of several extreme right-wing organisations which are in the forefront of opposition to gun controls.

Mr Craig Lovejoy, of Silhouette Militaria and Frontline Firearms, had two SKS weapons for sale for $350 and $550 and two SKK sporting versions priced at $650 and $595.

Following a 1991 Federal ban on their importation, "they're hard to come by," said Mr Lovejoy.

Another dealer, who asked not to be named, said: "I've had two phone calls from Tasmania today from collectors who want to sell. You can guess why, and who can blame them. Ninety-nine per cent of our sales of military-format weapons are to Queenslanders who want them for shooting pigs or paper punching – target shooting."

In a statement yesterday, the Queensland-based Firearm Owners Association of Australia said: "A few hundred murdered by nut cases is infinitesimal in comparison to what Mao, Stalin . . . have committed."

COLUMN 8

A SCAM that could be nasty . . . On a train from Central to Bankstown the other morning, a man came through the carriage where Anne Merrick, of Rozelle, was sitting, announcing he was a ticket inspector. In his early 30s and dark-complexioned, he wore navy blue trousers, a grey jumper, sunglasses and a police-style cap with white and blue checks. The "inspector" found one young man without a ticket, and announced he was being booked. "You can pay $20 now, or $100 in court," he said. The young man paid $20. Anne sensibly challenged the "collector", asking for ID, which, of course, he didn't have, and he left. Anne was quite right, says the SRA. Its collectors wear suits, have big badges, and issue infringement notices. Police do not check tickets.

IT WAS Saturday night, and 20-year-old Allyson was off to a fancy dress party – but, as a police constable, her choice of gear was a little suss. She was one of Robin Hood's merry band, wearing a cutaway sack as a jerkin, tights, a cap and with a quiver of "arrows" over a shoulder. Driving along Erskine Park Road, St Marys, she came upon an accident, and stopped. And that's why, folks, if you had driven by, you would have seen a Sherwood Forester directing traffic around the site until her more conventionally uniformed colleagues arrived to take over.

GOOD to see the RAAF has a sense of humour. It's advertising in the *Port Stephens Examiner* for recruits . . .

So, if you are between 6 and 30 months of age, have sharp teeth, fur, and are a German Shepherd and have been desexed, then you are the dog for us . . .

MORE on what drivers do besides drive – Kylie Knox, of Randwick, nominates her most alarming motorist. At the wheel of a van weaving down Anzac Parade, Maroubra, with head tilted back and eyes closed, one hand on the wheel, he was trying to put in eye drops. Barbara Jools, of Neutral Bay, drove just ahead of a woman driver flossing her teeth – try that with one hand. Nancy French, of Cromer, while on the Newcastle expressway, saw a driver wrapping a large box in gift paper.

Bank of Melbourne

1 Year Fixed

Residential Investment Special

7·75 % p.a. Fixed for 1 year New loans only

■ Or 9.5% p.a. fixed for 2 years. Then rollover to our low Home Loan Variable Rate.

■ Call 131 575 for a Personal Banker to visit you at your convenience.

Terms, conditions and charges apply.

263 George Street, Sydney, 2000

HOME DELIVERY (02) 282 3800

ISSN 0312-6315

WEATHER **TODAY Sydney** 15 to 20. Cloudy with a few showers. Light to moderate east to north-east winds. **Liverpool** 13 to 19. **Richmond** 12 to 19. **NSW:** Rain in the central and northern parts. Showers in the south. **Sunrise** 6.30 am **Sunset** 5.14 pm.

TOMORROW Sydney Showers with an expected maximum of 21. **NSW:** Rain or showers along the coast and central and northern inland. Fine in the south-west. **FULL DETAILS** Page 23.

INSIDE

Agenda 13
Amusements 20-23
Arts 16,17
Business 25-30
Classified index 46
Crosswords 23
Editorials 14
Law Notices 42
$2 Lottery 5948 .. M 12
Obituaries 31
Opinion 15
Personal Notices 31
Sport 42-46
Stay in Touch 24
Television 24
World 11,12

PHONE

Editorial 282 2822
Classifieds .. 282 1122
General 282 2833

↑ Death came in a Volvo: Martin Bryant's distinctive yellow Volvo abandoned in the Port Arthur car park after the massacre. The surfboards were permanently fixed to the roof-rack.

← A nation mourns: *The Sydney Morning Herald's* front page on May 1, 1996.

⬆ Brush with death: Gary King at the Forcett Shell service station where he served Bryant on that fateful Sunday.

⬅ Targets: David and Sally Martin, owners of the Seascape guest house, were first on Bryant's hit list.

➡ Aftermath: Police scour bushland around the Seascape guest house for evidence.

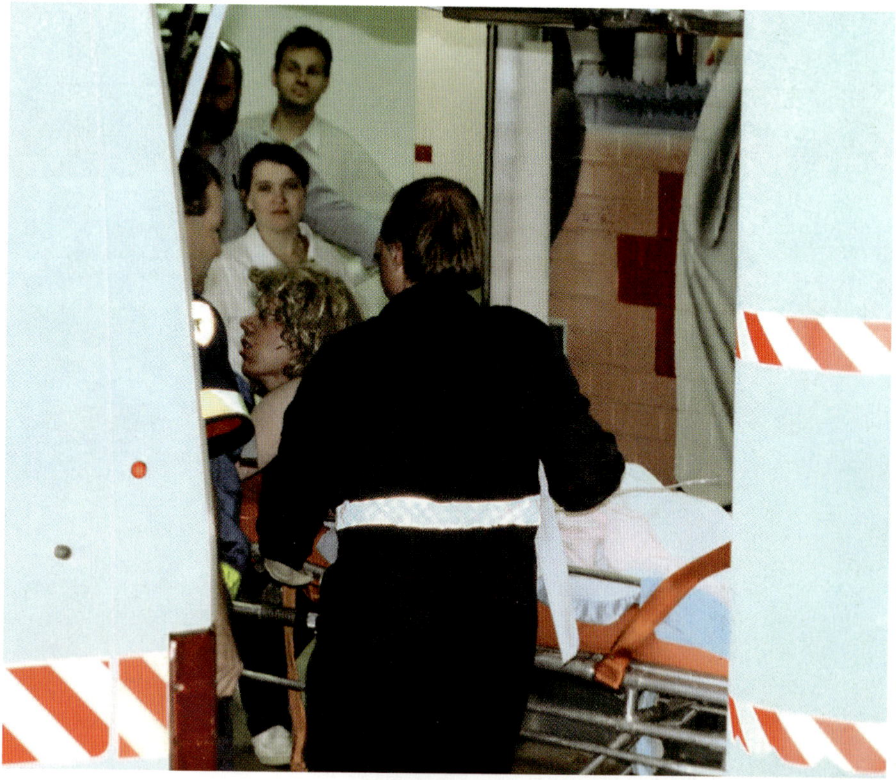

↑ Caught: Bryant, suffering serious burns from the Seascape fire, arrives at hospital.

→ Life: Bryant's cell at Risdon Prison. He has since been moved to the prison hospital.

← Siege: The Seascape guest house, top, still smoulders the morning after Bryant, who had holed up there, set it alight.

← Two minutes of madness: The Broad Arrow Cafe, epicentre of the massacre. Most of those killed were shot at point-blank range.

↑ Profound loss: The coffins of Nanette, Alannah and Madeline Mikac at their funeral. Of all the victims, the sheer callousness of their murders provoked the most community outrage.

← Innocent victims: Nanette Mikac with children, Alannah, 6, and Madeline, 3, and husband Walter, the only surviving member of the family.

↑ Healing: Up to 5000 people attended a memorial service at Port Arthur following the massacre.

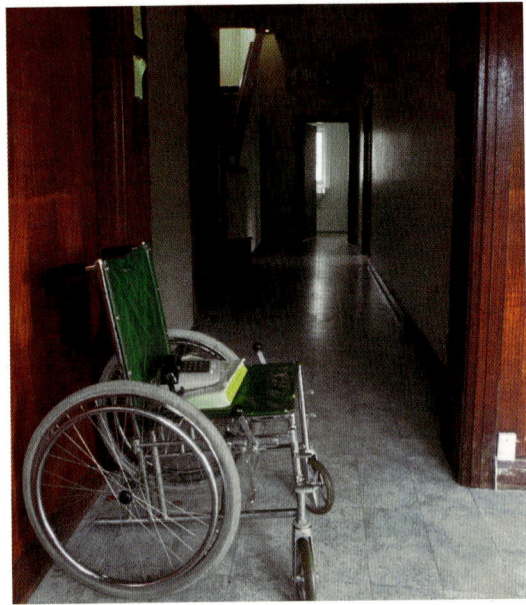

↑ Killing fields: The ruins at Port Arthur, where Bryant hunted down more victims after leaving the cafe. As shots rang out, some visitors thought it was a re-enactment and moved towards the gunfire.

← Second home: Inside the house at Clare Street, where Bryant lived alone in his final days of freedom. In the foreground is Hilza's wheelchair. The elderly mother of Bryant's late companion, Helen Harvey, had been left in it for days on end in agony with a broken hip.

← A lonely place: The Harvey house in Clare Street, where Bryant hatched his murderous plan. There police would find an arsenal of weapons and ammunition, some secreted in the bodies of pianos.

↑ Life-changing case: Defence lawyer John Avery, who would persuade Bryant to plead guilty to all 35 murders, thus sparing the victims and their families the ordeal of reliving the massacre in a long trial. Not long after this picture was taken, Avery too would find himself behind bars for embezzling from clients.

→ The expert: Forensic psychiatrist Professor Paul Mullen, who assessed Bryant's mental fitness to stand trial, says the perpetrators of civilian massacres around the world share many common traits.

⬆ Inside the mind of a killer: One of six drawings Bryant did for lawyer John Avery, which also included the massacre scene. This one depicts his secret place in the hills near Murdunna where he practised with his rifle. The red circles are the cardboard targets he hung on trees. The signposts point to the dirt track off the main road to Port Arthur. To the right is Eaglehawk Neck and the ocean. The blue figures appear to be sunbakers on the beach.

station near the white Corolla, forcing the person into the boot of the BMW, as you've described, and shooting the person that was still in the Corolla and then driving to Seascape …"

"Did that person die?"

"Yes."

"Mmm."

"At Seascape before driving down the driveway, we believe you shot at several cars driving past. Then you went down to Seascape."

"I didn't shoot anyone."

"You didn't shoot anyone?"

"No, not at all. And you reckon you've got dozens of witnesses."

"Certainly have." He was challenging them now.

"Where are they? Have you got any other photos to show me?"

"Do you want to see the photos? They're not very pleasant."

Bryant doesn't answer.

"You're in a little bit of trouble Martin, aren't you?"

"I dunno, I s'pose I am. I'd like to get hold of some bail money."

"There's no chance of that."

"I'd love to just get out of here now. Live a norm, a normal life. Will I be allowed to do that?"

The question is pathetically naive.

"Well that's not a question for us. What do you think your chances of that are after hearing what we've said?"

"Well, I shouldn't have gone and kidnapped him and the BMW. It's the wrong thing … I don't know why I stole the BMW in the first place. I wish I'd …" His voice drains away.

"Do you think people should take responsibility for their actions, Martin? Accept the consequences of what they do?"

"Yeah, I do. I s'pose I should for a little while for what I've done. Just a little while and let me out, let me live my own life. I'm missing my mum. I really miss her actually, what she cooks up for me, her rabbit stews and everything. She's not even allowed to bring a little bit of food for me, that, that's a bit upsetting. Mmm."

Bryant retreats into his own thoughts again. The police have what they came for. It is time to wrap up.

"Martin, unless there's anything else that you want to tell us, we're going to stop the interview now. As Mr Warren explained to you, this is the last opportunity you'll have to speak to us. You'll be at your next court appearance, charged with 35 murders and approximately 20 attempted murders and several wounding charges as well. You'll also be charged with the arson of Seascape. Do you understand all that?"

"How many months will it get me?"

Months? The guy must be kidding or off with the pixies, although the shrinks reckon he is sane. Paine keeps his thoughts to himself.

"Well, that's not a question I can answer. I hope we've explained things clearly and you understand the gravity of the situation."

"It's great to have someone to talk to. And you guys won't be in again?"

"No."

"I'll miss yas." Is he serious or teasing them? It is difficult to know.

"Now what's going to happen now, after we finish the interview, is you'll be introduced to a senior police officer, who will ask you several questions about the interview procedure..."

"Now?"

"Yeah in about, in a couple of moments."

"Might even bring me tea in here."

Now the bloke wants his dinner: "Well, I'm sorry, we can't give you any."

"It's sad."

"Certainly is Martin."

"Especially the ones that were injured."

"I might add, with all the people that were shot, were either shot with those two weapons closest to us over there, your weapons."

"Yeah ... Mmm. I'm not signing anything. Not until me lawyer sees me. I'm sure you'll find the person who caused all this. Me."

The bastard sits back in his chair and points to himself.

"I don't find that a very funny statement at all Martin, to be quite honest."

"You should've put that on recording."

"Oh it's still recording. Like I said to you before Martin, we are looking at the person responsible."

Bryant has fucked himself with that little comment. And he knows it.

"I must need a lawyer then ..."

"You tell me. We'd really like to know why mate because you know, I mean, it's ..."

"I'd really love to help you out but I can't. Have you had other trouble like this, dramatic?"

"Not on this scale, no."

"No. S'pose it happens, doesn't it?"

CHAPTER 20
Helen

Helen Mary Elizabeth Harvey was born into a world on the cusp of a terrible drama. The only child of Lorimer and Hilza Harvey arrived on May 16, 1933, as the world slowly clambered out of the Great Depression and teetered on the horror that would be World War II. In Germany, the new Chancellor, Adolf Hitler, was creating his Gestapo and burning books, in the United States, the failed experiment with Prohibition was about to end; in India Mahatma Gandhi was starving, again, for justice for his people.

The baby was announced into the world without a name, simply as "a daughter to the wife of LE Harvey". Her death, half a century later, would pass in a similarly invisible way – and yet circuitously spark a momentous chain of violence that would leave an indelible mark on modern Australia's psyche – and spark a courageous prohibition of another sort.

This strange granddaughter of David Hastie Harvey achieved little of note in her life. It may appear an unfair assessment but it is clear the remarkable financial legacy that fell her way was spent to feed her burgeoning eccentricities – and indulge an angry fit of pique in her will, leaving her considerable assets not to the family she believed had ignored or abandoned her, but to another strange soul, her one and only friend.

Helen Harvey did manage to hold down an office job with the Tasmanian Railways for a few years, according to all accounts, but at the age of 28, after the premature death of her father, quit to spend the rest of her life with her mother in the imposing family home, Wibruna, at No.30 Clare Street, New Town. The Harvey family enjoyed naming houses and farms as flamboyantly as David Harvey named his children.

Lorimer, the youngest, had bought the place after he sold the orchard at Margate, all financed from his substantial share in the legacy of George Adams and his own father. The reason for selling up and moving back into town is not recorded but economic uncertainty probably drove it. Farming was hard work, and its profits marginal at best. Besides, he didn't really need the money when he could rely on the steady income from the Adams estate so the last years of his life were lived in relative obscurity.

Lorimer died in August 1961, leaving an estate officially worth £135,904, equivalent to $3 million in 2008. Like those before him it is difficult to know its true value, given the nature of the trust set up to manage the Tattersall's distributions. In his will, written two years before his death, Lorimer insisted that the Adams legacy be continued. He wrote:

> *I declare that my trustee shall not sell or alienate or part with my interest in the late George Adams Estate including the business of Tattersall's Sweep Consultations but shall retain possession thereof during the whole period the same shall be in existence and provide further and I declare that my Trustee shall not sell or alienate or part with my interest in any real estate belonging to the estate of the late George Adams.*

Lorimer left the house to his wife with the provision that "my Trustees shall keep the premises in good repair". He also left his wife a modest annual income of £600 ($14,000) from the trust fund. Daughter Helen would receive the same amount. But the heavy emphasis through the entire document is the value of the Adams estate, his share of it and an insistence that nothing should be allowed to change, at least without the consent of a majority of his brothers and sisters.

There were few joys in life for Helen as the years progressed. It was more of an existence for a woman who appeared to struggle with mental health issues at a time – and in a society – when they were more likely to bring shame than succour. If she had thoughts of a husband and children, they disappeared as she plunged further into eccentricity, obsessive hoarding and an increasingly chaotic, and unhygienic life inside the home. Considering what was about to unfold, it seems incongruous that in November 1970 she actually complained to Tasmania's Minister for Health, Nigel Abbott, about a sewerage leak on her property. Perhaps it was the name Harvey which prompted personal action but whatever the reason, government records show that the secretary to the Minister, R.E. Maher, immediately referred the matter to the Director-General of Health, stating in a letter on November 25 it appears the City of Hobart has done all it can in the circumstances, however, the Minster would be glad if someone could look into these matters.

Within a week there was a reply, signed by the Director-General J.R. Macintyre stating that his officers and the council had inspected the property and found that the problem was coming from a leaking pipe in the house in the street behind the Harvey property and would be repaired.

The irony is that she would end up being the source of numerous complaints over the years from neighbours as the once impressive property was overrun by a combination of neglect and obsession. Behind the overgrown garden and weed-infested lawns was a growing menagerie of animals, cats and dogs in their dozens, which overwhelmed the house and its two increasingly incapable occupants.

The theatre was one of Helen Harvey's few outlets, and at some stage she appears to have been involved in amateur productions. There is one published photograph of her: a fleeting image picked out of a crowd in fancy dress, probably from a production of *The Mikado*, her dark hair piled high with a flower clip holding the bun in place. The picture is blurred but the faces around her are all facing the camera, suggesting the photograph was posed rather than captured during a moment of the performance. She has a slight smile on her face, as if pleased with herself. The features are clearly those of her paternal grandfather, David Hastie Harvey, with a prominent jaw-line and a short, stout build.

By the mid-1980s however, Helen and her ageing mother were virtual recluses within the square white walls of Clare Street; a faintly art deco structure perched well above the street as if peering down on its less well-to-do neighbours but forever hidden behind a garden that was almost as neglected as the two women within.

Helen and her mother ventured out of their home only to walk the dogs: two physically different women, the elder tall and handsome and the younger short, fat and plain. They might have been sisters but the neighbours never knew for certain because the pair kept to themselves. Some read it as arrogance, others a shyness or simply being a bit odd. Helen would buy food in bulk for the cats and dogs she collected by the dozen, fed on the best quality steak from the surprised but enthusiastic butcher at the end of the street.

They were bower birds, collecting not only animals but two or three of pretty much everything they owned, even two pianos, which lay at opposite ends of the house, unused apart from being a dumping ground for rubbish or a perch for a lounging feline. There were multiple television sets, each with a VCR player (and spares in case they stopped production) as well as a vast collection of videos, which Helen bought in twos or threes. She liked musicals mainly – titles such as *A Star is Born* and *The Sound of Music* – and the films of her youth such as *Random Harvest, Gentlemen Prefer Blondes, Seven Brides for Seven Brothers, National Velvet* and *The Swiss Family Robinson*.

The shopkeepers in the small collection of stores on New Town Road regarded Helen as an eccentric but essentially harmless character; heavy-set, missing a couple of teeth, with a whiff of body odour, combined with ageing clothes desperate for a wash and some air. She loved to chat while buying quality steak by the kilo for her dogs, often talking about her Hollywood "friends" Errol Flynn and Rock Hudson, with whom she insisted she was in contact – meaning she wrote them the occasional letter. The shop assistants played along and never challenged the tale by asking where she addressed the envelopes nor her insistence that Hudson often replied. There was another butcher who happily delivered to her home after she phoned orders to the shop. He was paid cash on arrival, often $100 or more, for orders that would include eight kilos of top-quality rump steak and up to 10 kilos of topside.

At the chemist she would occasionally buy perfume and other small items but mostly packets of tape and absorbent gauze bandages, 10 at a time – to dress her mother's ulcers she told them. From the late 1980s, Hilza Harvey was virtually confined to one room of the house where she spent most of her time in a chair. How the pair managed to take care of themselves was anyone's guess. Unlike the thousands of elderly men and women in similar, lonely situations around the country, the difference was that Helen was only in her 50s and, unlike most pensioners, had plenty of money.

....

As the crow flies it was roughly 400 metres from the Bryant home at No.65 Augusta Road to Helen Harvey's house in Clare Street. The two roads actually join as they forge into Elizabeth Street, which runs down the hill into the city, but the short cut is through Raluana Lane alongside the house, turning right into Joynton Street, which runs behind the hospital then left into Honora Avenue, which ends in a T-junction at Clare Street. The Harvey home was several houses to the right.

According to Carleen Bryant, it was Martin who found Helen one day in early 1987 while wandering the neighbourhood streets, as was his wont, during lonely afternoons while his father Maurice was at work. More likely, it was Maurice who found a job for Martin. Now almost 20, he was treading water but existing with an established routine of mowing lawns and vegetable rounds but always on the lookout for new customers. He (or his father) noticed the overgrown grounds through the iron fence, and decided to knock at the door. The woman who answered agreed that he do some work for her, and a friendship was forged, almost on the spot. Perhaps they had an intuition about each other, an echo that both struggled with the misunderstanding of the outside world, and what began as a regular lawn mowing visit turned into something much more important. The two had found companionship in a world that otherwise ignored or rejected them.

Soon, Helen provided Martin with regular work doing the gardening and odd jobs such as feeding the 40 or so cats living in the garage. There were already 14 dogs living inside the house, including an old, blind Doberman, pugs kept in cots in the kitchen, three Chihuahuas, a terrier and a Pekinese. They had the run of the downstairs rooms and a van out the back while Helen and her mother seemed happy to live confined to the upper level of the house in two bedrooms on opposing sides.

Carleen watched her son come home in overalls smelling of ammonia, and wondered how he could stand it. She refused to see two like souls, choosing instead to view Martin's friendship with Helen as him helping her – *giving her someone to talk to*. The truth was that the two misfits had forged a bond, and this was a two-way street. Martin had found someone who didn't see the contradictions that turned others away; a good-looking young man with an easy grin who revealed his disabilities, social and intellectual, the minute he opened his mouth. The forensic psychiatrist, Professor Paul Mullen, asked Bryant about the relationship with Helen Harvey after the murders:

> *He describes Miss Harvey as having been his only real friend. He said from the outset they got on well together. He enjoyed being with her. The relationship with Miss Harvey appears to have been that of a helpful and affectionate child. It was not a sexual relationship.*

The tragic consequences of their relationship, however, began very early. As the friendship moved from employer-employee to friends and then constant companionship, Helen's mother, Hilza was left increasingly alone inside what was fast becoming a filthy hellhole. She had been moved downstairs into the kitchen at some stage, and it was here that the old woman was forced to sleep, upright on a chair, writhing and wriggling in a bid to gain relief from an undiagnosed and untreated broken hip for most of the last two years of her life. The explanation given to Carleen by Martin was that the old woman couldn't lie down because she was in too much pain. Neither could they shift her into a car to take her on an outing because she screamed in agony as they tried to move her. They insisted, too, that she refused to allow a doctor in the house. Helen would telephone Martin in the early hours of the morning to ask that he come over because her mother had had an accident, soiled herself and needed changing. Carleen, in the benign naivety that is her primary characteristic, wondered at her son's resilience but never set foot in the Harvey house to see what was happening in the place where her son spent so much time.

Maurice Bryant didn't intervene too much in their affairs either. Helen, for Martin's beleaguered parents, was a blessing in many ways because it freed him from the increasingly difficult task of watching and keeping a handle on his son. While Martin was with Helen there seemed to be a lull in his erratic behaviour. He finally had a friend, mismatched in age but obviously not in spirit, and for him the details of their relationship hardly mattered.

That period of brief respite would change in dramatic circumstances in June 1990 when someone must have made a report to the health authorities: medics arrived to find both Hilza and Helen in need of urgent hospital treatment with infected leg ulcers and living in abject squalor in the kitchen, surrounded not only by roaming animals, but unwashed dishes and saucepans and bowls with mould so high it was climbing out of the oven. The room was so crowded they had to clamber over furniture just to reach the older woman. Seventy-nine-year-old Hilza Harvey was an abject horror of neglect, sitting untended with her broken hip and withering slowly in the kitchen on her chair. As horrified as they were, the ambulance officers cast no judgment on the situation other than two women "who lived with other priorities". The "nice young man who helps us" was ignorant and incapable rather than neglectful.

Carleen's response was equally frightening:

> *Is it any wonder this poor woman was in so much agony? Just think how much money Helen had saved the government caring for mother at home, maybe thousands of dollars, but it meant her broken hip could not heal.*

Hilza's deterioration was rapid. After several weeks in hospital, she was moved to a nursing home but died at the end of July. Helen, who spent several days being treated herself, was now alone and without a home. For the third time in as many years, the local council issued a health order on the property. Martin Bryant's efforts in the garden had, at best, been minimal and, as the friendship blossomed, disappeared altogether. One order, in 1988, demanded that the overgrown garden be cleared, then inspectors returned in February 1990 when a neighbour complained about the smell of the 50 animals, which were by then roaming the house and grounds. Helen Harvey had been ordered to cull her menagerie but had not done so four months later when she and her mother ended up in hospital.

This time the RSPCA was called and most of the animals were taken away while Helen recovered in hospital. A clean-up order was also placed on the house, and Maurice Bryant took it upon himself to take long service leave and attempt to co-ordinate the job with his son. It took three months to scrape the filth from the floors, walls and surfaces of almost every room. A dozen skips were filled with rubbish while Carleen, who took care and even housed Helen after she was released from hospital, recalled having to individually clean the muck off Helen's collection of 1300 videos on the front lawn of her home in Augusta Road.

Helen's entire wardrobe had to be thrown away. It was as if her previous life was removed, allowing her to start again in a pristine environment with a new live-in companion, Martin Bryant.

CHAPTER 21
Taurusville

After Hilza Harvey's death, there were no constraints on Helen and Martin, not that they had ever really made any sacrifices to take care of the old woman. Her demise was indicative of their own disabilities, in the old sense of the word. They did not set out to harm her but simply did not have the life skills – or the mental ability – to understand what was needed. The older woman and her younger companion were oblivious to their effect on others, as if divorced from the reality of a life built increasingly on largesse and waste fuelled by obsession. Neither seemed capable of anything but the vaguest understanding of money, not that it mattered. It was Helen's fortune which seemed to flow in an endless stream, the cup refilled each month by the Adams-Harvey legacy.

The strange couple spent days wandering the shops looking for new ways to spend money and add to the growing collections at home. Their ventures were most often in the afternoon after a leisurely lunch in a local restaurant. Sometimes Martin pushed Helen in the wheelchair bought for her mother but rarely used. At other times they drove.

For Helen, Martin was the human stray who had wandered into her life and could be led around more easily than one of her dogs. He was pliant company although it was clear to those who knew them that she cared for him. No one knew what they talked about in private but those who watched them day after day did so without question. They seemed to fit together, not neatly nor appropriately, but they had each other. For some who did not know them, the young man was seen as her son; others wondered about the relationship but preferred not to pry: it was clearly platonic, although Martin would later admit to some kissing and cuddling. But this was not about sex – Bryant would insist later that he used prostitutes every month or so – but about being accepted and loved by another human being. Helen Harvey, like Martin, had also suffered the humiliation of constant rejection but, in her case, it was by family. It would take her death to reveal the level of her particular animosity.

Car dealers, like the butchers earlier, loved the funny couple. Registration records would show "The Tatts Lady", as many of the shopkeepers referred to her, also collected and hoarded cars, buying 50 in her lifetime; some during a splurge in the 1970s but most in the few, strange but happy years with Martin Bryant. Tasmanian Transport Department officials catalogued the spree in amazement during the desperate scramble for information in the days after the massacre. Their research would show that some vehicles were kept a few months, others a matter of weeks and, occasionally, just a few days. All this by a woman who took 19 attempts to get her driver's licence. Carleen told of Helen's reluctance to get behind the wheel years later, seemingly to counter evidence of her son's bizarre and dangerous habit of leaning across the driver and yanking at the steering wheel.

The couple's visits to local car dealerships were greeted with curiosity and anticipation; the short, chubby and domineering matriarch followed by her blond puppy. As they walked around the yards, Bryant would comment on the cars in stock – "That's nice," or, "I'll have that one." More often than not it was enough for his senior companion to buy the vehicle. Colours meant little, nor the make although the cars were always small.

At times, she bought a new car at the beginning of the month only to sell it a few weeks later simply because she had run out of money for food. Then the next monthly cheque from her estate would come in and the folly would be repeated. On one occasion, she bought a car for $28,000 then backed it into a tree. Martin made some attempt to repair the damage, covering the indiscretion with house paint and then sold it for $7000. They never thought twice about it.

Carleen, unquestioning as always, watched it all with bemusement:

Helen then started changing cars every four months. The car yard dealers would clap their hands when they saw her coming. Most of her cars would need to be fumigated before reselling, because the dogs would relieve themselves inside. One dealer was not a happy man. Even after fumigation the stench stayed in the van. There was really nothing wrong with the vehicles that she replaced. Helen may not have liked the sound of the radio, so the car was sold. Perhaps she couldn't understand how to operate something; the car was sold. If her whim said the car was too big or too small, on to the market it went. It was the same with cameras and video cameras. Helen couldn't understand how they operated so she would buy another. She spent thousands of dollars. The main thing was that Helen and Martin were happy. Our hope was that the Lord would take care of them.

While Carleen prayed, oblivious in her own way, it was becoming clear that Helen and Martin may have been content but they also needed help – and Maurice Bryant's life was about to reach a watershed. In 1991, at the age of 62, he accepted an early retirement offer as reform on the Australian waterfront targeted older men like him and his mate, Ron Harmon. The package was generous and might have been the change he needed to fight the burgeoning depression he had long tried – and failed – to keep at bay with alcohol. His dream had been to enjoy his retirement years working with the local maritime museum but yet again, he had been forced to step into his son's life.

Only this time it would prove to be a tragedy.

Flush with funds and ever generous, Maurice offered to take Martin and Helen to New Zealand for a couple of weeks holiday but by the time they got there, he found himself trying to manage two difficult people who struggled to function within their own, familiar routines and environment but who flailed in unfamiliar surroundings. Maurice's kind plan had been to take them to a farm stay, allowing the two to enjoy the company of animals. Health authorities had restricted them to two small dogs, a silky terrier and Pomeranian, and one cat, and both Helen and Martin insisted they missed their menagerie terribly. Carleen recalls her husband calling to tell her that Helen and Martin were constantly complaining about the bedding and the food but the likelihood is that he simply had underestimated the couple's complex disabilities and behavioural problems. He spent the trip wishing he could simply leave everyone behind and take the next plane back to Tasmania.

At home, however, there were big problems, too. The marriage had been strained, mainly by Martin's problems – and the couple's entirely different responses to his needs. Maurice was constantly on guard, vigilant, ready to step in to restrain Martin's excesses yet denying the depth of his son's problems while Carleen withdrew, swinging between benign sufferance and high anxiety.

Over the next few years, they would spend more and more time living parallel lives but apart. Some read their decision as a separation of sorts, and later there were those who admitted to believing Maurice had begun an affair with Helen Harvey. It was more likely that Maurice was simply seeking some peace; trapped between two worlds of such equal need and high distress that he, too, in the end, would succumb.

In fact, Helen would become a rival for Carleen, but not for her husband's attentions so much as those of her son. As capable as she was of running a home, Carleen had been unable to manage the relationship with Martin. Now, another woman had stepped into the breach, not as a girlfriend or wife but as a friend, one who understood and valued him for who he was, unconditionally, perhaps even as a mother would. The fact that Helen was the opposite of Carleen – utterly dysfunctional – meant she did not try to control his behaviour. Martin preferred Helen's company – and its inherent freedom – to that of his mother, and so the unravelling was about to begin.

Out of the blue one day, Helen Harvey announced that she wanted to leave town and buy a farm. The trip to New Zealand, as difficult as it had been for Maurice, had inspired another bright idea in Helen, one that would help to alleviate her frustration at not being allowed to keep animals at Clare Street. She would simply create a rural ark where no one could question her or how many animals she chose to put in her menagerie. Maurice found them a place at Copping, a village halfway between the city and Port Arthur. He knew the owners of the 29-hectare property where he had often stopped to buy fruit for Martin to sell on his rounds. It was on the market for $130,000, and occupied the lower slopes of a hill, which were largely cleared of trees to run sheep or cattle, and overlooked a sweeping bend on the highway. The dense Australian bush on the other side of the road hinted at the panorama that would have existed before European settlement.

Clearing had begun in the mid-19th century under the orders of the man who would give the area his name, Captain Richard Copping, around the same time Martin Bryant's great-great-grandfather, Richard Cordwell, by then emancipated, was working to create a new life. There were two dams on the property, the larger positioned at the bottom end of the hill to catch the natural run-off, and the second one, a little higher, behind the three-bedroom weatherboard and iron-roofed house, which had been built in 1905 but was now in dire need of a spruce up. It was basic but functional enough to suit the odd couple, who had no interest in luxury and simply wanted plenty of space and land. They took possession of Taurusville, as they called it, in late October, leaving Clare Street as it was so they could move on a whim between the city and the country. The first animals were bought within weeks of moving in to the new house, as Carleen recalled:

We knew it wouldn't be long before Helen started buying more animals. Guess who had to pick up and deliver them? First Maurice was to bring three donkeys to the property for Helen. Then over time, about nine small ponies were added; most of them were wild and had never been handled. Then a third dog and more cats ended up inside the house, and out in a shed. Three purebred cats with long coats lived in Helen's bedroom, on the bed and around her neck. It amazed me that she didn't choke from all the loose hair.

There were already three aviaries on the property and, with about 30 canaries and budgerigars, it didn't take Helen long to fill the third one with different species of parrots. There were also about 10 cages in the sunroom. Maurice asked Helen never to buy goats or pigs. Helen wanted a Great Dane. Martin would see them for sale in the Mercury [newspaper] but always said to Helen that there were none. Thank goodness!

There were also fowls left on the property. Martin and Helen enjoyed going to the Hobart show. There she bought a prize rooster, then a bantam rooster. The bantams would run free and it was not long before they multiplied in number. The previous owners also left three peacocks, which roosted in a shed.

When Helen saw the pigs at the show she couldn't resist buying a piglet, a cream one with black spots. She said it was too cold outside and so she asked Martin to let the piglet in to sleep on his bed. The little one wet the bed and that was the last time the pig slept there. That piglet grew into a very large porker. Each morning Martin would cook rolled oats for that pig and then take him for a walk on a lead.

These scenes, surreal and eccentric but ultimately interpreted as happy by those around them, however, masked a much more sinister shift in Martin Bryant's psyche. The annoying, sometimes destructive and antisocial teenager known around his old haunts in Carnarvon Bay was changing, his moods darkening and becoming more erratic. Behaviour that could previously be ascribed to his inept social skills and intellectual shortcomings was deteriorating: stupid pranks began to make way to outright threats and an increasingly quick-to-flare temper. Outside the school environment – and in the company of a woman whose own psychological make-up lay well outside the norm – there was no one to observe or understand the import of the changes. The young child and adolescent, who had been assessed regularly and rigorously by educational and medical professionals in his early years, had not been reassessed since he had left school seven years before. The prescient words of Dr Cunningham Dax – warning that the development of a schizophrenic illness was possible – represented the last official appraisal of the schoolboy's psychological state. Now, the unhappy, destructive teen had escalated and turned into an unpredictable and furious young man.

It was not to be his parents or Helen to raise the alarm and insist that he undergo a new assessment. Indeed, Martin Bryant may never have been reassessed at all had it not been for the requirements of the social security system – and even then, the chilling assessment that would allow him to remain on the disability pension was attached to his file and forgotten:

Father protects him from any occasion which might upset him as he continually threatens violence ... Martin tells me he would like to go around shooting people. It would be unsafe to allow Martin out of his parents' control.

The prognosis from the family GP, Dr Bernard Mather, was equally grim:

Bad. He can only slowly worsen and will eventually be institutionalized.

For Maurice, the ever-patient father, it was confirmation of his darkest fears. The quietly spoken, unassuming Englishman knew that Martin was getting worse as he grew up. It was he who had taken on the role of a restraint; he had become the human equivalent of the leash his wife had used to tie the child to the veranda and keep him under control. Increasingly fearful and despondent, in November 1991 Maurice Bryant filed a will with the Public Trustee's office. The document, succinct and without emotional flourish, recognised that his son would find it difficult to manage life in the event of his father's passing. Maurice bequeathed the New Town house to Carleen or, in the event of her death, its division between his two children. Martin would require extra resources and so he left him the proceeds of the superannuation fund held with Commonwealth Life Policy No.10311246, worth more than $250,000, when he died.

Maurice must have told Helen Harvey about his will because three weeks later she filed her own, naming Maurice Bryant as a trustee. It was a defiant document, written with a clarity that others would not normally see in her eccentric facade, cementing her sense of alienation from the rest of her family. Like Martin, Helen felt both misunderstood and rejected. Indeed, her will begins not by stating to whom she would leave the various parts of her estate – the two properties, the animals and, of course, the Tattersall's legacy – but who would not be recognised: *I direct that no member of the Kalbfell or Harvey families shall take any benefit from my estate as I believe they are capable of providing for themselves.*

She also appeared to shun the Harvey name, and rather than choosing to be buried alongside her famous relatives at Cornelian Bay, she stipulated that she be buried in the grave of her maternal great-grandfather, John Gustav Kalbfell, and his wife Amelia. She also wanted provision *for my loyal friend the said Martin Bryant* to be buried in the same grave on his demise.

And it was to this very same young man, to *my friend Martin Bryant for his own absolute use and benefit*, that she left her fortune. That phrase would be repeated four times in the paragraphs where she bequeathed her worldly goods, her livestock, her animals and birds, her Clare Street mansion, the Taurusville farm and her Tattersall's income. Martin Bryant, the increasingly unstable misfit, became a multimillionaire in waiting.

CHAPTER 22
A Lawyer's Brief

If John Avery ever had a flash of sympathy for Martin Bryant – and a flash is all it would be – that moment came in early October 1996 when the Hobart lawyer's new client was wheeled into the interview room at Risdon Prison. Avery would later admit he was nervous about meeting the man accused of murdering 35 people but when he sees this man-boy, swathed in bandages and manacled to a wheelchair as if he has the physical capacity to leap out, attack the guards and escape to continue his killing spree, it seems absurd. He makes a mental note to himself to ask the prison to back off.

Acceptance of this Legal Aid brief is both the biggest opportunity of his life and its biggest professional risk. David Gunson, another prominent local lawyer, had been briefed originally but withdrew for ethical reasons. Gunson had never elaborated but it is widely assumed that he had been placed in an untenable position when Bryant confessed the killings but then insisted on entering a not guilty plea.

Avery had considered the request for a few hours but knew he couldn't really decline. He copped flak about his decision almost immediately, and most of his colleagues were already signed up to handle compensation claims from the victims. But Bryant had to have a lawyer, and the nation would be watching.

The lawyer is torn between fascination and revulsion, between the need to fashion a careful legal strategy and the sheer human desire and curiosity to find out why. What he knows without doubt though is that Tasmania should not have to relive the horror of a trial in which each and every charge of murder – all 35 of them – will have to be heard separately, calling families, witnesses, police to relive every moment of the horror again and again.

Somehow, he needs to establish some sort of rapport with the guy, and Bryant is immediately suspicious: "As long as you're not working for the police. I turned around and said to David [Gunson] one day, 'Are you working for the police, David?' and he said, 'No, no, I'm working for you, Martin.'"

Avery smiles reassuringly at the young man. "Well, there is no way we're working for the police, I can tell you that. Let's just talk about what I am here for. I have reviewed your case, and I now know as much as I need to know about it. I have gone through the statements that I think are appropriate, and I now know the weight of evidence against you, right."

"Yep."

"Now, having done all that, I have formed the view that I am prepared to act for you subject to a few limits, or a few conditions, right. Now I want to go through those and see whether you're content on that, right. First thing is that I think if you want me to act we've got to be frank with each other. I won't bullshit you but equally there are no games that I want you to play, right. Understand that?"

Avery wants to set out the ground rules with this bloke, who has already lost one lawyer and led the cops on some fantasy journey back in July when, somehow, he decided to deny involvement in the killings but admitted kidnapping.

Bryant nods as he continues.

"I will want to get from you, not today but in the next day or so, full instructions, right. And finally, I don't want you to have any false expectations and I won't give you any, right. Now within those broad parameters, do you want me to act for you?"

Bryant is like a puppy wagging his tail. "Yep, yeah, yeah."

"You're happy about that, that we talk frankly with each other? I'll do what I can for you but you've got to be frank with me, right?"

"OK. Will there still be a case? I mean, will there still be a trial?"

"Well, we'll talk about a trial or what we're going to do in a moment, right. Now for the next thing is: Do you understand legally why Mr Gunson can't act for you any more?"

"I think because there's no defence …"

It is clear he doesn't understand. Avery tries to explain. "Well, it's not really that. Let me just explain something to you in simple terms, right. If someone is charged with assaulting someone; let's use a simple example: there's a fight in a pub and someone punches another person and he is charged with assault. If that person goes to a lawyer and says, 'Yes, I punched him but I'm going to go to court and say I didn't do it,' it puts the lawyer in a position of conflict because he can't allow his client to go to court and lie."

"Oh yes." Bryant is nodding again.

"Right, now David Gunson, I gather, has found himself in an ethical problem because of what you have told him and what you want to do. Now, having said that, if you want me to act I will do so and I will appear in court tomorrow and tell the court that I am now acting for you and we will proceed down that path."

"Oh good."

Avery breathed a sigh of relief. The initial problem was over and, whether Bryant understood or not, he had been upfront and professional. If the bloke made a confession and then recanted again, he'd have no option but to walk. He hoped he could make Bryant see sense. First though, he had to ensure he was being treated fairly.

"Now, are there any parts of the evidence or anything like that that you haven't seen or you want to see again? Let me just give you examples. There's a video interview when you were interviewed in July that seemed to go all afternoon. Have you seen that interview?"

"No, I haven't."

"Have you read the transcript of it?"

"I have read the transcript, yes."

"Right, well I think I should at some stage show you that interview, right, or parts of … I think you should see."

"I think I know the part … the part where I pointed to myself."

Avery nods: "The part when you pointed to yourself and said 'Me', right."

"That's not going to help me." It is a statement rather than a question. Bryant knows he has made a blunder by being cocky.

Avery is almost mocking: "Not going to help? It is going to put you right under. But all I'm saying is if you want to, I can arrange in due course for you to see that."

Bryant shakes his head. "No, I don't really want to."

"You don't want to see it, OK. Are there any witness statements you haven't seen that you would like to see?"

"I've got them all."

"You've got them all? Have you read them?"

"Yes."

"Right, have you heard the negotiating tapes when you were on the phone?"

"Yes. I couldn't recall that that was my voice."

"Well, if you like I can bring them over sometime and play them on this recorder, right, and you can say, 'Yes, that's me,' or, 'No, it's not,' right. Because there is a lot of information on those and a lot of indication that you wanted to go in a helicopter for a ride, all that sort of stuff, but if you want to we can play them for you. I don't want you saying, 'Oh, I'm not sure about that.'"

"OK."

Avery pauses again. He is past the second roadblock. Bryant has seen all the written material and challenged nothing. And he isn't interested in the police tape, probably because of his fuck-up at the end. It doesn't make much difference really. It is time to move on.

"Has David Gunson discussed in detail what the psychiatric reports reveal?" Avery asked.

"Not really. All I've heard from David, he said that everything seems to be all right, everything seems to be all right in there."

"All right, well that is something else we will need to discuss in detail. In broad terms, they say there is nothing wrong with you, you're not mad!"

"No."

"Well you know that anyway, don't you?"

"Yeah."

Another problem out of the way; he is not claiming insanity but it opens up another opportunity. Maybe he can convince Bryant to draw what happened; unconventional, he knows. He might even be accused of trying to cash in on Bryant's infamy, but he'll deal with that later.

"All right, OK. Let me just ask you something. One of the things that came out when I was reading the psychiatric material is what you used to do at school and what you liked doing. I think your best subject seemed to be art."

"Art, yes."

"Do you want to do some about this? Do you want to do some drawings?"

Bryant is puzzled: "It's been ages since I was at school. I haven't done any since I was at school."

"Well, I might like you to do some, right?"

"What, today, or …"

"No, no not today but if I bring some paper over, what do you prefer, crayons or something like that?"

"Yeah, that would be fine, yep."

"We can start, if nothing else, to piece this together even through some illustrations or something like that, right. I collect art so I would like you to sort of start …"

"Oh good."

"OK, so do you think you might be interested in that if I get you some paper and crayon and you can start piecing all this together through your hands, right?"

"Yep."

"OK, all right. Let's turn to your case. It's pretty obvious that it all points to you being guilty, doesn't it?"

Bryant doesn't flinch. "Yes"

"I mean, let's be frank, we can't invent stories that you weren't there or anything like that. If you follow the evidence through and you have read those statements, they have you at Seascape, they have you, it would appear, killing the Martins, leaving and going down to Port Arthur etc etc. Now all that seems to have come out, doesn't it? I can't magically say none of that happened. I can't magically find a defence that you were in Hong Kong or somewhere else."

It is a speech; an alternative to accusing the guy outright, which isn't his job. Bryant has to reach the conclusion himself if it is going to be a valid confession.

He is subdued now: "Mm, that's right."

"But today isn't the purpose of going through that. When I next come back … you and I will talk."

"Yes."

"And I repeat, we're going to look each other in the eye, and I don't want any stories or bullshit. You're going to have to start putting your mind as to what you're going to do here for the rest of your life. Whether it's basket-making or sewing up policemen's trousers or whatever, I don't know. That's something you've got to wrestle with right?"

Bryant doesn't argue: "There's a lot of activities here … art classes or whatever."

"And we'll talk next week about whether you're going to go to trial or whether you're going to plead guilty."

"Yep."

"I am not here to make you plead guilty … but I'm not here also to say we're going to run a long trial just for the sake of a long trial. It doesn't do you any good and it doesn't do the broader community any good, right. You've got to come out of this now with some respectability, right?"

There, he has said it, hopefully in terms that this bloke, as simple as he was, can understand. But the reply indicates there is another motive beyond innocence and guilt:

"I just want to hear all the evidence and what other people have got to say about me."

Avery tries to cut him off: "Oh, we'll talk that through. You've got the statements and we'll go through that and …"

"No, I mean in court." Bryant is insistent. He has virtually agreed by consent that he is guilty and the evidence is overwhelming, but he wants his day in court.

Martin Bryant wants to relive his rampage.

"All right, well let's leave it at that today. You want me to act. I'll act for you, right. I'll be back in a couple of days and we'll have a couple of hours going through what happened, what you did, why you did it. Right, and then we'll talk about trials …"

It is Bryant's turn to cut Avery off. He isn't ready to move on:

"Will that actually be a statement?"

"Well, it will just be your instructions to me, right. I'm your lawyer. I can't pass it on to anyone. I won't be saying what you said. Lawyers' discussions with clients are privileged. They can't go somewhere else and tell someone."

Bryant persists: "I don't know if I can recall being down there. I can't recall a lot of what occurred but we can talk about that."

Avery gives in. If Bryant wants to talk about it, fair enough: "Well, we'll see where we go, all right, but I mean the reality is you've certainly made lots of admissions to lots of people that it was you."

"Yeah, on the video. That was when they left the room and came back. I must have said something like that, but I don't recall … I don't recall pointing at myself."

The lawyer is emphatic: "Well, you did. I've looked at the video."

"Well, that's strong evidence, that's more or less …"

"Admitting it," Avery chips in. "That's a total confession, that's what it's called."

"Will that go to trial?"

Avery is getting nowhere. It is like hitting his head against a brick wall.

"If you have a trial, that's the first bit of evidence they will put up. They will play that video. I mean, that's the best bit of evidence they've got, isn't it? Martin Bryant pointing to himself and saying, 'I'm the mass murderer.' They don't need much more, do they?"

"No," Bryant admits.

"Anyway, we don't have to talk that through today. The purpose of today, I repeat, is to see whether you're content with me as a lawyer. To deal with it and that we are going to be frank with each other and not set any unreal expectations. I'm not going to come in here and say you're going to be out next year. You won't be having any rabbit stews with mum, I can tell you that."

"They are trying to brainwash me to not having a trial."

Jeez, the bloke is still at it. It is going to be a struggle. "Well, I am not going to try and brainwash you on anything. If you want to have a trial, we'll have a trial. All I am saying, we have to look at what a trial is going to be about, and we've got to look at the inevitability at a trial that you will be found guilty."

"Would I be found guilty if I wasn't on that video screen?"

"I would have thought there was enough evidence to convict you without that. Heaps and heaps of people saying you're it, you were there, they've even got a photograph of you off the video walking round with a gun at Port Arthur shooting everyone. So you're pretty distinctive."

"Yes ... A person should have a balaclava on."

There is another admission. He appears to be regretting an oversight. "You should have had a balaclava on, yeah, yeah."

"It wouldn't have probably made much difference."

"Well, only just to say he's the fellow with the balaclava. So I think it's pretty inevitable that you will be found guilty whether by pleading guilty or having a trial, but by pleading guilty, I suppose, you are going to save a lot of people a lot of heartache and a lot of trauma, make your family feel you've done the right thing, make the community at least think you're not a monster."

"A monster! They probably think I am now. I don't know."

"I'm sure they do ..."

"An evil monster."

CHAPTER 23
Copping

Sue Featherstone waited a few weeks before introducing herself to the new neighbours, the slightly odd pairing of a middle-aged frump and her young sidekick. They clearly weren't related but the notion of an older woman and her young lover simply didn't ring true either.

Sue was intrigued. She and husband John had farmed at Copping for years and known the Blackwell family next door very well, often buying their raspberries to make jam. One day, she and daughter Kylie ventured across the dirt path that separated the two properties to introduce themselves to their new neighbours and to ask if they might continue the raspberry tradition. It was as much an excuse to say hello and have a little squizz as anything else.

The reaction, at first, was friendly. The young man who answered the door invited them in and made them a cup of tea. But before they had finished, his mood changed without warning and the women were herded back out the door with a threat: "If you come back again, I'll shoot you."

From that moment on, Martin Bryant took on a persona vastly different from that of his youth: he became a man to be avoided at all costs but out of fear, not pity.

A few months later, it happened again, this time to John's brother, Barry Featherstone, who ran a nearby property. In the days after the shootings, Barry would relate his clash with Bryant in florid detail to the media, describing his visit to the property to do some work. More than 12 years later, John can still recall the details with clarity.

It was about 8pm when Bryant answered the door. Miss Harvey appeared to be in bed already. Bryant, in a vile mood, demanded to know who he was and then ordered him off the property, threatening not only to call the police but his lawyer too if he ever returned. Featherstone, a much bigger man, stood at the door in amazement at the young man's fury: "I could've knocked him arse over head," he said in one account.

Instead he left, got in his car and drove to his home nearby: "I get to my place and he's followed me. He pulls up in the car and starts yelling, and I hop in his car and tell him he's on my property now and I'll go him. He starts bawling like a kid. It was incredible."

Helen Harvey came to see him the next day with Bryant in tow. She apologised for Martin's behaviour and insisted the two men shake hands, but the damage was done. The neighbours watched Bryant with growing concern, avoiding him at all costs and refusing the occasional, eccentric offers of friendship. He was unpredictable, erratic, changing from the foolhardy schoolboy to temperamental, spoiled brat – or worse – in seconds. Some remembered a wild-eyed boy who appeared to take delight in firing his air rifle at tourists as they stopped to buy apples at a stall on the highway. Bryant's dress changed, too, from his preferred white overalls and red cardigan to the natty pretensions of the country squire, complete with cravat, when the whim took him. For some neighbours, his penchant for roaming the properties in the dead of night became a palpable fear as he was hardly ever seen but the dogs would bark madly, sensing an intruder, and then they would hear the sound of gunfire – the air rifle Bryant carried with him everywhere.

For Helen and Martin, home may have changed but the rhythm of life did not. They still rose late, wandered listlessly, shopping and eating, often leaving their car full of animals parked in the local village. The odd sight of a car with dogs, cats and even miniature ponies jammed in the back seat began to disturb locals, the couple's strange behaviour adding to the mystery of their relationship. Rumours abounded, fuelled too by their habit of leaving cash strewn around the house, under books and secreted, in big rolls of notes in odd places such as ice-cream containers. What the odd visitor saw in the house only added to their mystique although, in truth, much of what was left around the place was due to carelessness rather than strategy.

Many neighbours saw Bryant as overly protective of his older companion, while others remember a placid, obedient character who trailed behind "Miss Harvey" when they went into the nearby town of Dunalley and roamed the local antique store or bought enormous garbage bags full of lettuces for the pigs. The shop owners observed similar behaviour to those seen by their counterparts back in Hobart: Helen was a kind of sergeant-major; a short and dumpy woman who barked orders, which her companion accepted without question. Martin, at least in these situations, appeared simply to be a nice-looking, polite young man who nevertheless exuded a palpable sense of aloneness.

Occasionally, the two would also drift down as far as Port Arthur, most often on a Sunday when they would join Maurice and Carleen for a roast lunch, after which they would head back to the historic settlement for tea and scones at the Broad Arrow Cafe. Helen, purse stuffed carelessly with notes, would invariably buy several things from the gift shop. They rarely went back to Clare Street.

There was another side of Helen, which revealed candidly that she was aware not only of the role she played in managing her young companion but of his impact on his parents. She explained frequently to neighbours that he lived with her because of a difficult relationship with his parents. She was "like a mother" to him, she said, because his parents could no longer handle his behaviour, and had given him the pet piglet to sleep with to calm him down. Carleen was simply never mentioned, while Maurice was a background figure, keeping a check on things but happy to have washed his hands of their day-to-day affairs, at least for a short while. Carleen remembers vividly a clash she had with Helen during a Sunday lunch, a clear indication of the continuing tension between the pair:

> On one particular day, Helen claimed that she owned a farm in the midlands of Tasmania, and that a manager was running the property. She said that she had a bear there. I told her not to talk nonsense. Helen replied that it was true. I continued to disagree saying it was not permitted to have an exotic bear in Tasmania. However Helen jumped out of the chair and said, "I'm going home" so off they went. She was a great storyteller. Maurice and Martin would say to me "You know it's not true so why disagree with her?" I said I could only put up with so many of the lies and exaggerations.

When it came to stories about Martin's increasingly difficult behaviour, there was no exaggeration: Martin had become a dangerous, potentially lethal passenger in a moving car. She simply could not predict when the 25-year-old, who had still not learned to drive and would never attempt to get a licence for fear of failure, would reach across her and wrench the steering wheel. It was the reason she had taken to crawling along the gentle but narrow country roads, never travelling above 60km/h. Twice she had run off the road while trying to fend off Martin, once running up against an embankment and the other time into a drain. A farmer came to help them haul the car out. She told another farmer while on a visit to buy cattle that he had pulled at the wheel on the way down that day: "What would you do with him?" she sighed benignly.

Bryant's school friend Greg had witnessed similar scenes. Once, he had been in the car and watched horrified as Maurice Bryant tried to wrest back control when his son reached over the seat and tried to grab the wheel. Paul Williams also recalled that Martin was always placed in the front passenger seat whenever the family drove anywhere. If Maurice drove then Carleen sat in the back and if Carleen drove then Maurice did so, apparently forever wary of their son and ready to hold him back if he reached over to grab the wheel.

The difference was that Maurice was a strong man, and Helen, despite her bulk, found it difficult to wrestle away a strapping and determined young man. Martin's was not a death wish but a sudden, childlike impulse, one he could neither control nor suppress. Worse still, he had no ability to understand the potentially fatal consequences of his actions.

Martin also appeared oblivious to external stimuli such as pain and the cold – a characteristic often seen in children and adults with Asperger's. As a child, he had flirted and played with fire, could dive without hesitation into freezing water, loved to catch crayfish without gloves and was not bothered by heights or taking risks. Now, he not only appeared to fear nothing but also felt very little, viewing the world through a childish, cartoon-like prism, one where the coyote bounces back to life despite falling off a cliff while chasing the roadrunner or being blown up by dynamite. But in real life, a car hurtling out of control can kill – and people do not walk away from a shotgun fired at point-blank range.

Maurice and Carleen were toying with the notion of another overseas holiday. The Carnarvon Bay property had become all but obsolete – the kids didn't want to go there any more – and so, they decided to sell up and make better use of the money. On a fleeting, four-day trip to Sydney in September 1992, as the strained couple browsed the shopfronts along the Manly Corso, they noticed a travel agent advertising a package trip to London, flying out of Australia and returning by cruise ship, the Canberra. Maurice immediately imagined reliving the momentous journey that had brought him to Australia 40 years before on the Orcades. They booked the trip there and then – but would never get to board the flight.

Maurice had always worried about Helen and his son driving after dark. Apart from Martin's dangerous habits, she was not a good driver, and a car full of animals only exacerbated the situation. In April, the couple had another accident, this time near Copping, when she braked sharply to avoid a kangaroo, and the two cars behind her, anxious to overtake the slow driver, ran up the back of the car. The damage was minimal but Maurice pleaded with the couple not to go out after mid-afternoon. Of course, the warning went unheeded.

On October 20, they loaded three dogs into their white Mazda 121 and headed north for Sorell to do some shopping for groceries and feedstock in one of the larger towns along the highway. It was after 5pm when they started back for the farm. Sunset was still more than an hour away but the light was fading as the sun lowered towards the hilltops behind Hobart. As they entered a straight, uphill stretch of road just over a kilometre west of the town of Copping itself, something happened. There are those who believe without doubt that Martin probably succumbed to another impulse and reached over and grabbed the wheel, forcing the car to the wrong side of the road. Bryant himself told police that Helen Harvey had been distracted by dogs fighting in the back seat, and his last recollection was turning around to look back at the dogs and Helen veering to cross the double white lines and straight into the path of an oncoming Ford sedan. When police arrived at the scene they found Helen Harvey dead behind the wheel, her neck snapped by the impact. One of the dogs lay dead in the back seat and another on the verge. The third had survived and would be found back at Taurusville a few days later. Martin Bryant was in the passenger seat, barely alive with serious neck injuries: X-rays would reveal two fractured vertebrae.

The Mercury carried a small story at the bottom of page 3 the next day under the heading "Woman killed in collision". It stated simply that a middle-aged woman had been killed in a head-on collision:

The female driver and a male passenger in the dead woman's car were admitted to Royal Hobart Hospital in a serious condition.

The bereavement notice posted by Maurice Bryant in *The Mercury* newspaper a few days later was poignant in its simplicity:

From quiet homes and first beginning
Out to undiscovered ends,
There's nothing worth the wear of winning
But laughter and the love of friends.

Strangely, the poem, written by the French-born, English poet, Hilaire Belloc, formed part of a compilation of work titled *The Bad Child's Book of Beasts*.

The next day, a verse from a Henry Wadsworth Longfellow poem *A Psalm of Life* appeared, placed by the funeral director, not family.

Life is real! Life is earnest!
And the grave is not its goal;
Dust thou art, to dust returnest,
Was not spoken of the soul.

Helen Harvey died unmourned by her family but deeply missed by the Bryants. While they would benefit financially, her passing would also bring them incalculable tragedy.

As the family struggled to come to terms with Helen's loss, Lindy Bryant, the little sister so often forgotten in this family's tragic saga, had been working as an apprentice chef near Port Arthur. A mature young woman, her father asked her to step into the fray. The relationship with her brother had always been difficult, not only because of his jealousies and frustrations but because he had demanded so much of her parents' time and energy. What was left for her? She was even cut out of her father's will despite the fact that he knew that Martin would be well cared for financially by Helen Harvey, in life and now in death.

Still, she became a pivotal force during her brother's recovery in hospital to the point where he later recognised a significant and positive shift in their relationship. Maurice had offered to pay her a wage to look after her brother, and she quit her job at the Fox and Hounds to be there when he returned from hospital. Locked into a metal brace that kept his head and neck still and in a specific position for three months, he would then spend another two months in a leather brace.

While Martin was in hospital and out of harm's way, Maurice began clearing the farm of stock, preparing for what he told the neighbours would be its sale. Martin was not coming back, he insisted. The Featherstones and others were only too happy to help while Maurice either shot or sold off the disparate collection of farm animals and pets. When Carleen arrived a few days later to begin cleaning the house, she found new litters of cats and dogs in almost every room. She called the RSPCA, which had to shoot several dogs because they had become feral.

Martin, meanwhile, settled back into the family home at Augusta Road to see out his convalescence. Neighbours recall he appeared relatively content, walking around looking like a spaceman with his neck in a brace with two steel rods pinned into his skull. He was also more chatty than usual.

Yet again, what Martin exhibited externally did not tally with what he was undergoing internally. He had lost Helen, his best friend and maternal companion, and her loss had a profound impact. Martin began to regress, desperately seeking new relationships to replace the old. This time, he turned his attention to much younger children and began pestering kids as young as nine to join in their games. He wanted desperately to play Nintendo with a 10-year-old who lived the other side of the rotting tennis court behind the house, and pursued him relentlessly.

At times, adults feared there may be a sexual connotation to his behaviour but it was far more likely that he was trying to connect with human beings more akin to his intellectual abilities, which at the time were measured roughly equivalent to those of an 11-year-old. Even so, younger children wouldn't have a bar of him, again rejecting his attempts at friendship: "The kids were wary of him," one neighbour would recount. "They understood instinctively that he was someone to stay away from. He was just a little scary."

Contrary to Maurice's insistence that his son was not going back to Copping, however, Martin began returning to the property in March 1993 as soon as his leather brace was removed. Without the guidance of Helen Harvey though, he began to cause trouble with the neighbours and further afield. One clear morning not long after his release from the neck brace, Martin boarded a coach bound for Hobart from a stop on the nearby highway. Halfway through the journey, a ruckus blew up when a young girl complained to the driver that Bryant had put his hand up another girl's skirt.

The driver stopped the bus and ordered Bryant to sit at the front where he could be watched until they reached their destination: "He was stroppy at first but quietened down after a while," the driver told a local newspaper following the shootings. The young man had been "chucked out" as soon as they reached Hobart. Characteristically, Martin Bryant had absolutely no sense of the impact of his behaviour on another human being and was waiting at the stop ready to board for the return journey. When the driver refused to take him on board, he reacted violently. In defiance, Bryant then hailed a taxi and had it follow the bus while he hung out the window, waving his fist and swearing at the driver and his passengers.

The incident was reported to Dunalley police but, like so many complaints made before, nothing was done.

CHAPTER 24
Call the Police

Maurice Bryant was planning another trip to England but unlike their earlier, ill-fated plan, this time he did not want to take Carleen. It was mid 1993 and Martin was dividing his time between the Copping farm and New Town. He had also received word of his vast inheritance, a remarkable turn of events for a boy from a family that had always worked for its simple but middle-class existence.

Maurice and Carleen were also comfortable financially: Carnarvon Bay had been sold in March, its part in their lives now a distant – and not always pleasant – memory. The proceeds were supposed to fund a more mobile retirement, filled with travel and a dose of the adventure that Maurice had always craved.

For now though, he felt desperately in need of a break. Their travel plan the previous year, an attempt to help them restore the struggling marriage, had again been wrecked by Martin, and Maurice too was feeling Helen's loss deeply. Only this time, he seemed to have lost the will to find a solution.

A few weeks after Helen's death, Maurice had felt so low that he had gone to visit the family GP, Dr Bernard Mather, complaining about a sense of constant anxiety and encroaching sadness and depression. It was the second time in six months he had asked for help, unusual in a man usually so stoic. The first time was in May, around Martin's 25th birthday, and then the doctor had given him a script for Valium to help him sleep. It was not enough. This time, in the aftermath of Helen's death and increasing worry about Martin's future, Maurice went back for more help. Mather prescribed Prothiaden, a tricyclic antidepressant, and gave Maurice two scripts, enough to last three months. He advised that he take one 25 milligram tablet twice during the day and a 75mg tablet at night.

Tragically, Maurice did not continue with the course of antidepressants.

Instead, he decided to head overseas, not with his wife, but with Lindy. It was as if the father of two had suddenly understood just how much his daughter had missed out on due to her brother's difficulties, and Maurice had decided he wanted to make up for her lost childhood. So much attention had been lavished on Martin, either managing his behaviour or extricating him from the repercussions, that Lindy had been largely left to fend for herself, alone. There were horse-riding lessons and weekends at Carnarvon Bay but the young girl's normality alongside Martin made it easy to forget that she was a little kid and needed attention, too.

The increasingly sad father turned to taking his daughter out for restaurant meals where, inevitably, the conversation would drift to talk about his fathering. She reassured him that he had been a good father, not realising that he had started to talk in the past tense – "had he been" a good dad rather than "was he being" a good dad. Neither Lindy nor her mother could possibly have understood the importance of the phrasing at the time. Indeed, Lindy was about to embark on her own first, adult journey, turning 20 in July and readying to leave Tasmania for the mainland to begin a job on the Gold Coast as a chef.

It was during their trip to Europe, in London then Paris, that Lindy perceived that her father was in the grip of a serious, clinical depression. At one point, Maurice became disoriented and Lindy was forced to take him to hospital. They managed to continue on their trip but it was clear he would need immediate medical help when they got home. The depression, masked over the years to a large degree by his self-medication with alcohol, had finally burst through to the surface. Maurice did indeed go to see his doctor when he returned to Hobart – on July 5 and August 3 – but both times he asked for treatment for a viral throat infection but did not raise the depression again.

In spite of his burgeoning internal desperation, Maurice was still trying to keep his son in check. He knew it was impossible for Martin to manage the fortune he had inherited without some help and feared he would fritter it away if he were not around to stop him. Maurice decided that a court order, under the Mental Health Act, was the only way to take control of Martin's financial affairs and have them managed independently by the Perpetual Trustees. This way, his son would be given a stipend which he could spend as he wished but the money would be doled out in a controlled way to ensure it lasted for life.

This was not the only arrangement Maurice was organising. Secretly, he had put their joint bank accounts in Carleen's name alone and signed the bills for household utilities over to her.

Although Carleen would not discover the changes until it was too late, she did note a difference in her husband. He looked tired, defeated, and she despaired that his retirement, so full of promise with plans to visit countries such as Egypt, had turned instead to an endless burden of watching, controlling and fixing problems created by their son. He'd been the backbone for everything, not just for Martin but Helen too, and the two, bereft of most life skills had relied on his practicality and capable approach. At least Maurice had managed to convince Martin to sell the farm after Helen's death, although the young man insisted that he wanted to delay this until the summer, after he had ploughed some fields.

In fact, the family GP had also seen the young man, who was desperately fighting his own demons and grief following Helen's death. Twice he complained to Dr Mather that he, too, was riddled with anxiety and had problems sleeping. And he was also prescribed tranquillisers, medication he took three or four times a week.

That was the last time Martin Bryant would seek any medical or psychological help.

While Maurice began spending weekends alone at Copping, Martin decided to return to his old haunt at Clare Street. Carleen's memoirs make no mention of the increasing difficulties in the marriage, focusing on the last few weeks she spent with Maurice in early August 1993. Every Saturday, she was in the habit of taking her mother and a couple of friends from the Jutland retirement village out to lunch at a seafood restaurant near the docks. Maurice had never accompanied them, until August 6 when he suddenly agreed to go with the women:

Maurice was so quiet ... so burdened, sad and depressed. I held his hand as we walked into the restaurant.

A few days later, just before midday on Friday, August 13, Maurice Bryant drove to Copping for the weekend. Carleen was due to drive down the next day, while Martin had plans to catch the bus and meet them for a meal before his parents headed home. They had found that this was a way of maintaining contact with the boy without immersing themselves in his world again and risking yet another altercation. Martin was known to have made threats against his father, too, although no one ever took those seriously.

Carleen didn't question the time her husband wanted to spend alone but became anxious when he telephoned about 7.30 that evening. He sounded particularly quiet and withdrawn:

Over all the years when any of us would travel to Port Arthur, we would always telephone to say we had arrived safely. On Friday evening Maurice telephoned and said very little other than "I love you." At the time I was surprised, as he had not said that before when calling, and so I assumed he had had a few drinks. Sadly this would be the last time I would speak to my husband.

Maurice made another call that night; to daughter Lindy in Queensland to tell her he loved her. He did not make a call to his son.

The next morning a man came to the front door of the Copping farmhouse to answer an advertisement for the horse float. No one answered but pinned to the door was a note in Maurice's handwriting: "Call the police."

By mid-morning, police had scrambled to the property, bringing in 20 cadets and local rural fire service volunteers to help scour the hillside. It took two days to find the body. Maurice Bryant was lying face down in almost three metres of water in the dam at the back of the house. His body was weighed down with Martin's diving belt strung bandolier fashion around his neck and across his torso. There was a strip of the antidepressant drug Serapax in his pocket. Eighteen of the 30mg tablets were missing.

In his report to the corner, Constable Garry Whittle concluded:

"I examined the deceased's body and failed to locate any marks of violence on the body. From the enquiries I have concluded ... it would appear the deceased took his own life."

Lindy rushed back from Queensland and identified her father's body while Carleen sobbed in the kitchen. No one saw the young man crying or grieving, later feeding spiralling rumours that Martin not only may have had a role in his father's death but in the accident which had killed Helen Harvey 10 months earlier.

Investigations cleared him of any involvement in either death. Maurice Bryant, wracked by a sense of increasing helplessness in the face of his son's problems, had taken his own life. The post mortem examination revealed he had two antidepressant, prescription drugs in his system – dothiepin (the Prothiaden he had been given nine months earlier by his doctor), and diazepam, otherwise known as Valium which had been prescribed for Martin. The water in his lungs showed clearly, the coroner, Edward Vickers said, that 64-year-old Maurice had drowned. Vickers's conclusion was succinct: "I find that Maurice Bryant died by drowning, consistent with suicide."

Police would review the case after Martin Bryant's rampage three years later but quickly reach the same conclusion.

The funeral notice on August 18 read:

> BRYANT, MAURICE – *Suddenly passed away on or about August 13, 1993, dearly beloved husband of Carleen and devoted and treasured father of Martin and Lindy. The loss we are feeling cannot be explained. Our love for this man will never leave us. And all our good memories will always stay. No other man could give all the love he did. Oh Dad why so soon? Your love will always be in our hearts. Although we never really said goodbye, one can only question why. Goodbye for now but not forever. Sleep peacefully now.*

The following day there were simple notices from family in Britain and another from Freda Cordwell describing her son-in-law as "a true gentleman". Martin Bryant chose the music for his father's funeral – "a certain piece from the American Civil Army", as Carleen described it without naming the piece. But her son, she said, was too traumatised to attend:

He had lost not only a wonderful father but also his true friend. The real friend he had for certain, in contrast to the friends he didn't have.

Others read Martin's absence differently, seeing a man who didn't seem to understand that his father was dead. He had smiled and joked during the police search for his father, preferring to mow the lawn at the farm and listen to music on his Walkman than to help look for Maurice. And he appeared to show no remorse.

John Featherstone was one of those who looked on perplexed: "He was dressed in those bloody white overalls and had a headset on. He walked up and down with a Whipper Snipper sort of slashing at the grass but cutting nothing but a few blades of grass every now and then. We knew there was something wrong with this bloke. You could write a book about the fellow. He had three or four different personalities."

Or one very flawed personality.

Again, Martin Bryant had revealed without doubt that he was incapable of empathy – and a stranger to consequence.

CHAPTER 25
All Alone

Martin Bryant was now alone in a world he believed ignored, ridiculed and even feared him. In the space of 10 months, he had lost the two people his mother would describe as her son's best friends but who, more accurately, were the only people who had ever managed to keep him under some semblance of control. The strain had emotionally tortured and finally killed his father and contributed, albeit accidentally, to the death of his beloved Helen Harvey. Indeed, the notion that the young man deliberately killed either made no sense at all because Martin Bryant did not crave money, just companionship.

Forensic psychiatrist Professor Paul Mullen would tell the court:

> The death first of Ms Harvey and then the suicide of his father stripped away from Mr Bryant the two main sources of support and stability in his life. The acquisition of a level of wealth, which even with the intercession of the Public Trustees was beyond Mr Bryant's capacity to comprehend, let alone manage, may well have contributed to the subsequent increasing disorganisation in his existence, rather than forming a basis for stability as presumably had been hoped by Ms Harvey and his father when they bequeathed him this wealth.

When Lindy returned to Queensland after the funeral, all that remained of Martin's previous life was his mum, Carleen. Their relationship had long been problematic, the tension between them highlighted by his decision not to move back to Augusta Road but to Clare Street to live by himself in the house he had shared with Helen just a few streets from the family home. He didn't want Carleen interfering and telling him what to do, and yet he accepted her help to clean the house on some occasions and happily looked forward to her cooking him meals for him at other times. He was like a teenage kid, halfway between childhood and adulthood, self-centred and entirely unaware of his mother's own struggle with loss, grief and her place in the world.

Martin Bryant's loss was close to complete. His world had changed dramatically – and with it his behaviour as he struggled to establish an identity without Helen. He attempted vainly to rekindle his own version of the happy times but it didn't seem the same wandering the streets shopping, dropping in to cafes and restaurants for a leisurely meal. It all just highlighted his isolation and deep loneliness. Helen had driven their activities, been the dominant force in their spending, their search for activities, their communication with others. Now, she was gone and so was his father. There would be no more help and encouragement to go lawn mowing or selling vegies door-to-door without Maurice to organise and motivate. Not that Martin Bryant needed the money – it was more about having a place in society, something to do, an identity of sorts. Instead, he was rudderless, floating without a goal or his dad's gentle moral compass. As Stella Sampson, his former teacher, would later tell the media: "My personal view is that his dad kept him in check, and when he died he didn't have that restraining influence any longer. I felt that dad was the linchpin that kept them all together, kept everything on an even keel."

Bryant's struggle for acceptance was displayed dramatically in his ever-changing attire. Gone were the overalls and cravats he had favoured around Copping. The farm was abandoned to memory, allowed to fall into disrepair and finally sold. Instead now, he would appear at a Glenorchy cafe for afternoon tea in the grey linen suit and lizard skin shoes of a *roué*, the outfit topped with a rakish Panama hat. He would tell the sympathetic ladies behind the counter at the suburban shopping centre sandwich bar that he was carrying a briefcase because he had a job earning $400 a week. On other days, he'd appear at a pizza restaurant looking like a surfie, with wild hair encased in a badly tied bandana and pink-rimmed, John Lennon-style sunglasses. It was as if the child in him had raided the parental wardrobe to play dress-ups, the costumes garish in their attempt to ape adults he didn't really quite understand.

There was also an unforgettable electric blue suit with flared trousers and ruffled shirt he wore to the upmarket North Hobart restaurant where he was a regular. The owner, Chris Jackman, recalled the response: "It was horrible. Everyone was laughing at him, even the customers. I really felt suddenly quite sorry for him. I realised this guy didn't really have any friends. He was like a child, trying to impress everybody. He struck me as a very eager sort of young guy, like a Labrador puppy. Always having something to say, always trying to impress."

Bryant struck his neighbours at Clare Street the same way. Harry and Anitra Kuiper had recently moved into a house in Bedford Street directly behind No.30 Clare Street, which had initially appeared empty. Then Martin Bryant showed up, keen to be friends. At first, as they later told journalist and author Mike Bingham for his 1996 book *Suddenly One Sunday*, the Kuipers allowed their three children aged between nine and 13 to play with the rather odd man at the back and even make short visits across the fence to his house. They came home with stories of a house much less tidy than their own with lots of TV sets and unopened boxes containing video players, even a dead rat on a window sill and dirty kitty litter trays. The vigilant Kuipers kept a close eye on events even as the friendship blossomed. Martin would occasionally take them on outings into Hobart for ice-cream and to the movies, and showered them with gifts, on one occasion buying huge water pistols for "wars" in the garden, which had returned to its natural, tangled state. He seemed to be the biggest kid of them all, intellectually at least, and at last felt on a par with his playmates.

Then Anitra Kuiper began receiving telephone calls from Carleen Bryant, warning her against allowing the children to become too close to her son. More chilling still, she warned Anitra to ban the children from getting into the car with Martin, who by now was driving himself for the first time. He had bought an old yellow Volvo and strapped a surfboard permanently to the roof-rack. The problem was that he did not have a licence, later telling police he had always been too fearful of failure to sit the theory test.

The relationship with the Kuiper family ended suddenly after six months but it was not because of Carleen's intervention. One day, while at his house, Bryant suggested a game of cards with the children. The pack of playing cards was printed with naked women: it was enough for Harry Kuiper to ban his children from ever going to the house again. Bryant's pleas of a misunderstanding were ignored.

Martin now turned his ever more desperate attempts to find companionship to older women in a bid to re-create his old life with a new Helen. His relationship with Carleen continued to grind and founder in the background. Anitra Kuiper remembers him telling her that Carleen was trying to move in with him: "She's always telling me what to do, and I'll have to do all this stuff I don't want to do," he complained, later blaming his mother for the problem with the Kuiper family.

Yvonne Briggs was 50 years old, lived down the street and had just separated from her husband when Bryant walked up to her in the street one day and asked her out on a date. She later told *The Sydney Morning Herald* she had been flabbergasted that a young, good-looking man would find her attractive. She declined, thinking it was a cruel joke but when he asked again a week later she agreed.

"He came and picked me up. We went dancing one night at a place down Elizabeth Street in Hobart and the second time to the Wrest Point Casino. He didn't seem like he'd harm anyone. He seemed very genuine. He would open the car door and things like that.

"He seemed to have a lot of money. He'd take out $100 notes," she recalled, adding that he had been polite and kissed her on the cheek before thanking her for going out with him. He told me: 'I'm very lonely. It's awful to be lonely and to have no one.'"

And yet there were also increasing instances where he would make inappropriate advances to young teenage girls, seemingly unable to comprehend just how inappropriate – and at times frightening – his behaviour could be for others. He made an advance to the Kuipers' daughter, there was the incident on the bus from Copping, and several reports of him approaching young women in the street and asking directly if they would sleep with him.

The problem was that just as his interest in older women was about companionship and friendship, Bryant's approaches to young girls were overtly and solely sexual. As psychiatric testing would later conclude, Bryant's mental development, judged as that of an 11- or 12-year-old, explained why he sought the company of children and played their games – but also why he sought very young girls as his physical, sexual contemporaries. Indeed, when he finally began to find girlfriends, they were always aged between 16 and 19 – even when he was in his late 20s.

A scrawled note – the wording for a classified personal advertisement – was later found inside his kitchen:

> Lady companion for scuba diving, tennis, camping and wining and dining for an attractive, slim, caring, 29 year-old male. Genuine replies only please.

The note showed his intense desire for friendship and the re-creation of his past life. It also demonstrated that Martin Bryant was capable of writing, even if it was mimicking the wording of other ads he had read.

∙∙∙∙∙∙∙∙∙∙∙∙∙∙∙∙∙∙∙∙∙∙∙∙∙∙∙∙∙

If the company of children was enough for games, it wasn't enough to satisfy Martin's need for a real friendship. In December 1993, flush with funds, he decided to venture outside the little world of Hobart and see what he might find elsewhere. He had been paid his first regular stipend from the Tattersall's coffers and bought himself an air ticket, first to Melbourne and then on to Singapore. He managed to stay away just three days before returning home. In April 1994, however, not long after selling the Copping farm, he went a little further. This time he travelled to Melbourne, took a flight to Bangkok and continued on to London. He stayed for six days before flying on to Sweden then back to Britain on April 30 before flying on to Los Angeles on May 3 and then back to Melbourne on May 7.

His mother watched with trepidation:

> After Maurice's death it was not long before Martin sold the farm. Martin had lost his two best friends and was feeling even more lonely and lost. He became very restless and decided to travel to Europe. Martin would only be away for three weeks. I worried for him, because he had

never travelled alone before. So of course I was very pleased and relieved when he arrived home safely. I was very anxious to hear about the trip and most interested to hear about all that had transpired. However I was to be disappointed. He had very little to say when questioned.

The mother's instincts were correct. Her son was troubled but she simply did not have the ability to bridge the widening gap with a young man whose quest to try to find friendship was becoming ever more desperate.

His decision to travel, and to choose long-haul flights across seas and continents, was not about adventure but the drive for companionship. He had no one, his attempts in Hobart had been rejected again and again, and at least in the air, strapped into a business class seat 30,000 feet above the earth, the person beside him had to stay and listen to him. His air travel became his way of buying 24 hours of chat and company. Police would later use airline logs to find and interview the many passengers who had found themselves sitting next to Martin Bryant. All would recall the same, difficult experience: he would invade their personal space, talk into their faces and simply would not shut up.

Increasingly, there were also emerging questions about his behaviour abroad. He had raised suspicions in the city of Hereford, England, when he checked into a hotel, then changed his mind because the room was "too hot" and checked into a nearby guest house. More seriously, his luggage was checked on the way back into Australia and found to contain pornographic videos.

Martin was gone again on July 10, just a few days before Hobart coroner Edward Vickers formally found that his father had committed suicide. This time he flew to Sydney then Frankfurt followed by Vienna and Copenhagen before returning to Frankfurt on July 17 and then back to Sydney on July 22. It appeared to police that he was, again, more interested in being in the aircraft with his hapless fellow passengers than the destination. In November, he flew again, from Melbourne to London via Bangkok but this time he was away for three weeks, returning to Australia on November 30.

The pattern of short stopovers returned in early February 1995 when he flew from Melbourne to Auckland. Four days later, he went on to Los Angeles, then from Miami to Frankfurt for six days before returning by the same route, spending a few days in Los Angeles and Auckland before returning to Melbourne. In mid-April he flew to Melbourne then Sydney before going on to London via Bangkok. He then travelled to Germany and Poland before returning to London and, two days later, back to Sydney.

In June, it was Hobart to Melbourne then Melbourne-Bangkok-Frankfurt. After a fortnight, he returned, this time via Singapore. Just three weeks later, he was off again, bound for Los Angeles, where he stayed for six days before flying to Tokyo for just 48 hours before returning to Melbourne. Less than a month later, he flew to Kuala Lumpur, where he lasted two days, and flew from there to Bangkok and then back to Sydney and Hobart.

In the two years between the end of 1993 and the end of 1995, Bryant had spent more than four months flying overseas, visiting Europe six times and the United States and South-East Asia three times as well as New Zealand and Japan. The summary of his domestic travel over the same period would take three pages to list, travelling to Queensland and South Australia but most often to Melbourne where he loved the zoo as some sort of a replacement to the farm.

But had the travel filled the void?

No, he would tell Professor Mullen:

> He described his various attempts at national and international travel as disappointing. He said he usually undertook these trips because "I wanted to meet up with normal people" but apparently "it didn't work". He travelled to such places as London, Los Angeles, Amsterdam and Bangkok and in these various cities tried to strike up conversations with people that he encountered. He said that he would go to what he referred to as cafeterias and sit down next to someone and try and engage them in conversation. He was distressed and enraged by the frequency with which people would move away from him or in other ways reject what he saw as his friendly advances. Mr Bryant stated that the best part of his international trips was the long plane journey. It transpired that the attraction of the long aeroplane journey was that he could speak to the people next to him, who presumably being strapped to their seats had no choice but to at least appear friendly. Mr Bryant became quite animated in describing some of what he regarded as the more successful interactions with fellow travellers on the journeys to and from Europe and the United States. This account is confirmed by statements obtained

by the police from passengers who found themselves seated next to Mr Bryant. Next to the journeys themselves, Mr Bryant listed the sex video shops in Amsterdam as the greatest pleasure he had derived from world travel. He denied using brothels and prostitutes while overseas. Mr Bryant made the majority of these trips through Melbourne where he was fond of riding on the trams and of going to the zoo.

CHAPTER 26
The Truth

Tuesday, October 8, 1996, was hot and sticky. A portent of the summer ahead, John Avery thought to himself as he made his way through the heavy traffic heading for the showgrounds at Glenorchy for the opening of the annual Royal Hobart Show, then across the Derwent and along its eastern bank to Risdon Prison. This will be the Hobart lawyer's third visit to Martin Bryant, and time is running out. Unless he can persuade the bloke to change his plea, the town is in for another horror ride in a month or so when the trial is scheduled to start. The Crown is preparing 200 witnesses to give evidence if necessary, bringing them from across Australia, Europe, the United States and Asia. They all hope it will not come to this and that Bryant will relent. But this is a personality no one can decipher. They are all at a loss.

Martin Bryant is guilty of the world's worst killing spree by a lone gunman. He has been identified numerous times in dozens of ways by hundreds of people and yet he is holding out, pleading not guilty and even giggling in court. His statements to police behind the scenes so far are as confused as his bizarre demeanour – a mix of outright denials, part truths and confused attempts to build an alibi which wouldn't stand up to the slightest scrutiny.

Avery knows only too well that his own conversations with his client – taped and transcribed – are privileged and will have no legal standing in a court of law, no matter what he says. The contents of those talks will end up lying hidden in a cardboard box and locked in an office cupboard for more than 10 years before the most critical elements emerge in public: his is the only record of a full admission and the only complete picture of Bryant's confused, selfish and detached state as he prepared and conducted the carnage.

Avery and his offsider James Hannon pass through security at Risdon and find their client. He looks better than he had the previous week. His burns are healing, not that the seething public hatred outside would care. He seems more at ease now, too – or is it a warped amusement? There are times when the young man is so clearly impaired that it is like talking to a silly kid, and yet there are other times when he exudes a manipulative superiority. Who is toying with whom? It is difficult to know sometimes.

Avery begins the conversation with a warning. This is their third meeting, the ice has been broken and there is clearly some rapport between them now. But he isn't going to mince words.

"I really want to start talking about the serious matters, and I remind you what deal we struck, that I wouldn't give you any false hope and you would be frank with me, and we would see how we can help each other. Remember the deal?"

Bryant responds with childlike enthusiasm. He is desperate to be taken out of the prison hospital where he feels he doesn't belong. He isn't crazy, don't they understand that? "Yes, that's right," he replies. "Will the day come, do you think, when I will be allowed out of the hospital and into the main prison?"

Avery isn't going to promise anything. He has to hold the whip hand for as long as possible. "Well, that's for someone else to determine but certainly depending on how this goes we will do what we can to help you in that regard, in other words …"

Bryant interrupts: "I don't think the psychiatrist's reports are saying that I am unstable at all."

"Well, not really, no."

Avery, like others, had been surprised by the psychiatric assessments. They are dealing with a cluster of problems that together are far more complex than a diagnosis based solely on old-fashioned notions of sanity.

"Now, I want you to carefully go through with me the events of that day, right. I'll kick it off but it's really got to be your instructions to me because I'm your lawyer and I've got to act on what you tell me, right. As long as I don't think you're telling me absolute bullshit, right?"

"No, I'll tell you what happened," Bryant promises.

But the young man doesn't, instead repeating his claim of going surfing that morning at Roaring Beach, a secluded windswept stretch of sand 15 kilometres west of Port Arthur, looking across to Bruny Island. There are several problems with his story. The weather was beautiful – sunny and mirror calm – but no swell meant the conditions were all wrong for surfing. No surfer in his right mind would bother making the trip on such a day. Even more obvious was that he didn't take a wetsuit or a towel let alone any wax for his board, something he has already conceded to police a few months earlier. As for the guns in his car, he claims to have taken them to fire at home-made targets attached to trees in a bush hideaway somewhere past the village of Murdunna. But none of the times match.

Avery listens patiently. They are getting nowhere:

"After that I left and got a toasted sandwich at Nubeena and a coffee and that was about, what time was that, it must have been 12 o'clock."

"Right, so where did you go after that?"

"I drove around. I thought I'll go into Port Arthur."

The story has changed. He has previously denied being at Port Arthur but now he has not only gone to the historic settlement but paid his fee at the toll gate and parked his car at the water's edge near the tourist buses.

"Then I thought to myself, 'I'll go in and have something to eat and drink,' so I went in to have something to eat and drink at the cafeteria, sat down outside and, um, I could just hear a few people, there was a few people talking outside.

"I thought, 'Oh golly, there's this Oriental couple in there.' I had my gun in the Volvo, and I thought, 'I'll go down and get my gun ... I'll put my gun underneath my jacket.' I had a long jacket on ... I went in and sat next to the Oriental couple, and I thought, 'I'll shoot them.'"

Avery has his opening. The time has finally come to get a proper account of that day out of Bryant. He stops his client:

"You do accept you did shoot other people there, I assume?"

Bryant shakes his head: "No, I don't."

"Well, who else could have if you didn't?"

"I don't really know."

The story rambles on. Bryant admits again that he had taken a hostage and driven to the Seascape guest house before setting fire to the BMW. The rest he can't remember. He had woken in an ambulance.

Avery stops him again: "All right, well we'll go over this in a minute. There seems to be evidence that what you're telling me is not true, that you firstly went to the Seascape cottage that morning and shot the Martins."

"No, that's not true."

"All I'm saying is the evidence goes much further than you shooting two Oriental people, doesn't it. You know that and I know that. It was you shooting 35 people, right, and there's no way we're going to satisfy the court you didn't, right."

Bryant stares but doesn't deny the statement. "How long will it take, do you think, to come to prove that I'm guilty? Will it take long?"

Avery presses: "Well, not very long I would have thought because the evidence is overwhelming against you, right. Now, I'm not going to press you today as to what your plea is going to be because it's not my purpose to change your mind. My purpose is to point out to you the facts, and the facts will show, I have no doubt, that you did what is alleged."

"Yep."

"Right, now either you are deliberately lying to me or you consciously can't remember some aspects but it seems to me that sooner or later we have to accept the reality of what's going to happen, right."

"That's right."

"See, we are simply not going to be able to show you weren't there because people, everyone identifies you. You're an identifiable person, right?"

Bryant laughed: "Yeah, in the Volvo with the surfboard on top. Someone even took a homemade video of me reversing out."

"Now it can't be anyone else, can it?"

"No."

"I mean, we'd be away with the fairies … I mean, there might be other fellows out here in this hospital who are away with the fairies, but you're not?"

"Definitely not."

"You're fine in the head, right?"

"I'm fine. Yep."

"What we've got to do is get in your head and find out why you did it. I don't know whether you know why you did it?"

"No."

"How long had you been planning it?"

"Oh, a couple of years."

"So what were you planning, to shoot one person, to shoot a million people or …?"

"A couple of people."

"And I suggest it got so easy this day you ended up shooting 35. Is that really what it was about?"

"Yeah, I don't really know."

"I mean, you didn't go there thinking you were going to shoot …?"

Bryant pauses, realising he is taking a risk: "Is this going to be said in court?"

Avery reassures his client: "No, this is your instructions to me, right."

Bryant is placated: "Oh, I see, that's all right then …"

"We'll talk about what you, what we put in court, right."

Bryant nods. He can speak freely.

"My intention was to kill the Martins …"

••••••••••••••••••••••••••••

Three days later, Avery is back at Risdon, and running out of time. It is one thing to get Bryant's confidential confession inside an interview room but another entirely to convince him not to pursue his real desire to relive the crime in court purely for his own enjoyment and infamy. Avery might talk to the court-appointed psychiatrist, Professor Paul Mullen, to get a sense of his client and how to reason with him, but for now at least he will persist.

Bryant is waiting, eager to show his lawyer the drawings he has made. There are six laid out on the table when Avery walks in. "I did do some drawings. Are they large enough, do you think?"

Avery is noncommittal but pleased, a school master directing his pupil. "Well, let's have a look. Right, so what's this one?"

"That's where I did my target shooting, usually between Murdunna and Eaglehawk Neck."

"Right, right."

"This is more important, isn't it," Bryant says, pointing to another. "This is where the Martins, where the Seascape guest house is."

"Right, so this is the Seascape guest house here."

"Yep, that's the top; that's where [the hostage] was, there," Bryant says, pointing at the stick figures which represent his victims.

Avery stays cool, despite his excitement at this breakthrough. "Right."

"The police allege that I was shooting out at them, I can't recall."

"Right, OK, the Fox and Hounds?"

"The Fox and Hounds; that's the car that was parked near the main house, the Seascape guest house, and there's the two smaller houses on the property."

"Right, so this is just an exploded version of this, is it?"

"Yep, and that's the Martins. That's where I shot them, on the bed."

"Right, right, OK, well that's fine …"

"Are they big enough?"

"Yep, yep. No, they're fine."

"And another thing … I remember shooting people around the bus but I don't recall going on the bus."

"You don't recall going on the bus? All right so, OK …"

"And I recall, um, shooting people in the cafeteria but I don't recall injuring anyone at all."

"Right, all right."

"I recall them dying."

Avery changes the subject. He has to get back to the plea. "What's your current feeling as to how you want to plead? Have you given any further thought to that?"

Bryant looks up from the drawings: "I don't really know. Can I plead guilty to some and some not. Am I allowed to do that?"

"Well, you can plead to some and not guilty to others. What sort of ones do you think that you might want to plead not guilty to?"

"To the injured."

Avery is stunned. Bryant is prepared to plead guilty to 35 murders but not the 20 who survived. It doesn't make sense. "The injured people?"

"'Cos all I can recall is people sitting down in the cafeteria. I don't recall anyone running out, just the people that I've shot, sitting down, and they all just died."

"So what you're saying, you accept that you killed people but you don't think you injured, or you don't remember injuring people?"

"I don't remember injuring …"

"Other than the ones that you killed."

"That's right."

So Bryant is admitting what he can remember, or at least what he intended – mass death. But why? Why did he want to kill so many?

"The other thing I just wanted to ask you," Avery continues, "I think I did talk to you last time about this. How long do you think, looking back in your mind now, you'd been planning this?"

"Oh, about one, two years."

"Had you ever sort of had a dummy run before or almost got to doing it before?"

"No, never. It's only been … since after Christmas this year."

"Right, that you seriously thought about it or seriously started thinking about it?"

"Yeah."

"What did you think you were going to get out of it? I mean, you must have known you were going to get caught."

"I thought I'd either get caught or get killed, and I thought of killing the Martins. I thought that if I killed the Martins I would go to jail for life, right."

"Yeah."

"And I thought, well, if I kill a lot of people, it really won't make much of a difference."

"In other words, if you kill 10, it's not much difference as far as the time in jail to killing one person."

"That's right."

Avery takes a deep breath. It is time to finish this. Time for his client to accept his fate and stop the nonsense.

"We'll work along the basis that you're probably going to have to plead guilty to the people you've killed, right?"

Bryant seems surprised: "What, to all of them?"

"Well, I mean realistically I think, but …"

"Hmm."

"Because I think you know as well as I do that I think you're going to be convicted of that, don't you?"

Bryant laughs. "Yeah that's right."

"And there's no sort of sense us thinking we can pull rabbits out of the hat."

The stupid smile falls from Bryant's face. "Will you actually then make a statement in writing to that, or what happens?"

"Well, I mean, it depends on which way we end up going. If you were to plead guilty … the Crown still has to put a lot of evidence before the court to tell what happened. What we would have to do then, you and I, is work out what I'd say on your behalf."

"Yep."

"Now you could tell the world through me whatever you want to about it or you could say, like some people in this situation, 'I'm not going to say anything.'"

"What happens there?"

"You might want the world to know what motivated you to do this or you may not. You may say, well, I want everyone to know. That's something you've got to think on – whether you want me to tell the world what you've told me."

Bryant hesitates. He knows the lawyer is right; that he is going to be found guilty. What he wants is to ensure he can relive it and show the people what he has done, so he can be powerful again.

"Yeah … I might come out in court and tell everyone what happened. I don't know. It might be the best thing to do, mightn't it?"

"We'll worry about that later, right. That's something you and I have to work through as to whether you say it or I say it on your behalf."

"Exactly. It might upset the people more if I say it."

"Well, it might. I mean, it might be more diplomatic for me to tell the world what you want to say rather than see you smiling and grinning and you know …"

Bryant laughs: "Yeah, I might let them know."

CHAPTER 27
Money and Guns

Maurice Bryant had been right. His son could not manage his unexpected wealth. Martin's spending had started to become more than a niggling worry before Maurice's careful reorganisation of the inheritance. Now that his father's gentle influence was gone, his spending threatened to turn into a serious drain. Not only did Martin choose to fly business class but booked expensive hotels and ate in equally pricey restaurants on overseas jaunts that were becoming a monthly habit. He had also developed a routine of withdrawing big amounts of cash and splashing them around indiscriminately, on one occasion dumping $10,000 on the desk of a travel agent and challenging her to, "Send me somewhere." Another woman would tell police that he threw $2000 in cash in front of her, smiled widely and said, "Let's go to lunch."

The money was just another tool he used to try to break the ice with people, to try to impress them and buy a little attention. It is something most of us try at one time or another in our lives but in Martin Bryant's case, the way he did it, his behaviour was so odd and so far outside the norm – even for a rich eccentric – that it only served to highlight how outlandish he was and ended up having the opposite effect, pushing people away.

For Maurice, always cautious and, by nature, organised, this level of profligacy and indiscriminate spending would have been a torture to watch.

But Martin did not read his father's careful planning as a protective act but as yet further rejection.

It was late January 1996, and he had decided to fly to Melbourne then Sydney and on to London via Bangkok again. He stayed in London for six days before flying back to Melbourne on January 29, taking advantage of a standby flight from Heathrow. While he waited, Bryant turned his attentions to Rachel Lee, a 23-year-old psychology and law student, who, by chance, also came from Hobart and was waiting for a flight home.

Within a few minutes, he excused himself and went away to make a phone call. When he came back Bryant announced that he had just spoken to his mother:

"I just told her I have met the girl I'm going to marry," he told her. Rachel would later tell police of a rambling, occasionally troubling conversation that went on and on throughout the flight. She found she couldn't escape the attention of this intense young man who tried to engage all those around him indiscriminately but was mostly ignored. It seemed he didn't understand that his actions came across as inappropriate: too friendly, even sleazy.

She didn't feel threatened, she explained, but felt it odd, particularly when he told her he had a big house and she could move in. And the fact he was flying halfway around the world after spending just three days at Disneyland "because it was raining" added to her discomfort.

Bryant also talked about the impact of his father's death, boasting of the large amount of money he had been left, but also how the loss had stunned him to the point where he hadn't been able to work since. He was lying about the work of course, never really doing much more than the odd gardening job or selling vegetables door-to-door with his dad. But he chose to cover his own inadequacies – and made up the story to normalise himself – while chatting up a girl. It showed not only an unexpected level of self-awareness but the true depth of feeling about losing his father. Rachel described his behaviour as "intense", a world away from the buffoon who laughed and chatted to police as they recovered the body. Bryant's laughter, his physical responses at the time, were not those of a man who did not care about his loss but rather, an inappropriate response to stress and fear. He did not view the death of his father as funny, quite the opposite – he knew he had lost one of the only people in the world who cared for him unconditionally and he would now be left alone among people who couldn't stand being around him.

The search for answers about Martin Bryant, what made him do what he did when he did, is wrapped up in a confluence of these events, moments, incidents, vignettes which, through his eyes, meant layer upon layer of rejection over a backdrop of loss and grief.

The truth is, however, that Martin Bryant's choice of date – April 28, 1996 – was as random as his personality. While the core of his anger lay with the Martin family and Sally in particular, the decision to kill and avenge his losses occurred when they did simply because the human restraints that had held him in check – Helen's friendship and his father's patient control – had gone. There was no anniversary, no momentous single psychological event that sparked the flame, nor a day of any particular significance at Port Arthur itself. Martin Bryant simply wanted attention.

The search for answers cannot be seen solely as a young man born with a personality disorder, intellectually impaired and struggling with autistic traits. His genetic load was the baggage he carried with him into life. What occurred around him, a devoted and vigilant father who effectively managed him – and an heiress mentor and eccentric friend – were equally important, creating a cushion that for a long period of his life protected him from reality. More importantly, they acted as constraints that impeded or at least diffused and gave an outlet for his most obsessive tendencies. Once Helen and his father were gone, Bryant was left to his mounting frustrations, his angers, his resentment of rejection and social misunderstanding. All he had left, was the money, which gave him an outlet to continue the strange pursuits that gave his life some meaning.

That was until early 1996.

The most significant clue to what pushed Bryant to violence would emerge during his interview with the two detectives, Paine and Warren, at the prison. As they scrambled to cover the vast canvas of events in the three hours available to them, the two officers stumbled on what appears to have been the last straw for the pathetic young man before them. As they chat about money and his extraordinary spending habits – "I'd rather spend it than keep it," he told them – the subject of his expensive travelling habits comes up. "You've certainly spent it on those overseas trips," quipped Ross Paine offhandedly.

"Yeah, spent a little bit," Bryant agreed, adding: "Unfortunately, I couldn't go on any more otherwise I would've gone away in May. I was informed nicely that I wasn't able to go away for a long time, for about 12 months, which upset me greatly."

John Warren was intrigued. "Why's that?"

"'Cos maybe once or twice a year because I only have to accumulate and, and just couldn't go away on any more trips for a while, but that upset me a lot, yeah."

Warren probed further. Bryant was clearly not happy about something: "When you say it upset you, what ...?"

Bryant thought for a moment: "Mmm, just threw me back 'cos I didn't have anything to do."

"Right. Who, who actually told you that?"

"I wasn't able to go on a trip probably for six months, and that was oh, the people, Perpetual Trustees, a lady that looks after my money."

"Right. Did you have a regular contact with her?"

"Yeah, we phone up whenever I needed something to talk about ..."

It seems infernally simple, a natural human desire to have something to do, a role to play in life, something that provides structure to the days and a reason for being. This young man has not only lost the two people who understood and tolerated him but, in his mind, has lost the last outlet that allowed him human interaction; his prisoner-passengers were gone, too.

Maurice Bryant would never know that the financial protection mechanisms he set up to protect his son a few months before his death may have lit the fuse that led to massacre.

On October 11, a few days after finally extracting a confession from Bryant, John Avery decided to retrace his steps and go back over a few details.

"The other thing I just wanted to ask you – I think I did talk to you last time about this – how long do you think, looking back in your mind now, you'd been planning this?"

Bryant was vague: "Oh, about one to two years."

It crossed Avery's mind that Maurice Bryant had killed himself just over two years earlier. It is possible, indeed quite probable, that the loss of Helen Harvey, compounded by his father's suicide, may have set off the young man's own quest for oblivion.

Bryant had said before that he was prepared, indeed expecting, to be killed by police.

"Had you ever sort of had a dummy run before or almost got to doing it before?"

"No, never. It's only been ... since after Christmas this year."

"Right, that you seriously thought about it or seriously started thinking about it?"

"Yeah."

There it was again. Something happened early in the year which had upset him enough to transform dark thoughts of revenge into an actual plan, and the only incident of any significance in this time of Bryant's life was the decision by Perpetual Trustees to rein in his spending by curbing his travel habits. He'd made his last trip in January.

....

In late 1993, probably October or November – and just as he was attempting to come to terms with the death of his father – Martin Bryant bought his first, serious rifle. Although he had been given an air gun as a teenager and wreaked havoc through the Port Arthur community, his indiscriminate firing had frightened but not harmed anyone. This firearm was an entirely different proposition – and his father was no longer there to keep a leash on him. The weapon, a semi-automatic, gas-powered rifle known as an AR-10, had been favoured by Portuguese paratroopers during the Angolan War of Independence in the 1960s and the Sudanese military during the country's first civil war in the 1960s and '70s. Several thousand were imported to Australia in the 1990s and sold through gun shops or advertisements in local newspapers. Bryant bought his from a paper, with cash, no questions asked. Just like his unlicensed driving, Bryant did not have a firearms licence either. He had never fired anything but the air rifle.

In the two months that he searched for his semi-automatic, there were more than 30 rifles advertised in the classified pages of *The Mercury* newspaper – Winchesters, Rugers, Brunos, Mausers and Brownings – most complete with scopes and even ammunition. Only one ad specified that prospective buyers had to hold and produce a licence. Bryant responded to an advertisement on November 14, almost invisible squeezed between ads for a refrigerator and a roof-rack:

RIFLE .308
With scope $600 ono

There were no other details other than a Hobart telephone number. Far more chilling was the story on the front page of the same edition: "VITAL CLUE Death Rifle targets killer" screamed the headline. The story detailed a police breakthrough in the search for the notorious backpacker killer in NSW, pinpointing a connection between the attacker and a US-made Ruger .22 rifle. Just a few months later, they would arrest the serial killer Ivan Milat.

Inside, there was double-page coverage. The headlines – "Hitchhikers told to take extra care", "How they died" and "Killer will strike again" – were chilling. Martin Bryant read the advertisement inside the paper to buy his first rifle – the coverage in the paper that day also included a profile of "a sadistic madman" put together by the forensic psychiatrist, Professor Paul Mullen. Three years later, he would be called in by the courts to decide if Martin Bryant was sane. Mullen declared Milat was probably working alone:

"It is difficult to generalise but these sorts of people are not usually good at working co-operatively. They tend to be loners," he wrote. "One of the mistakes people make in a situation like this is to assume that someone committing crimes like this must be mad ..."

Rifle bought, Bryant hid his new toy in a padlocked cupboard beneath the stairs of the Clare Street house, away from the eyes of his mother, who still came over occasionally to clean the house or deliver a meal. Bryant, contemplating his future, ruminated about his lost friendship with the Kuiper children, his travels, especially the overseas jaunts. All had placated him as they provided interaction, friendship of sorts or, at worst, regular human interaction. Left to his own devices, idle, disconnected and increasingly alienated, his mind turned back over and over again thoughts of retribution for his loneliness.

Now, grounded and angry, he began the quest to assemble an arsenal.

Life, however, provided the occasional, unexpected joy. In April 1995, Bryant met 16-year-old Janetta Hoani. The connection came through his mother, who regularly attended a church in North Hobart and had befriended the young girl's mother. The two made friends almost immediately, and Bryant, whose only previous sexual contact other than a few short-lived liaisons had been with prostitutes and escort services around Hobart, had finally found his first real girlfriend. Janetta loved his manners, his clothes and his independence, even Bryant's childlike manner, which she interpreted as endearing and refreshing, seemed loveable and showed a kind of vulnerability. And he was rich and liked to splash his money around: "He had long blond hair, he had blue eyes, he had huge muscles ... and he was rich, God," she said.

Bryant took her to restaurants where staff recalled the couple behaving like little kids, rolling a ball between them at the table. Janetta, not much more than a child herself, looked so young that one night a waiter asked her for identification before serving wine. Bryant was outraged, standing and grabbing the waiter by the wrists: "How dare you do this," he yelled trembling. He read the legitimate question as a slight on him, one that destroyed his credibility in the eyes of those watching and fuelled his paranoia. Janetta looked on, perplexed and slightly scared. Even though he was prone to strange and sometimes disturbing behaviour, she went away with him on at least two trips to the mainland and was a frequent overnight visitor at Clare Street.

The relative happiness was not to continue though. Towards the end of 1995, during a diving trip off the isolated southern tip of Tasmania, trouble struck. The couple had launched Bryant's two-metre Zodiac at Recherche Bay and motored out into choppy seas around South East Cape towards a cluster of tiny islands. Despite the rough conditions and tiny boat, Bryant had quelled Janetta's fears and persuaded her to come out with him. He seemed to show no fear but the young girl was terrified, pleading with him to turn back. He ignored her pleas and drifted off Hen Island, a pristine seal sanctuary, before finally agreeing to turn back to shore. It was quite late in the afternoon and as he manoeuvred to return to shore, the 25 horsepower outboard motor cut out. Bryant would later recount to police what happened over the next few hours: "The motor actually stopped. Went through one tank of petrol, put the other tank on the hose and one. It was the connection inside the motor had fallen off. I kept on trying to start it, it just wouldn't start. I was starting to get cold feet; my feet were starting to freeze up and I was shaking. My girlfriend was shaking. It was nearly dark and we actually had a couple of flares and that ... saved us. It was just luck that a fishing boat came along otherwise I wouldn't be here ... me girlfriend wouldn't be definitely because she didn't have a wetsuit on."

The near-death experience was finally enough for Janetta. A few weeks later, the couple flew to Surfers Paradise for a few days but within 48 hours of coming home, she ended the relationship. He had been "acting weird", she would say later, even questioning his sexuality. Although they met a few times around Hobart, she rejected Bryant's pleas to get back together.

He was devastated.

This would also be the last time that Martin Bryant would venture out on to his beloved water. One by one, his attempts to re-create the few treasured memories of his life fell foul of his own inadequacies. The last – boating and diving with his patient father – was now gone, too. In early 1996, Bryant sold the boat he'd paid almost $9000 to fit out a few months earlier for barely half the price. With what was left he bought guns and ammunition:

"And that's how I paid for my AR-15," he told police triumphantly.

The Colt AR-15 was a version of the M16 used by the US military during the Vietnam War. With a magazine holding 30 bullets at a time, the lightweight weapon was a killing machine. Like the AR-10, there were thousands imported into Australia and hundreds of registered owners before the bans imposed nationally by the Prime Minister, John Howard, after the Port Arthur killings. The great majority were also sold through newspaper advertisements and mail order although some were bought through gun shops.

Bryant would tell police he bought his at Guns and Ammo, a store just 300 metres from his front door, where for $5000 the owner Terry Hill threw in a scope and 80 to 100 rounds of ammunition. Bryant insisted he wasn't asked for a licence. After all, he didn't have one. Hill, who had known Bryant since he was a teenager, has always denied selling him any guns.

Nonetheless, Tasmanian gun laws at the time allowed any adult without a conviction for violence to own a gun for life. The only stipulation was that it be updated with a new photograph every 10 years.

Over the next three months, Bryant would return to buy boxes of ammunition, rifle cases and even cleaning kits for a .30 calibre and a 12-gauge shotgun, not just from Hill but another shop.

CHAPTER 28
The Final Descent

Carleen Bryant was trying to move on, her life fragmented by the sadness of the loss of Maurice and the continuing anxieties thrown up by a son she found difficult to understand and who continually rejected her. In October 1994, she sold the Augusta Road home, bought almost a quarter of a century earlier to raise a family, and headed back to the northern fringe of the city where she had grown up.

It was not a hard decision to make in the end. The house was a constant reminder of what had gone wrong and was physically falling apart. In several rooms, the ceilings were caving in and the plumbing had backed up after a water pipe burst. The house had begun to look the way she felt: tired, drawn, at the end of her resources, emotional and physical. It was Maurice who had been wedded to the place originally, although he'd also flirted with the idea of selling when the kids had grown up and finding a house at Battery Point, down by the Derwent.

She decided to follow his lead and began hunting for a house with river views. She found it at Berriedale, 10 kilometres north of the city centre, where she fell for a two-storey house with expansive views up and down the river. At night the lights seemed to dance on the water as cars flashed over the nearby Bowen Bridge that runs across to Risdon. It seemed the perfect compromise between Maurice's dream and a return to the sanctuary of the suburbs, just over the back fence from the Cadbury factory where she was working when she fell pregnant with Martin and a short drive from St Paul's Church at Montrose where she had married Maurice.

The first heavy rains destroyed the dream. The lower bedroom flooded, and the plumbers told her there was little they could do: the floor was below ground level and likely to flood again. Worse still, the house had a flat roof, a feature Maurice had always warned her about in a wet climate such as Hobart's. The problems only seemed to highlight her shattered and lonely life. Financial security seemed hollow without a family to share it with. Lindy was gone – now at the tourist mecca of Byron Bay on the NSW north coast – and engaging with Martin was almost impossible. At most, they could share a meal and a few words or she could visit his house to give it a tidy-up while he was away on one of his overseas trips.

She had started to worry about him more than usual, particularly after he came home from the last trip, in January 1996. Call it a motherly instinct but she could tell when he was agitated and under pressure. He was restless this time, obviously worried about something, fretting and uptight but not willing to share the problem or discuss it with her. Instead he was brusque, almost rude, when she ventured over, demanding immediately to know how long she intended staying and making it clear he did not want company.

His manner was also changing around the neighbourhood. The neat but garishly dressed figure with the largely sunny, if simple demeanour was seen rarely now, replaced by an irritable character, frequently angry and prone to sharp exchanges: arguments became daily occurrences, usually about trivialities, from encroaching branches into his now unkempt front yard or temper tantrums at the local hairdressers who trimmed the ever-lengthening blond hair. It was as if he had given up on an external life, given up on engaging with the outside world except to battle with it.

In some ways, the young man had finally surrendered: he was drinking heavily, to fill in the time and the void of his loneliness, usually while watching TV, videos or listening to music, some of them obsessively, over and over again. He usually started drinking in the late morning and imbibed more heavily in the afternoon, typically making his way through half a bottle of Sambuca and a similar amount of Bailey's Irish Cream. The alcohol he favoured fed a sweet tooth, like a little kid in a lolly store. In the evening, it was sweet wine such as moselle or port, which he bought by the cask from the Talbot Tavern bottle shop on New Town Road. When he went shopping for alcohol, he would park the Volvo in the aisle of the drive-through and get out to wander through the shop. The staff would remember him as a regular who never went inside the hotel and rarely conversed with anyone – a quiet, softly spoken customer, but one all would describe as strange.

Bryant's sleep was also disturbed, his insomnia fuelled by burgeoning anxieties that the Clare Street house was haunted. The ghosts, he told psychiatrist Paul Mullen after the killings, sometimes kept him awake at night. He found it hard enough to go to sleep, let alone with the sounds of spirits moving around downstairs, bumping and banging.

There were two of them, he thought. One of them was Helen, he was certain, but he wasn't quite certain about the other except it was a woman; Hilza perhaps. They spoke sometimes; nothing much, a few fleeting words or phrases like "come on" or "here", as if he was being summoned. He couldn't tell for sure, or if they meant him any harm, but even so it was frightening to be alone while they were here. He was scared of ghosts. Was he mad? Were these hallucinations an indication of a mental illness?

When Bryant raised these fears with Mullen, the psychiatrist told him he didn't think so. They were brief, passing and did not fall within the pathological spectrum, like the person whose paranoias might think they hear coded messages from television or radio. What was clear was the young man's growing sense of desperation and solitude:

> Later in the interview Mr Bryant became more frank. He talked of the extent to which he thinks about the distress and the rejections in the past. He said that he tries to live day by day, but acknowledges that frequently thoughts about past rejections, and what he recalls as his victimisation at school by bullies, intrude. He has become more caught up in these thoughts about past indignities over the last year. He said he became increasingly unhappy and angry because he had no real friends. He said, "All I wanted was for people to like me." Their failure to respond to his overtures led him to feel "that I'd had a gut full". This culminated in the months before the tragedy in a sense that there was no future for him, that he would always remain lonely and rejected and that he would be better off dead. The picture that emerges was not suggestive of a depressive illness. It was a pattern more reminiscent of an angry and distressed man having

increasing difficulties coping with his social isolation and his various disappointments. Nevertheless in this context Mr Bryant came to the conclusion that life for him was not worth living. He began to consider suicide for the first time about a year ago. He said, "about twelve months ago I decided I'd had enough". The thoughts of suicide became more prominent in recent months.

Bryant's music and film tastes were as diverse as his character. He loved the Elton John soundtrack to the movie *Lion King* (of which he had several copies) and British 1960s pop icon Cliff Richard. Just as innocent was his favourite movie, the 1995 Australian triumph *Babe* about a pig that wanted to be a sheepdog. Of all the 1300 videos in Helen Harvey's collection, he preferred two martial arts action movies. The Steven Seagal movie *Under Siege*, made in 1992, was a violent story about the hijacking of a US warship. Likewise, the 1985 Jackie Chan movie *The Protector*, about a karate-kicking New York cop investigating a crime in Hong Kong, which, in the style of Chan, was comical rather than violent. Martin also had a dozen or so pornographic movies and magazines – most bought from adult stores on the mainland.

What was dangerous, on the other hand, was his growing collection of military magazines, replete with stories about weapons, military tactics and survivalist activities.

His travel plans curtailed by the financial managers, Martin began to ruminate and hatch a new plan, one almost as expensive as his long-haul flights but much, much more dangerous. Over several weeks, he obsessed day and night, consolidating and accumulating the funds available to him. He still had access to the two bank accounts, which were used to disburse his allowances, and in March withdrew $13,150 from one account and $1100 from the other. He also began selling significant assets through auction houses, including his beloved boat and outboard motor, raising a further $9800. In total, he accumulated more than $24,000, much of it spent on firearms and ammunition.

In the midst of this dark pursuit, Martin might still have been diverted – or at least distracted – from the inevitable. Following Janetta's departure, he had made one final, sad attempt to rekindle the last few satisfying parts of his life. While his attempts to replace Helen had failed as the older women in the neighbourhood continued to reject his advances, he reversed roles and lodged a newspaper advertisement for a gardener to take care of Clare Street. But this time, the young man was hoping that the person who would answer the ad would be a young woman.

Among those who answered was a 20-year-old horticultural student, Petra Wilmott, who was so petite that she looked barely 14. According to friends, this was matched by a naive, childlike quality which, coupled with her appearance, immediately engaged Bryant.

Just like his meeting with the maternal soul mate, Helen Harvey nine years earlier, the two connected immediately. Petra lived with her parents at Nicholls Rivulet, a 40-minute drive south-west of Hobart, and was studying at TAFE but finding it difficult to secure regular work. Bryant hired her on the spot and they would meet several times a week, the role of the gardener falling by the wayside to be replaced by that of a girlfriend. Bryant took her to restaurants, to the movies and Hobart clubs such as Regines at the Wrest Point Casino. Petra regarded him as a gentleman but could see that the young man was difficult to read and a mass of behavioural contradictions. Petra Wilmott only granted one media interview following the shootings: "He didn't have many friends, he was gentle and kind and he'd look after me," she would reflect. "Around me he was different. When he was around other people, he would change."

Although she remembered him talking about guns, she never saw one in the house. And despite his love of action movies, she also recalled him walking out of the cinema during the movie *Casino* because he could not stomach a scene in which a man had his fingers crushed.

Most telling, and tragic in retrospect, was her belief that Bryant may have been motivated by frustration born of boredom: "Maybe he was looking for action. He'd say that sometimes. Like we'd drive around an accident scene, and it just looked like he was looking for action. He was bored."

•••••••••••••••••••••••••••

Although life had turned for the better, Bryant was an obsessive and, like many of the young men studied by forensic psychiatrists following similar, indiscriminate shootings, would not be swayed once a thought had crystallised in his mind. Petra provided friendship and companionship, a respite from the relentless loneliness, but the notion that life was no longer worth living – and the people he believed had led him to this feeling or contributed to his sense of hopelessness – began to dominate his thoughts.

In the middle of this pathological descent, two significant events exploded and received saturation media coverage.

In late February, Hobart had been transfixed by a kidnapping case. The city had already been horrified 18 months earlier when an eight-year-old boy named Ben Morrison was wrenched at gunpoint from his frightened parents, locked in the boot of the family car and driven away from his Mt Nelson home by two abductors in the dead of night. The motive was ransom but the men panicked when they thought police were on their way to the city motel unit where the boy had been secreted. The little boy was dumped on a city street 18 hours later, terrified and bound with a pillowcase over his head but otherwise unharmed. The abductors, James Michael Deane and Geoffrey Terrence Bean, were caught shortly after as was the mastermind, Jeffrey Peter Radloff, who was described during his very public trial as "ruthless, arrogant and evil".

Bryant's careful attention to the case as it unfolded on television and was analysed in minute detail in the newspaper would become clear following the shootings: he recognised the police officer who questioned him about his abduction, killing and secretion in a car boot of Glen Pears as a senior detective on the little boy's kidnapping.

Indeed, Detective Inspector John Warren, who headed the CIB's eastern district, had been a prime force in the Morrison case. He had been assigned to interview Bryant the night after the shootings but was unable to because Bryant was so heavily sedated. The next morning he'd gone back past the phalanx of mainland media and the local mob howling for blood outside the hospital and tried to talk to the gunman again. This time Bryant had refused to participate, stating only that he wasn't there and had been unjustly accused.

On his third attempt, Bryant appeared willing to co-operate, to a point.

"So you drove away in the BMW?" asked Warren's offsider, Inspector Ross Paine.

"Yes," answered Bryant, admitting to the kidnapping but insisting this does not necessarily link him to mass murder.

"With another male person?" Paine continued.

"Yeah, he was in the boot. I put him in the boot of the car."

"How did he get into the boot?"

"Bit like the Ben Morrison case isn't it?" Bryant commented.

Warren interjected: "You remember the Ben Morrison case, do you?"

"Yeah."

"What do you remember about it?"

"I remember I saw you on television and I saw you that day at the Royal. I thought you were connected with Ben Morrison. Yeah, I thought that was rather dramatic.

"'Cos Radloff's in here," Bryant added.

Inspector Paine jumped in, not sure he'd heard the name correctly.

"Who's in here?"

"Radloff, the man that was involved in the Ben Morrison ..."

"Have you met him, Martin?"

"No, I've only read things about him in the paper, mmm."

"What sort of things, ah, do you think about him?"

"I don't know. Funny guy. I think things went wrong with him. Like they did with me ... and later on you'll think twice why did, why did you do these things ..."

The kidnapping was not, however, to be the only influence. There was a second, even more horrifying and violent event that ultimately would shape and colour Martin Bryant's perception of himself wreaking havoc as a potential violent criminal. Just six weeks before he embarked on his own carnage, on March 13, 1996, the world was horrified by the brutality of an unemployed former shopkeeper and scout leader named Thomas Watt Hamilton who walked into the primary school of the small Scottish town of Dunblane and in a matter of seconds, murdered 16 children and their teacher. Another 10 children and three teachers were injured. Armed with two 9mm pistols and two .357 Magnum revolvers, Hamilton entered the school gymnasium where he opened fire on a class of five- and six-year-olds. He then left the gymnasium and from the playground outside continued firing into a mobile classroom where a teacher, realising something was wrong, had managed to barricade the children inside and hide beneath their desks.

Although the venue, targets and weapons were completely different, the massacre would be eerily similar to Bryant's actions: trapping a crowd of people inside a cramped, confined space, the quick and indiscriminate fire carried out at point-blank range, the killing of as many as possible as quickly as possible, and the final, terrible continuation of the spree from a longer range outside in the open air.

In October, Bryant would raise the Dunblane massacre with his lawyer John Avery, who was trying to understand if his client had been influenced or inspired by other crimes:

"You'd heard about all these people who did that?" he asked. "I mean, you talk about the Hoddle Street massacre and Milat. You'd heard of all these fellows?"

Bryant nodded: "Yeah and … Dunblane."

Avery stopped for a moment: "I haven't heard of him, where's he?"

"The Dunblane massacre. The children."

Avery suddenly remembered: "Oh, Dunblane. Yes."

"Oh! That was the worst one in the world because he did a lot of children in. Would you say it was worse?"

"It's not up to me to say but do you think that's worse than what you did?"

"Yes, yes, I think so because they were all schoolchildren, 16 of them."

"Did you admire him for that?"

"I actually thought he'd had a sad sort of life and things went wrong with him, and he went out and was going to start up a scout group or something. I think they found out that he was interfering with the children."

What Bryant did not reveal to his lawyer then was that within days of reading about Hamilton's spree, he had chosen his own day of retribution. Bryant did not aim to copy that crime, nor was it his inspiration. He felt Hamilton was a kindred soul, a fellow outsider and victim of society's injustices, but he did not use him as a model, rather Dunblane enabled him to choose a date for his plan.

Bryant decided, with the stroke of a pen on a kitchen calendar, that Sunday, April 28, would be the day that he would show the world that his mistreatment, his rejection, his loneliness would not be taken lying down. He marked the day he would kill himself – but not before leaving a mark on the world he believed hated him. Like so many people tortured by obsessive personalities, this would be one decision he would fear and want to abandon but his nature would not allow it. Abandoning a plan so obsessively laid out was not an option for a personality driven by compulsions so powerful.

....

Scott Goldsmith had two connections with No.30 Clare Street and its occupants. His parents lived at No.27, directly opposite, and as an officer with the Public Trustee, he'd had frequent dealings helping Helen and Hilza Harvey administer the George Adams Estate over the years. It was a problematic professional relationship and one he would never feel comfortable discussing publicly, given his oath of office. As a neighbour, Miss Harvey was just as difficult, a recluse who rarely spoke to others as she methodically walked the streets with her dogs. Her friend Martin was even stranger, particularly when he moved back into the house after Miss Harvey died.

Scott was troubled by several things but made a real effort to connect with a young man he could tell was struggling alone. Occasionally, there might be polite if perfunctory exchanges in the street. Once Bryant even introduced Scott to his new girlfriend.

"He was polite and well spoken," Scott said in the aftermath. "Never aggressive, but he had a strange look. His eyes were sort of blank. It's a look you always remember. He was obviously very lonely. There were very few people going in and out of the house. I felt sorry for him. And I made a point of talking to him. When I saw the girlfriend I thought that might settle him down."

But one day in early April 1996, Scott had a different encounter with the strange man. Walking past the overgrown Clare Street property, he saw Bryant standing on the garden path staring out into the street. Habitually, he walked over to say hello:

"I said something to him – I can't remember what it was now – and he stopped and just stared at me, a real steely sort of glare that looked right through me. I thought, 'This boy is having a bad day.' He said something that I couldn't catch and moved away up the path."

A few days earlier, on March 27, Bryant had retrieved the AR-10 rifle he'd bought three years earlier from its hiding place and took it into Guns and Ammo asking if it could be repaired. Terry Hill and assistant Greg Peck were working when he walked in with a package wrapped in a towel.

"Something is wrong with it," Bryant said abruptly, presenting the package muzzle-first, akin to handing a knife over blade-first. Hill unwrapped the towel to find the gun fitted with a clip containing 15 rounds of high-velocity .308 Winchester ammunition. As he worked the action, another live round ejected from the breech of the weapon. Hill sent him away.

Martin Bryant had also been seen hanging around Port Arthur again. In early April, he parked outside the Dunalley fruit store where he and Helen used to shop and bought some tomatoes. The owner told police he had noticed the surfboard on the roof and asked if he was headed for the beach but Bryant waved him away saying he was just looking around.

On April 15, he and Petra went shopping at the Myer store in the centre of Hobart. Bryant wanted a sports bag for his Tai Chi classes, he told her, and then measured the length of the bag with a tape measure he'd taken with him. As he turned back to speak to the shop assistant, she heard him query if the bag had strong handles because, he added blithely, "It will be used to carry ammunition, which will be heavy."

Bryant did not choose to brood and lounge inside his house drinking nor did he watch much television in the last week before the massacre. A timeline stitched together from witnesses, police and media accounts reveals a frenetic pace as he prepared for the moment he believed would finally make him relevant to the world.

On Monday, April 22, he drove to the local pet shop where he had been many times, parked the Volvo out the front and went inside to strike up a conversation with the owner, who would later say that Bryant was "acting weird and saying funny things". The only thing he would manage to recall specifically, however, was the odd comment: "There's a lot of Jap tourists around here today."

Around 10am on Tuesday, April 23, Bryant drove to Bishop Street, New Town, turned down a long gravel laneway and parked outside a drab block of brown units. Inside No.44a, Stewart Woods ran a thriving business repairing, reconditioning and selling old guns. Bryant began browsing for weapons, asking about the price of an AR-15 rifle. Woods told him it would cost $3000. Bryant walked away.

On April 24, Petra came to visit Bryant – but not before he had been to Guns and Ammo where he bought three boxes of Winchester Double X shotgun shells. That night he and Petra went dancing at Regines nightclub. They drank heavily and Martin, in high spirits, was dressed in jeans and wearing his rakish Panama hat, his blond hair slicked back in a pony tail.

The next morning – Anzac Day, April 25 – he and Petra drove out to the historic village of Richmond, 30 kilometres north-east of Hobart, ostensibly to try out a new camera. He tried unsuccessfully to take a photograph of two tourists. Instead Petra photographed him in front of a bed of roses pruned for the coming winter. He was wearing a white-ribbed fisherman's jumper, his curly hair unkempt, an uncharacteristically grim expression on his face. While browsing through one of the shops, Petra heard him asking about tourist numbers. He commented again about the number of Japanese tourists and made a glib comment about "WASPs", which she assumed was slang for white or European tourists.

There was one more trip that he would make when they returned to New Town. Leaving Petra at home again, Bryant drove to the local supermarket where, by chance, he met Nancy D'Alton, a neighbour of his grandmother, Freda, who lived in a nearby retirement village. Nancy had always felt there was something offputting and "lame dog" about the boy. When he asked her to join him on a picnic to see Helen Harvey's property at Copping, Nancy declined because of a previous commitment to her grandchildren but then asked Bryant candidly why he looked so annoyed and angry about her response. There were two versions of his reply but both, in hindsight, were signals, warnings of what was about to unfold.

The shorter response was: "Nobody wants to listen to me or let me help them. One day I'll do something to make them notice me."

The longer version, detailed in her statement to police, was terrifying: "Oh I don't know. Nobody ever wants to listen to me or go with me. I'm getting fed up with this. I'll think of something and everybody will remember me."

On Friday morning, Bryant left Petra at home and drove back to Stuart Woods's unit with the AR-10 rifle he'd previously taken to Hill, asking him how much it would cost to repair the gun. This time he left the weapon behind.

Then, he drove to Liverpool Street in the city where the bus company, Tigerline Coaches, had its offices next door to the Royal Hobart Hospital. The owner, Don Hazell, would recall the weird young fellow whose behaviour was both agitated and queer, a demeanour he could only place with a drug user. Bryant wanted to book a seat on the bus to Port Arthur which left at 11am on Sunday, planning to arrive at the site around 1pm, in time for lunch. When Hazell told him there was a bus at 9am but not at 11am, Bryant became angry and stormed out. By the time he caught up with Petra again, he had calmed down enough to take her to lunch down by the docks at Salamanca Place.

On Saturday, April 27, Bryant went to see his grandmother, Freda Cordwell, in her little unit at the Jutland retirement village, a few hundred metres from the old family home in Augusta Road. He was saying goodbye: "I followed him to the door, and then he turned around, kissed me and said goodbye," she said in the aftermath.

"That's all I'm going to say. I loved Martin."

Freda, wife of the alcoholic, depressive and often violent Albert Arthur Cordwell, died in December 1998 at the age of 90.

That night, Bryant and Petra drove out to Berriedale to have dinner with his mum. They had milled among the tourists at Salamanca Place again that morning, browsing and buying vegetables for Carleen. But it ended up being an uncomfortable few hours. Bryant was drinking heavily, appeared agitated, abrupt and outright rude to his mother although, to Petra, it felt as if he were almost play-acting. The young couple escaped to go nightclubbing at the casino.

Scott Goldsmith happened to be at the Wrest Point Casino with his girlfriend. He noticed his blond neighbour with the odd smile walk towards him along the corridor which led to the main bar. He decided to force the guy to say hello.

"Watch this bloke; he's a bit strange," he whispered to his girlfriend. It was clear Bryant had spotted Scott and was determined to avoid conversation.

"I kept moving sideways to force him to walk past me and stop but he kept moving as well," Goldsmith recalled. "By the time we came face to face he was pressed up against the wall. He put his head down and shoved right past me. He said nothing."

It was not the last time Scott would see Bryant.

The next morning, Sunday April 28, Scott got up later than usual, probably as a result of his late night at the casino. Just before 10am, he wandered out the front to retrieve the paper from the front lawn. He glanced up to see Bryant's familiar yellow Volvo with the surfboard strapped to the roof appear from behind the white house across the road. Bryant was at the wheel as he made his way down a gravel driveway to the side of the property. He glanced quickly left and then right and turned towards the city. He did not appear to be in a hurry: "I watched the bastard go," Goldsmith said shaking his head. "I watched him go."

CHAPTER 29
Through His Eyes

The day of death begins with a lie: "I'll see you tomorrow." With a nonchalant goodbye and no real expectation of seeing her again, Martin Bryant waves off his girlfriend, Petra Wilmott, and walks back inside the big, square white house to begin preparing for mass slaughter.

It is just after 8am on Sunday, April 28, 1996. The couple have been up for several hours, showered and had a leisurely breakfast before Petra went home to her parents. It was unusual, she would later say, because Bryant had set the alarm the night before for 6am. It was the first time he had done so in the few weeks they'd been together, and there was no apparent reason to be up so early, particularly after a lateish night around town. Not that she knew of anyway.

Carleen Bryant would say later she could sense unease in her son. She'd noticed it in the weeks since his return from his last overseas trip. The relationship with Petra had given him some stability but there were disturbing signs that something was wrong. She was right about his mood, not that she could have dreamed what was on his mind.

Bryant does not communicate with Petra either, offering only that he has "some things to do". This terrible day has arrived, the demons inside his mind bubbling and stewing and fermenting, but the details other than the first victims are still undecided. How many are to die will depend on how he feels after dealing with the symbols of his quiet fury, Sally and David Martin.

Bryant's car looks innocent enough, that ubiquitous surfboard strapped to the roof-rack of the yellow Volvo bought seven months earlier but still driven without licence. What is stashed in the boot cannot have been imagined: an arsenal including two sets of handcuffs, sash-cord rope, a hunting knife and several canisters of petrol. There is also the sports bag with three semi-automatic weapons and ammunition. The guns – an AR-15 semi-automatic .223 calibre rifle, an SLR military-style semi-automatic .308 calibre rifle and a semi-automatic Daewoo 12-gauge shotgun – have been secreted inside the house in the bodies of two unused pianos. This morning, in the haste, anxiety and excitement at what lies ahead, Bryant forgets another semi-automatic firearm and ammunition, leaving them lying in the hallway, haphazardly discarded among the mismatched furniture inside Clare Street.

Curious neighbours and marauding media crews would spy inside the house over the following week, noting all sorts of bric-a-brac, from a Christmas tree still decorated with baubles to a cabinet filled with dolls. In one side of a room, a set of dumb bells were scattered on the floor while an empty bird cage complete with fluffy, stuffed parrots hanging upside down on the perch was in another corner. A reporter would later describe the scene as "a lonely place".

At 9.47am, the time registered to the minute on the house alarm as he shuts the door, Bryant takes a few swigs of Sambuca and drives through the thin line of Sunday morning traffic down the hill from Clare Street towards the Derwent River, swings left on to the Brooker Highway to avoid the city centre and heads across the Tasman Bridge.

Obsessed, armed, his plan indelibly rooted in his mind, Bryant nevertheless spends the next hour looking for a reason to abandon his mission.

The drive to his destination is punctuated by stop after stop, every one brief but very public. The first is around 10.30am at a roadside newsagency at Midway Point, a small community perched between the two causeways that form a gateway to the spectacular Tasman Peninsula. Here he buys a $1.50 cigarette lighter and quickly departs, leaving his change on the counter.

Bryant pauses and parks again, just 10 minutes later, in the slightly larger township of Sorell where he buys a $1.40 bottle of tomato sauce from a supermarket. It isn't the purchase so much as the large sports bag he carries openly into the store that catches the attention of owner Spiros Diamantis, who watches him closely until he pays with small change and leaves.

In Forcett, barely 10 kilometres south, he stops for a cup of coffee from the Shell service station. Gary King remembers him because of his strange request – to "boil the kettle less time" – because a coffee he'd bought the previous week had been too hot. Bryant again pays with loose change – five and 10 cent coins – and leaves but not before announcing publicly that he is heading to Roaring Beach. At the Taranna Convict Bakery, Bryant stands with owner Christopher Hammond while he pumps $15 worth of petrol into the Volvo. Bryant tells him of his surfing plans as both men look out over peaceful Norfolk Bay.

Bryant's actions that day suggest that either he wanted to create a surfing alibi – not only naive but almost incredible – or that he wanted to be seen and deep down, wanted a reason to end his journey. The frequent stops made very little sense on the surface. He had walked into three petrol stations, filling up only at the last one. He'd bought small items at three venues, all of which could have been bought at just one. And why did he need tomato sauce or a lighter? He didn't smoke and he wasn't planning on eating a pie or cooking a barbecue.

It was, according to his psychiatrists, complex behaviour, suggesting that not only did he want to be remembered for what he was about to do but that he had accepted that he was likely to die in the act.

Martin Bryant expected to die with his victims and was putting off his own demise, searching, stopping, procrastinating in the desperate hope that someone, somewhere would give him a reason to turn around and go home.

The rising anger noticed by people such as Scott Goldsmith in the weeks before were not only of a man struggling with his obsession, fighting the demon that urged him relentlessly on towards his Armageddon but a damaged psyche that was simply incapable of straying from a set course. Since marking the event on his calendar in the days after Dunblane, Bryant's life had turned around and for the better. He had entered a new relationship, found the human connection he had craved for so long.

Suddenly, he had reasons to live, and yet the rigidity of his nature drove him towards the suicide deadline. The closer it got to April 28, the more anxious he became. He had wanted to die but now he was not so sure. Still, the date circled on his calendar drew him like a magnet.

There was no reason for the date, April 28. It had no significance when he chose it, merely that it was a Sunday when tourists would be at Port Arthur just in case he wanted to go on a killing spree after disposing of the Martins.

When asked why he had settled on that date by his lawyer, John Avery, Bryant answered: "It was a nice day." It seems an unfathomably cruel remark but for him, it signified nothing more than a shrug of the shoulders.

The answer meant little except to confirm that he had given himself a deadline. Even then he was still searching for a way out: the cigarette lighter and sauce were bought for no reason other than to give him an excuse to stop and try to engage with others. Like his long-haul flights, he wanted to find someone with whom he could strike up a conversation, perhaps even a person who might make a kind remark, respond to him and make him feel accepted, if only for a moment. When he bought the coffee at Forcett, Bryant walked outside and sat down next to a tourist who'd also stopped for petrol. The desperate young man tried to involve the man in conversation: here was a chance for the world to admit it was wrong.

If the man had exchanged even a few words with Bryant, it might have been just enough for him to turn around, put his terrible plan on the backburner. But like so many times before, his inane observations and the stupid blank grin got in the way. The man walked away from him, and from the warped perspective of Martin Bryant, he had been slighted yet again. His indignation had been reignited, and the world had been robbed of its last chance. Now it was a case of how many would die with him.

It is just after 11 o'clock when Bryant leaves Taranna, a place where his mother fondly recalled riding horses with his sister. About that time, Sally Martin is waving goodbye to the last of her overnight guests at the Seascape guest house. She turns and goes back inside where husband David is in the kitchen. Neither hear the crunch of tyres on the gravel drive a few minutes later as the yellow Volvo makes its way slowly to the back of the property, until there is a knock at the back door. Sally Martin starts as she recognises the familiar face of Martin Bryant. He is rambling about his girlfriend, who is apparently at The Fox and Hounds, the mock-Tudor motel a few kilometres further down the road. They want to book a room for a night.

"Will it be a single or a double?" she asks.

"Oh, a double I reckon," he replies.

Sally walks Bryant to an upstairs bedroom where he promptly puts his sports bag, containing the shotgun and rifles, on the bed. She is irritated.

"Don't put your bag on the bed. I don't want you to put your bag on the bed."

Bryant stares back, says nothing, but complies. "How's David?" he asks.

"He's just finishing his breakfast," she replies, and leaves the room.

Bryant watches her go, puts the bag back on the bed and pulls out the AR-15. "Gosh, she is such a straight, hard bitch," he thinks to himself. It just confirms his hatred of the couple, the lightning rod for all his ills. Here is the excuse he needs to kill.

A few minutes later, Bryant walks into the kitchen below where David Martin, celebrating his 72nd birthday, is sitting at the table. His wife turns around in surprise. "What's going on?" she says, seeing the gun.

Bryant stares at her. "I've got a few things to talk to you about. See, I'm here to rob you and take your jewellery from you."

He marches them into the front room – David Martin in front of his wife with a gag tied over his mouth – and orders the couple to lie face-down on the bed. Then, without hesitation, he places a pillow over their heads and fires, killing David Martin. Sally Martin is next, felled by a blow to the head. He then rolls her over and shoots her in the chest. It is over in a few seconds, the sounds of gunfire lost in the hills outside. In the country, a couple of shots in the distance are barely noticed.

It all seems so easy, Bryant feels his resentment ebb like the tides. He has often wondered what would happen when he finally got rid of the Martins. Would it be enough, or just the beginning? The idea of going to Port Arthur – "such a pretty place" – and killing lots of tourists appeals to him. It seems so appropriate given all the years of torment. He knew the laughter – "Silly Marty", they called him. Lindy had friends but he had no one. Then there was the humiliation of the Broad Arrow Cafe. Now, he is just going to go out and do it. He showers and leaves quickly, feeling "refreshed", he says later.

• •

Half an hour later, after visiting Carnarvon Bay and stopping to speak to Roger Larner, Bryant parks his car among the buses down by the waterfront and walks up to the Broad Arrow Cafe. He is suddenly hungry so he decides to go inside to buy something to eat. The killing can wait. He takes his juice and a can of fruit back out to the veranda, looks around, finds a table and sits down. It is perfect. He is in the middle of the tourists, which means he can simply sweep around in an arc, shooting.

Bryant barely tastes the food. He walks back inside, places his bag on an empty table, takes out the AR-15 and starts firing.

There is no time to notice the people or take in their fear. They are simply numbers, flies to be swatted. He laughs as he moves and shoots, rarely missing as he places the barrel against necks and heads, the muzzle searing circular tattoos around entry wounds. Diners cower beneath tables, behind counters, in corners, some sandwiched so tightly that two men will be killed with a single bullet.

Bryant has imagined that someone might lunge at him to stop the shooting, but no one does. One man claws at his legs to plead for his life. It is annoying. There should be a hero. He shoots the man.

Nor is there any blood, at least none that he notices when he thinks about it later. No names, no faces, no blood. Just noise: bang bang bang. Dead dead dead. He doesn't know how many. Maybe a dozen, he thinks later when his lawyer asks. It seems a stupid question: Why would he count? Just keep firing.

In his address to the court on November 19, 1996, Crown prosecutor Damian Bugg would spend an hour describing in detail the personal horror – face by face, bullet by bullet, and wound by wound – of the mayhem inside the cafe and the souvenir shop. But to Bryant, the faces, the people, those terrified souls, were nothing.

The thrill for him lay in the event itself, the momentary power, the absolute and utter control. The detail means zero. He pauses only to reload from a magazine in his pocket.

Bryant feels excitement, not sexual excitement, but a thrill like scuba diving or going fast in the boat of his childhood. He is powerful, and this is the most exciting moment in his shitty life.

He moves outside and starts shooting from the veranda towards people cowering behind one of the buses. There is no method, just a response to movement and the desire to keep going and kill as many as he can. He climbs aboard one of the buses parked near the water and starts shooting as passengers cower behind seats. Time is a blur.

He can see people running up towards the ruins on the hill to get away from him. From him, the all-powerful. "Run away," he thinks as he fires. They scatter like seagulls, "to get away from me".

He decides to take a hostage. As he drives up the hill, he sees a woman with a girl or is it two? He stops. She doesn't want to come so he shoots her and the girls. Was it one or two? He can't recall later when the lawyer wants to know the detail. The girl was small. She hid. He shot but missed and fired again. He remembers that, but not the faces. Names? There are no names.

Bryant leaves the bodies and drives to the toll gate. There is a gold-coloured BMW with four people inside. This will do. He stops and gets out of his car. A man gets out of the driver's seat of the BMW as he walks up.

"I'm gonna take you hostage," he says to the man.

"Oh, you can't take me hostage, I've got a bad heart," the man pleads. He is elderly.

"Well, here's something for your heart," he replies and shoots the man in the chest. As the man falls, Bryant moves across to the car and shoots the other three inside.

He still doesn't have a hostage, and he's somehow locked himself out of the Volvo. What about the BMW? The keys are in the ignition. He shoots open the boot of his car, takes a can of petrol for the fire he'll light later and drags the bodies from the BMW.

He still wants a hostage. There are people in a white car parked at the Stewarts Bay shop waiting to get petrol. He swerves off the road to cut off their escape route. A man gets out of the driver's seat.

"I'm gonna take you hostage," Bryant tells the man. He then spies a woman in the front seat and changes his mind. "I don't think I'll take you hostage, I'll take the wife."

The man panics. "No, don't take the wife, please don't take my wife."

"All right, I'll take you," Bryant says.

The man is scared. "Where are we going?" he asks.

Bryant isn't scared. He is in control. He is powerful.

"To Seascape guest house," he says, shoving the man in the boot.

Bryant looks around as he shuts the boot. There are a lot of people hiding inside the shop, looking out at him, scared of him. He could shoot them all but he is getting uncomfortable. His hands are sore from shooting.

It is time to go back to Seascape and finish things. He shoots the woman and leaves.

The Martins are still where he left them when he gets back. He doesn't have to rush. He gets the man out of the boot and sets fire to the BMW. He doesn't need it any more. He wonders whether he should have gone somewhere like Launceston but it doesn't matter. It is better to do things here, where it matters.

Bryant is hungry again. How about some eggs and bacon? The hostage might even like some. And a coffee. They can talk about things. The man isn't going anywhere. Later they can have wine or maybe some port. The Martins have a stash.

The hostage is in handcuffs. He has to listen and to talk. He has no choice, just like the passengers in the planes when he went to Europe.

••••••••••••••••••••••••••••

Lawyer John Avery seems amazed when Bryant later tells him of his encounter with the hostage.

"So he told you a bit about himself, his family?" Avery asks.

"Yes," Bryant replies. "He was keen on getting in contact with his parents who lived at Lindisfarne, and I said, 'You can't really do that at present because I have got you captive.'"

"So when did you dispose of him?"

"Ah. He got shot. The next morning. I don't recall anything else. I don't recall lighting the fire."

"What was the intention when you did that? You were going to go up in flames, were you, in the fire?"

"No," Bryant insists, his voice rising in protest. "I wanted to come out because I sang out twice, 'I'm coming out now,' loud from the upstairs to police. I don't know whether they heard me or not but I just raced out the back. I don't even know what door it was."

Avery sits back in his chair and looks at the figure on the other side. "So that was the end of it. Pretty sad, sinister tale isn't it?"

Bryant protests like a petulant child: "For me, too!"

His desire to be pitied as a victim sounds ludicrous, but not to him.

Avery ignores him: "Why do you think it got out of control? I mean, you said you really went there to kill the Martins but obviously you had gone there thinking you were going to kill some other people. Was it the excitement of it all?"

"It was the excitement of it all," Bryant agrees. "Does that make me mentally…" His words became a mumble.

"I'll have to ask the doctors but I don't think so."

CHAPTER 30
The Lawyer

Hobart's limpid skies say much about this island's isolation from the grime of the mainland. The air, even in mid-summer, is needle sharp, and the smoggy jaundice that mars big city horizons is nowhere to be seen. Just as absent is the amorphous hum of the large metropolis. It is not quiet, far from it. But sounds are vivid, distinct and can be heard individually, trapped and amplified by the hilly surrounds: the tinny ring-a-ding-ding of a single-cylinder motorbike, the chaotic grind of an early morning garbage truck, men shouting as they disgorge empty beer kegs from the cellar of a nearby pub.

Australians have long enjoyed a joke at Tasmania's expense, dismissive about its isolation, vulgar in their aspersions about its tiny population, slow wit and shallow gene pool. And yet modern Hobart is unrecognisable from the stereotype: petite, quick witted, it sings with a distinct life and tempo of its own.

Nature, of course, is omnipresent and offers a counterpoint to the human narrative. Just as Hobart's elegant, Georgian buildings mark out the city's human scale, the surrounding mountains define the sky, mysterious, dark and often shrouded in low-lying cloud.

Water, too, is ever present, visible at street corners, between houses, glimpsed between public buildings, through the gates of parks and gardens.

In bright sunshine, Hobart exudes cheerful optimism. When clouds obliterate the sun, the immediate chill is a reminder that the untamed squalls of the Great Southern Ocean and Antarctica are not really so far away. Indeed, Hobart's relationship with the water is anathema to that embraced by the rest of Australia: ask a local for directions to a swimming beach, and the response is often benign superiority. In Hobart, you don't swim; the water's there to be sailed, to be fished, observed from the window.

John Avery, Martin Bryant's lawyer, lives in Battery Point, one of Hobart's best known waterside quarters, a tiny village perched on the cliff directly above the sandstone warehouses of the old port and Salamanca Place. Here, the city's founders re-created a well-mannered English village, workman's cottages alongside terraces beside corner pubs. On the blocks commanding the best views are the homes of merchants, bigger stone or weatherboard residences with verandas, gates, gardens and even the odd viewing tower. Tiny cottage gardens abound with English lavender, roses and nasturtiums, bounded by picket fences and weathered stone walls. Memories of the midlands and Cotswolds elicit a momentary, geographic confusion.

Vivid in our mind as we walk the tiny streets are John Avery's interviews with Martin Bryant in the months after the massacre. We have read and reread the transcripts, straining to imagine Bryant's voice, to absorb and understand his lawyer's egg-shell walk to bring this client to a guilty plea without cajoling or undue pressure.

The terror that he might alienate the strange young man before nailing a plea is palpable even on paper: Avery's professional identity is in the national spotlight following the national tragedy, and as Bryant veers between eccentric charm and petulant tantrum, his lawyer's meticulous efforts to control his frustration are evident in every word.

Bryant's unadulterated narcissism is strangely compelling – as is his understanding that the decision he makes about his plea will not only define his future but that of his lawyer.

His client's complex nature – manipulative, childish, suspicious – is unadulterated but so, too, is his lawyer's mercenary understanding that these conversations with the killer, the pencil sketches he asks him to draw, his very relationship with this client may, one day, be worth money. Perhaps even big money.

We've arrived in Battery Point half an hour before the appointed time, and decide to slip into a cafe next door to the lawyer's neat brick bungalow. There is nothing salubrious about this house. Ten years after his defendant has been put away, Bryant's barrister is awaiting trial on charges of embezzling the funds of both clients and former legal partners. The For Sale sign on the modest home speaks volumes about the fall from grace. Over a quickly downed coffee, we muse about Avery's predicament and how much he might divulge about himself, let alone Bryant.

Our tentative knock on the door is followed immediately by a definitive "Gidday, how are you?" A 50-something man walks us briskly away from his house and out on to the street. A gesture directs us next door: "Let's go for a coffee," he calls over his shoulder.

The young woman behind the counter doesn't blink despite our return just minutes after leaving. As the soon-to-be disgraced barrister steers us towards a table in the deserted courtyard outside, the waitress's look of understanding speaks volumes about Hobart town. Here, everyone knows everything about each other but Anglo-Saxon dictums of privacy remain paramount.

John Avery is shortish, dressed nattily in baggy holiday shorts, a red shirt and black-faced diving watch. He has a florid face and a wide, engaging smile. It takes less than a minute before he throws himself into the confessional, and any anxieties we had about touching on his legal conundrum are wiped away by a memorable candour.

"I've wondered if I was Martin Bryant's last victim," he says without a skerrick of irony. "I remember the day after he was sentenced, I woke up early and just put my head in my hands and bawled like a baby."

Avery pauses, perhaps for drama.

"What? Relief?" we ask puzzled.

He shakes his head.

"Oh, you mean like some kind of jinx?"

"Yeah, something like that," he answers.

Mug in hand, Avery chats about his crimes. And they are crimes, not misdemeanours. Thousands of dollars skimmed from the accounts of clients but much, much more from the accounts of the firm. Matter of fact, he explains that he never believed himself to be stealing from clients, rather it was the belief that, "I was owed more as a partner in the firm than I was getting."

A jail sentence is a reality but he says he is not sure how long he might get; a few years perhaps. Somehow, the familiarity with prisons, with the criminal justice system over so many decades of legal work, allows him to face his future with disturbing fatalism: "I just want to get it over and done with," he says with a shrug.

For now, it's about treading water. The support of his wife and daughter, who accompanied him to court and helped him face his public shame, is a big fillip. His three sons have not taken the fall from grace so easily, the emergence of several earlier affairs have made it so much worse.

"My mum was amazing," he says of his mother's unconditional and loving support despite his crime. "The idea of prison ... she hasn't responded to that quite the same way," he adds quietly as another long black is placed in front of him.

Looking at Avery's craggy face, we wonder out loud if he remembers his reactions to meeting Martin Bryant for the first time. His answer is eerily similar to the notes we had scrawled the night before while reading his first record of interview with Bryant. "Did Avery, like most of us, imagine the killer, the mass murderer as a creature different from us ... a being who inhabits a frightening, crepuscular world but whose physical presence surely will hint at the evil within?"

Avery, a criminal lawyer with decades of experience admits he, too, entertained similar fantasies, describing sheepishly the expectation that he would be faced with a Hannibal Lecter-style character: "When I first saw him, he was in leg and hand irons ... In all my years, I had not seen anybody restrained like that," he said sipping gingerly at the hot coffee.

"But what I got despite the irons was just a big kid. Without his guns, he couldn't have hurt a fly."

Avery's observation, even a decade or more later, makes him pause a moment. He looked away, as if struck once more by the banality of the horror: 35 blasted to death by a simpleton with an obsession with guns.

It took a few moments for the lawyer to return to his train of thought: "He laughed a lot, and at the strangest times. I interpreted that as a kind of social unease, as nerves. We had some banter, we had a few laughs even, but I had to keep reminding myself that this person had done what he did."

Do you think he understood death? That he had killed people, maimed others? Avery's answer is immediate: "He understood death. But he had no empathy. To him, it was like swatting an ant."

What about insanity? Again, not a quiver of doubt: "He was not insane. It was clear he was not insane. He showed an ability to maintain a ruse during the siege. An insane person could not have managed to keep up the pretence of another, separate persona. He wanted attention. He craved attention. I have not told anyone this but there were times during our discussions when he said, quite simply, that he wished he had done more."

Avery insists his requests for Bryant to draw and sketch his crimes were designed as a kind of insurance, in case the written confession gleaned from the young killer on "the day of the Hobart show ... yes, I still have a copy, it's short, doesn't say much" was reneged at the 11th hour.

Placing his thumb and index fingers at right angles to indicate a gun, Avery looks up for an instant: "They're simple, just stick figures really ... shooting. He didn't leave much out."

For the next hour or so, the craggy former barrister continues to talk and answer questions. The conversation is remarkable and relaxed for a man who has lost everything, his pride, his profession, his significant social status in this small city. He talks candidly, mainly about himself, veering towards anxiety only once or twice when we press too far on what information he keeps stashed away. It seems the magnitude of the experience with Bryant is so indelibly printed in his existence, both as a man and as a lawyer, that another question prompting yet another memory renders it almost impossible for him to wrap up.

At one point, he mutters curiously about having been part of the legal "A team" and his discomfort at being relegated back to the "B team": could it be that like his client, there was something about being in the national spotlight, about the public gaze and interest that mesmerised and seduced him, too?

"I have to admit that I am aware of the value of what I do have," he says. "The artwork, the tapes ... but I'm still not sure what to do with them."

"Can we hear the tapes?" we ask in unison, with perhaps a little too much enthusiasm. The idea of hearing Bryant's voice, placing it out of our mind's eye and into the physical world, is tantalising. Avery deftly ignores the question, musing almost to himself, "The Law Society might pursue me still ... Do I want still more grief?"

"Do you really think they would bother after you have been struck off, face charges, all that?" we ask.

"There are some people for whom a principle is worth pursuing," he answers impatiently.

"I have thought of writing something myself. I kept a diary, of my own observations at the time ... I have a friend in New York who said to me, 'Send me his drawings ... there are people in the US who collect this kind of stuff. I'll sell it in a minute.'"

....

John Avery's pretrial conversations with Martin Bryant span some 20 hours. The overall effect is of a grown man attempting to talk a spoiled and erratic child into doing the right thing. What makes them mesmerising is hindsight: this intemperate brat is a mass murderer, not a teenager demanding to take his dad's car out.

Bryant held out for days; stonewalling, evading and trying to impress. Over and over again, Avery brought him back to the understanding that the evidence against him was overwhelming but it must be his own decision, not Avery's, to change the plea he made on his first appearance after which his first lawyer, David Gunson, had quit.

This exchange is typical of several between lawyer and client:

Avery: "I'm not going to put anything to the court you don't want me to. But you might want the world to know your story as to what led you to do this."

Bryant: "I don't know ..."

Avery: "If you plead guilty ... I will do the talking for you, right, but all I'm saying is even if that happens, the court and the world and your family, I suspect, will want to know what you say about it, and you will have to tell me what you want to say."

Bryant: "But even if I plead not guilty, I can tell them the story of what happened."

Avery: "Well, if you plead not guilty and you tell them the story you've told me, they will say what the heck are you pleading not guilty for? You can hardly plead not guilty if you think you've got a defence, and they'll say, 'This bloke's as mad as a hatter if he is now saying he did it and he is pleading not guilty.'"

Bryant: "Yeah, that's right."

When he wasn't sleeping in his specially built cell, Bryant spent his days reading witness statements over and over again, reliving the anguish through the eyes of others. And he wanted more.

In the minutes after Avery met his client in early October, Bryant asked if it were true that other lawyers did not want to represent him. Avery nodded: "I will be frank with you. I have already copped some flak for suggesting I will act for you because a lot of people out there see you as someone who shouldn't have anyone acting for you."

It confirmed what Bryant had been told by Gunson: "Hmm. That's right."

Avery pressed on: "But I repeat, I will do what I can to assist you but you've got to help me. Now are we clear on that? Can we strike a deal on that basis?"

"Yes."

"All right ... Anything else you want that might help us?"

"I just want to hear all the evidence and what other people have got to say about me."

"Oh, we'll talk that through. You've got the statements, and we'll go through that and ..."

Bryant cut him off: "No, I mean in court."

Not once in the weeks that followed, did Bryant express fear, sorrow or compassion for what he had done. Occasionally, his self-absorption emerged cleanly to reveal the depth of his pathology.

At one point, they were discussing his psychiatric evaluation. Bryant had confessed to attempting to lie his way into the prison hospital by pretending he heard voices. None of the psychiatrists had believed him:

"Well, you don't think you're insane do you?" Avery asked.

"No, of course not. Oh! I intended to go down there. I was excited that morning. I had all the guns ready. I had all the ammunition, I had a big box with about 600 rounds of ammunition in the back of the Volvo, big canisters of petrol. I was going to light up the whole, a lot of the historic parts. If I had of done that it would have been a disaster."

"What were you thinking though, that you'd become some celebrity, that you'd become important, that you'd be famous?"

"No, I just thought I'd kill a lot of people."

At the end of another interview, they were discussing what would happen in court. Avery said: "Look, the last thing I'm ever going to say to you is, 'Are you sorry?', 'cos I know you're not, are you?"

Bryant shook his head: "No."

"You're not going to con me and say you're sorry for what you did, are you?"

"No, I'm not."

"In fact, I suspect you're pleased."

Bryant nodded enthusiastically: "I'm excited, yeah."

"Does it still give you some excitement as to what you did?"

"Yeah, I don't know. I might come out in court and tell everyone what happened. I don't know. It might be the best thing to do, mightn't it?"

Avery's greatest difficulty lay in giving the narcissist enough leeway to satisfy his need for attention while sparing a shellshocked community the horror of reliving the massacre in a long and expensive trial:

"I had to hold his hand, to take him with me, but I always knew, right up to the end, that he knew he had the power and he could land me in the shit just as he had done to Gunson."

Then came the revelation by Bryant that he had known Avery and his family since he was a boy. It emerged as they discussed the death of Glen Pears, the man kidnapped and shoved in the boot of the car before being driven to the Seascape guest house and handcuffed inside the house overnight. He had been shot by Bryant the next morning, just before setting the place alight.

"Did you tell him you were going to shoot him?" Avery asked.

The answer was cold: "No, I didn't say anything. I don't even know where I shot him now."

Then he brightened suddenly: "Oh gosh! Have you still got your Mercedes?"

The question came from nowhere, as if it had been brewing in Bryant's brain and suddenly popped out. Avery was stunned. "Yes," he stammered.

Bryant was smiling now: "Yeah, it's a white one isn't it?"

"How did you know I had that?"

The answer chilled him: "Oh, you used to drive around – I used to see you driving around in it ... and your wife had the station wagon, didn't she?"

Avery tried not to show his surprise: "Oh yes, that's years ago."

"I think it's a Holden station wagon. I used to see her going up to the shop in Lenah Valley and the newsagency, and I used to see you going in and reading the magazines."

Avery's wife remembered Bryant, too. He used to come to the house selling vegetables and rabbits. He was weird, and she never let him come inside. The notion of Martin Bryant spying on them years before the spree was uncomfortable but served a useful purpose in the sense that Bryant felt comforted, as if they were friends.

And there John Avery ends our conversation. There are other, more pressing matters to attend to. Months later, we read that he has gone ahead with his plan to plead guilty to 130 counts of stealing and dishonesty. Between December 2001 and March 2006 while a director at the Moonah practice Avery Partners, he had apparently stolen more than $500,000 from clients and his law firm partners. His lawyer was, ironically, the same David Gunson SC, who repeats the same mitigating circumstances Avery had described in the cafe. He gets the sentence he is expecting and will be eligible for parole around Christmas 2010.

What also emerged in the plethora of publicity was the portrait of an engaging personality who collected art as a schoolboy, not just as a rich lawyer. A contemporary recalled that, as a university student, Avery told then chief justice Sir Stanley Burbury he was in law for the money but, as much as he collected the baubles such as an E-type Jaguar and Montblanc pens, he made his name representing working-class battlers in the northern suburbs and even winning a famous case in the Family Court representing a gay man who wanted custody of his son. Then came Martin Bryant, and his fall from grace on the way down from the summit of his own Mont Blanc.

We decide to call, perhaps speak with his wife and pass on our best wishes, but it was Avery who answered. He had one last night of freedom. The noise in the background was a going away party. "No sense in being morbid", he chuckles. It is difficult not to like the man and his attitude.

CHAPTER 31
The Psychiatrist

Professor Paul Mullen lopes across the hotel foyer with the surefooted gait of a man confident both of his import and his position. It is a warm, sunny day in Sydney and outside the hotel's plate-glass window, the sound of the sea mingles with the faint hum of traffic. Brighton-le-Sands is bathed in the gentle autumn light that manages to soften Sydney's worst architectural indiscretions.

Mullen, we smile to ourselves, is the forensic psychiatrist from Central Casting, papers in hand, just too good to be true. A full head of silver hair, handsome jawline, wide forehead, black turtleneck and trousers, funky Italian Persol glasses and, through the lenses, bright blue eyes. Elegant but deliberate and understated.

We shake hands, slightly stiff and unsure of just how this meeting will unfold but Mullen is cordial and leads us to the hotel cafe.

Until this moment, we have been unsure if the world-renowned, British-born, Melbourne-based psychiatrist would agree to see us, let alone allow a probe of this most infamous of cases. And yet he is integral to Bryant's story. Mullen is the expert who assessed the young gunman's state of mind in the aftermath of the killings and he is the man who sat with Bryant on behalf of the state of Tasmania and the Crown, to work out if he were fit to stand trial. This eloquent professor with the English accent infused with a hint of Kiwi vowels is probably the only man who can walk with us, down the mind-boggling road map that led a dim, disorganised but quasi-functional young eccentric to abandon his life and rain death upon 35 men, women and children.

We are at pains to tell him that the decision to return and rake over this atrocity was not one we took lightly. We have debated it ad nauseam, wrestling with ethical doubts about refocusing public attention on a man who not only murdered innocent human beings but did so, in part, because he craved attention. We are mindful, too, that Mullen himself has written a number of clinical papers which have examined the role of the media after mass homicide: he does not warn of copycat killings but argues a complex ripple effect in which saturation media coverage has been shown to influence obsessive behaviours over inordinately long periods of time. In a study titled 'Media and mass homicides', which he co-authored with three colleagues and was published in *Archives of Suicide Research*, he outlined a time link between these killings, beginning in Australia in 1987 with the Hoddle Street massacre in Melbourne, in which seven died, to Hungerford in Britain 10 days later when a gun fanatic slaughtered 16 people before killing himself. In another shooting spree four months later in Queen Street, Melbourne, eight died before the killer turned his weapon on himself. A second cluster occurred in 1990-91 when an assailant gunned down 13 people in Aramoana, New Zealand, and nine months later, a man slaughtered seven people in Sydney's Strathfield Plaza shopping centre in a similarly random way before killing himself. The murders of 16 in a primary school in Dunblane, Scotland, as we now know, preceded Martin Bryant's Port Arthur killings by just a few weeks.

Many months later, Mullen would tell us that in his studies of similar killings, the trigger thought for the act of mass homicide as a way to commit suicide often takes six months or even up to a year to coalesce: "You saw it with Virginia Tech. You were still getting imitators six to nine months, even a year later. It suddenly seems to be an attractive way to die. The man who committed Dunblane, Thomas Hamilton, was a rigid, obsessive man who felt he had been mistreated and he decided he was going to kill himself in a way that made the world realise how awfully he had been mistreated. These people always deny they are imitating but when you sit with them they know a lot more about these other events than you would expect."

Important, too, in our discussion is the potential effect of telling the full story on those who survived the horror and the families of his victims. Would it be cruel, perhaps even immoral, to probe an atrocity that destroyed and traumatised the lives of so many?

What about Bryant's remaining family, his mother, Carleen, and younger sister, Lindy? Had they not suffered enough?

Coffees ordered, Mullen begins, as psychiatrists do, by asking questions. What is it that we want to achieve by delving into this story more than a decade after the event? Is Carleen Bryant co-operating with the project? How much do we know about her? And what about the family history?

In fact, it had been Carleen who had sown that first seed of curiosity, we tell him. The long trek had begun with us, as parents, asking ourselves how a parent could possibly survive, let alone reconcile, such a crime? Did Martin Bryant's mother ask herself, "Why me?" Did she, in her darkest moments, question whether her boy was born with his fate indelibly stamped inside him or was it his childhood and adolescent experiences that led him to his action?

Could it be that there, by the grace of God, go all of us parents?

For an hour, we to and fro with the professor, glissing and toying with profound questions, from the nature of evil (he does not believe in the notion) to the possibility that there may now be room for a new, more sophisticated understanding of such terrible events; that the realms of neuroscience and the growing body of knowledge about the complex interactions between genes, life experience and opportunity that shape all our lives might provide new insight into what created Martin Bryant.

Society may have no room for compassion for Bryant but scientific – and a more sophisticated approach and understanding of violent crime – may allow us, as a community, to take preventative steps in future, action which might identify risky individuals and maybe even step in before the build-up of lethal, infernal, deadly male anger.

Finally, as the time comes for Professor Mullen to return to the conference in the hotel's meeting room above, he utters the words we have been fervently praying to hear: "Goodbye, talk to you again soon."

•••••••••••••••••••••••••••••

Eight months pass by the time we see him again, and hints of a new antipodean summer are visible in the buds on the cherry blossoms and in the hint of violet in Sydney's ubiquitous jacaranda trees. A humidity and warmth in the sea air signals that the wet season is just around the corner.

Our odyssey to scrape away, dig and reveal how this mass murderer came to be, to unravel, one by one, the ingredients that created Martin Bryant led us to Britain, back to Tasmania and to London again. We have become experts at navigating archives, trawling the births, deaths and marriages registers in two hemispheres, in Hobart and in the British National Archives near London's spectacular Kew Gardens. We've made nuisances of ourselves with the Tasmanian Supreme Court and haunted the Department of Planning's record files in Hobart.

Dusty old piles of newspapers are our friends, as are reels of black-and-grey microfilm. Endlessly, we pored over pages of newsprint and thousands of column inches of classified advertisements. For weeks we are catapulted back two centuries, wondering in awe at the fluid, meticulous, handwritten records of the criminal courts of 1880s London.

The cruelty of life for the poor in Victorian England is palpable, young men and women brutalised – and in turn brutalising others – in the quest for survival, their punishments rarely commensurate with the crimes. Like children on a treasure hunt, every skerrick of paper, every tiny detail – from the tattoo on the bicep of Martin Bryant's convict great-great-grandfather to the tiny ad for a gun the young man would buy and use ultimately to kill – became a prize, another piece in the enormous jigsaw growing beneath our gaze.

By the time Mullen agrees to see us again, the puzzle has taken on a finite shape but the story it tells still needs the psychiatrist to fill in key pieces he has gleaned first-hand. Again, he chooses a hotel coffee shop as our meeting place, as if the homogeneity of the surrounds might lighten the import of information shared.

This time however, we have plenty to report: the tale of five maternal generations, his mother and father's story, the web of odd relationships and rejections and the minutiae of his patient's decade-long breakdown. Mullen leans forward, his body language imperceptible at first but after a while he appears to be genuinely intrigued. A nod in some places, a murmur of assent and recognition, "uh huh", in others. As the sunlight glances off the harbour through the trees of Rushcutters Bay, it becomes clear at last that our quest into the past for answers fits neatly with what he knows first-hand. Better still, put together, we might even be able to add to his own detailed, forensic profile.

And so, we begin, with the most complex, vexed – and potentially painful – question of all: Martin Bryant's experiences within his own family. We know that Carleen and Maurice Bryant had toiled and struggled with their own personal demons as adults. We also know they fought valiantly to rear a clearly abnormal, increasingly troubled child. The finger of blame is often counterproductive, particularly in hindsight, but true understanding requires an unflinching gaze, and Paul Mullen pulls no punches.

Behavioural problems, he makes clear, can sometimes be common to more than one generation. Perhaps there is the possibility of a genetic propensity to express emotion in a particular way or to exhibit anger or frustration in a violent way. But the professor is at pains to state that in the end, biological leaning cannot be extricated from what is experienced and learned. And modelling within the family is critical: "To the extent that there is some vulnerability which comes down the maternal line ... the more important aspect is what sort of mother [Carleen] could have been for him," Mullen says quietly.

"The fact that he inherited 50 per cent of genetic material is one thing. But he inherited 100 per cent of her as a mother. This clearly is a lady who would have had enormous difficulty. That doesn't determine of itself whether someone is going to have problems. The sister is a very good example; she had the same mother and she coped. But you combine the vulnerabilities with which he started off in life and an environment created in large part by a mother who struggled and couldn't give him what he needed, and then you have the problem of someone whose innate problems are going to come through because there is no compensation. In fact, there is aggravation from the world in which he lives, which is determined, in his case, almost entirely by his mother."

Carleen did not fail to love her son but her own psychological make-up, her own childhood experiences and modelling of motherhood – of parenthood – meant she herself had difficulties relating to other people, let alone to a difficult child.

"Everyone who saw this kid from a very early age felt there was something not right about him. Now, whether that 'not right' was hard-wired, in other words he inherited it, or whether it was a mixture of some vulnerabilities he inherited and, for him, an inadequate, damaging environment in which he lived it makes a plausible combination. He's this kid who, probably through some anomalies of his own essential nature, has difficulty socialising, has difficulty coping with demands of other people, and the model he has is a mother who has similar if not worse difficulties, so someone who can't help him, who can't substitute, who may well have had enough difficulties relating to her own children, let alone other people. Although the father did his best, and struggled, he was inevitably away at work. His contribution, particularly when Martin was young, was going to be relatively marginal."

In a flash, Carleen's reading of Martin's problems – that he was misunderstood by the world, victimised by the cruelty of other children – falls into place. Martin's mum, like her boy, knew first-hand his feelings of alienation and bewilderment. She too struggled socially, knew intimately the confusion sparked when people reacted in unfamiliar or unexpected ways. As she wrote at the beginning of her manuscript:

> *For as long as I have been able to remember, I have never been a confident person. From my childhood to becoming an adult, I was always self-conscious.*

Great suffering in childhood, her own mother brutalised psychologically by an alcoholic husband and too stretched and distraught to really nurture her brood, all led to a sense of displacement and the shaping of a personality cowed and powered mostly by the desperate desire to please. Parenting is even more difficult when you were never properly parented yourself.

Martin's dad tried so very hard, too, but again, a traumatic childhood left its scars. Maurice's suffering – finding his mother dead, leaving home young – had contributed to his own well of sadness. "He certainly had an alcohol problem," Mullen says. "That's clear from what [information] we had. He was also almost certainly significantly depressed. The difficulty is knowing the interaction between depression, which he may have had for years on and off, and his drinking. Problem drinking and depression can go hand in hand. You are never sure which is driving which ..."

Mullen's gauging of Martin's father is that he had fought, even with himself, to accept that his son had intellectual limitations, and as time went on, the severity of his behavioural issues. "There's not much doubt that from a very early age the father thought there was something wrong with him. He was a mixture. He wanted him to stay in normal schools and he didn't want him to be separated, to be labelled. But at the same time he always seemed to be trying to protect him, to support him, to provide a whole lot of things he felt this kid needed over and above what a normal child would need."

This type of interaction also coloured the handful of relationships Martin Bryant had with women: "He really was limited in his choices. You had to feel sorry for him or be simple yourself to stay in any kind of relationship with him. He was so inept and interpersonally awkward that you have to ask yourself who could stay with him: the answer, of course, is an older woman who could treat him as a child [or] a woman who is so immature that she feels comfortable being alongside another child. To relate to this boy-man you would have to be maternal or also a child."

The years with Helen Harvey, Mullen says, were almost an unconscious attempt for the young man to create his own, tailor-made family, a core of stability and outward happiness and understanding he had not encountered before. There was clearly a relationship between Maurice and Helen, he says, but how it expressed itself will probably remain a mystery. But for the short period that the three were able to coalesce as a nucleus, Martin Bryant was happiest – and kept in check.

"It's almost as if the father and Martin were able to reconstruct a new family for Martin for a while, which actually seemed to work. Both Miss Harvey and the father seemed happy to treat Martin during that period as if he was a much younger child when in fact he was already a grown man. He was allowed to buy what he wanted, the multiple videos were an example: it was like taking out a small child. If he wanted it, he got it."

Martin's descriptions, the professor says, make it sound like an idealised childhood period: "The childhood of someone between the ages of five and 10, with the parties and the balloons and the trips to the [Melbourne] zoo. His memories of it were very much of a childhood, and yet it wasn't a childhood with mother and dad being Miss Harvey and his father."

Bryant's ability to describe his relationship with his mother, however, was very matter-of-fact. He was unable to enter complex analyses and, for him, "It just was."

"I got very little really out of him about his feelings for his mother ... although he could appreciate when people did things for him. He did speak very positively about the period with Miss Harvey and his father which, clearly for him, was the best time of his life."

Sadness, however, appeared to be outside the realms of his abilities, neither for the chasm between himself and his mum or for the loss of his dad. Mullen remembers that his response to discussion about his father's suicide was muted and not of "the level you would expect for someone" whose parent had taken his own life.

"He didn't have either the distress or the anger or the grief which you would expect to be expressed. Some people, understandably, get very angry with a loved one who takes their own life; it's the ultimate rejection in a way. Martin was aware that his father had made a lot of arrangements for him, and he resented those arrangements. My impression was that he was more upset that his father had done the sensible thing and made these arrangements that had ensured his son's future was assured ... that really pissed him off."

For Maurice, the decision to walk into the dam, weighed down with his son's lead diving belt, was not a cry for help or attention but the understanding that he had had enough. The symbolism of that last act seems almost too poignant: Maurice Bryant had been worn down by the weight of his son's needs to a point of desperation where death, with his son's lead belt, seemed the only way out. "It was a very determined suicide attempt," Mullen says simply.

•••••••••••••••••••••••••••

Martin Bryant is, of course, not the only mass murderer Mullen has studied. While massacres by lone killers are rare, most often the gunman dies in a contrived suicide. The odd thing in Australia is that two have survived – Bryant and 19-year-old Julian Knight, who shot 26 people in Melbourne's Hoddle Street in 1987, but was caught before he could turn the gun on himself, having run out of bullets. Mullen is a specialist in this area, too, the author of several significant clinical and research papers on a phenomenon he has dubbed the "civil massacre". He argues there are similarities too between the assailants studied in the seven cases in New Zealand, Australia and Britain. Like Martin Bryant, all these men were socially inept, utterly self-absorbed and ultimately, highly resentful. Each one exhibited a slow build-up of festering anger underpinned by an overblown and overwhelming sense of victimhood about the way other people reacted to them. Their crimes were hatched after long periods of obsessive rehearsing and reliving of the many slights endured and rejections and humiliations suffered throughout their lives.

In the minds of these young men, the outside world had spurned them, and while their final acts may have been triggered by impulse, all had long fantasised their revenge on a society they believed had deliberately shunned and excluded them. Almost all exhibited a fascination with firearms, which became external symbols of power and a means to wreak their fury. All ended up placing innocent, unarmed strangers in their sights.

Crucial too in their stories was the breakdown of support networks at critical times of their lives, leading to a contemplation of suicide or, at the very least, a psychological acceptance or preparedness for death. Just like Bryant when he lost his father and the beloved Miss Harvey, all these young men had suddenly been let off the leash after a lifetime being held in check by a handful of caring relatives, friends and occasionally, even by the unexpected fulfilment of a dream or ambition which stymied the self-destructive impulse, even briefly. Once these integral supports collapsed, the obsessive desires were resurrected, reawakening the wish to exert dominance on a world they believe had kept them powerless and was hostile and alienating. Mass homicide and an attempt at simultaneous suicide was the result.

"There is usually a long gestation period between the time someone plans something like this and the act itself," Mullen says. "In that period, Bryant's life had actually improved, and there were a lot of reasons for him not to go ahead. He was caught by his own rigidity and obsessionality.

"That is one aspect of his mentality which is easy to miss. Because he is dim, disorganised and untidy, you can miss the rigidity of this man, the obsessive rigidity. Once the killings started, he had to go through with it. The killing of the children beggars belief. What's going on is not an act of evil but the act of someone who is obsessive and rigid, who is so caught up with carrying out his plan that he is not even concerned or noticing the awfulness of the actual act."

Mullen is sceptical of suggestions that Martin Bryant fell within the spectrum of autism disorders including Asperger's syndrome: "It depends on how widely you want to define it but, typically, you don't find sufferers of Asperger's who desperately seek relationships with others. The problem with Martin Bryant is that he was a man who was incapable of effectively establishing and maintaining any kind of relationship, from the most superficial to one that approached any kind of intimacy.

"It wasn't for a lack of effort. I mean, there was this extraordinary pattern of behaviour where he would fly business class to London so some poor soul has to talk to him for 22 hours. That doesn't sound autistic. It sounds like someone who is profoundly socially disabled but desperately wants contact."

This desire was displayed to the last, and Mullen is convinced that even on the way to Port Arthur, his car boot loaded with weaponry and with a list of victims drawn up, Bryant had still wanted to be stopped. In his twisted way of thinking, given a kind word, a positive response on that terrible day, he was secretly hoping to give the world "one last chance".

When they talked in prison the first time, Mullen says, Bryant was still swathed in bandages covering the festering burns from Seascape. "Even as he was driving out to commit the first two murders, the impression I gained from him was there was still a bit of him that was unsure. There was a bit of him that was still hoping that, somehow, something would happen and he wouldn't go through with it. Part of the stops was the hope that something or someone would magically persuade him to turn around and go home."

Mullen's words sit between us, heavy, almost imponderable. The enormity of the crime in terrifying contrast with the triviality of what might have stopped it: a kind word from a tourist, an offer to share a coffee from a stranger. The psychiatrist breaks the silence first.

"The extraordinary thing is how you get from an odd relationship and an odd young man to an act of such mind-boggling horror ... it's very difficult for us to get our heads around this but here was one of the world's worst mass killers who has ever existed, and you assume that what they are trying to do is something awful, which is partly true, but he saw himself as the aggrieved person. It was the world that had driven him to this. It wasn't as if he really wanted to [murder] but he had no choice. So many people had been so horrible to him that this was what he had been driven to do.

"Even in that last journey you have the attempt to see if the world will be nice to him, which sounds extraordinary, but these people have to justify what they are doing to themselves. Few want to commit an act of evil. Bryant wanted to show the world that he was a powerful and significant person, which nobody had ever recognised. He expected to go out in a blaze of glory, paying back a world that had been so mean and nasty to him, and at the same time become famous."

Martin Bryant's intention originally, he told his psychiatrist, was to be shot down. When that did not happen, he aimed to die in a blaze at Seascape but when it got too hot, he got scared and ran outside.

"There were some bits which were fairly well thought out and planned, like the automatic versus semi-automatic rifle. He decided on the semi-automatic because the other was too unreliable. But then you had this ridiculous situation where he couldn't open the boot of his car to get other weapons out. At one level you get this carefully planned action and on another you get this sad, silly man who can't even get the basics right."

••••••••••••••••••••••••••

Mullen was born in Bristol in 1944, smack bang in the middle of World War II. He remembers being shy and introverted as a child, characteristics almost unimaginable in a man who exudes such quiet confidence.

The only son of doting, older parents, he has described his own childhood as slightly peculiar, reminiscing that he had decided his life's course by the age of eight, choosing medicine after long stays in hospital to cure a childhood deafness. Even the decision to specialise as a psychiatrist was made precociously, at the age of just 14. He laughingly ascribes his professional choice to teenage testosterone and "dirty books", uncovered in the locked bookcase of his family's north London home. While Emil Zola figured large, it was a textbook of case histories written by Sigmund Freud that ignited his interest, not because there was much sex – disappointingly there wasn't – but because the great psychoanalyst injected human beings with an intriguing complexity, suggesting and hinting that beneath the veneer of the everyday and the banal lay unseen layers, fascinating depths to uncover, hidden reservoirs of seething conflict and desires, forbidden thoughts and that unfathomable unconscious.

Mullen, like senior colleague, Professor John Gunn, whom we would later meet in Britain, studied in London at the pioneering Maudsley Hospital. He still remembers, with gusto, its chief medical officer's credo that not everyone who is slightly different is creative or able – but that no one who is able and creative is in step. Those early years placed Mullen among a group of extremely intelligent and able people, many of them odd he says, but all of them clever and, most importantly, challenging.

Freudian analysis, however, was not to be his life's path. This young doctor was too rebellious, too interested in asking questions and questioning, using a young, honed and often prodigious memory to prickle lecturers and highlight inconsistent theories. In the end, however, it was the notion of the unconscious – and the complexity of human beings that originally attracted him to Freud as a kid – that he rejected. "Human beings are rather more simple than we like to believe," he tells us many months after our first meeting.

Mullen graduated in 1968, a young medico imbued in the ethos and fashion of the era, driven by a love of music, complete with long hair, jeans, boots, bangles, the whole flower-power kit and caboodle.

Occasionally, he and like-minded colleagues volunteered their medical services at big rock concerts, reviving overdosed revellers and keeping an eye on the "trippers". He remembers the young doctors always confiscated drugs from their victims – but he reminisced, with a twinkle, that not all the substances were always destined for destruction. The aftermath of stints in the so-called "trip tents" also meant there were many kids facing court and needing psychiatric appraisal. Here, suddenly, was a job the budding shrink could do to earn a little extra income outside the public health system. So began what would be a lifetime's work, which would slowly move away from the misdemeanours of young, recreational drug takers to assessing and telling the courts about some of the most difficult, violent and complex criminals of all.

In the end though, it was an innate restlessness combined with the election of Margaret Thatcher that lured him across the seas like so many of his compatriots, to the Antipodes. He told a journalist some years ago that ultimately, the Falklands War was the last straw.

By then married and with a young family, Mullen decided to live and work in New Zealand for a decade. His English accent, still razor sharp all these years later, nevertheless can betray the characteristic vowel of the Kiwi.

Finally, in 1992 he moved to Melbourne, headhunted over the Tasman to establish what has become a pioneering and state-of-the-art forensic mental health facility. Since then, as a forensic psychiatrist and the clinical director of Forensicare, Victoria's service for criminal offenders with mental illness, the father of five has seen, heard and studied the secrets of those who commit the most frightening crimes known to humanity. And yet, again, it was not the complexity of these crimes that struck him but their banality, the deep and shocking realisation that killers are just people, ordinary human beings, often damaged by mental illness or traumatic life experience – they may have committed monstrous acts but the notion of them being "monsters" is something he simply does not accept.

Mullen rejects persistent rumours that Bryant may have committed other unsolved murders – such as that of Italian tourist Victoria Cafasso, who was stabbed to death on Beaumaris Beach, 200 kilometres north of Hobart, in 1995, or German tourist Nancy Grunwaldt, who disappeared in nearby Scamander in 1993 – let alone suggestions that he may have been involved in Helen Harvey's death or even his own father's demise. Mullen argues that such theories say more about human beings' need to explain the inexplicably random nature of the crime.

"You can understand why people want to do this. The obvious explanation of Martin Bryant is that he was some horrific killer driven by blood lust and evil, and therefore you want some precedent so you can see a build-up from the little crimes to big crimes, from murder to more murders so that it makes some sort of sense.

"It's an explanation that makes people feel comfortable. It's much more difficult to get your head around the fact that this was an angry man who saw himself as a victim, didn't want to go on living and decided to die in such an awful manner."

Mullen notes that even Martin Bryant's greatest asset – his looks – worked horribly against him. "One of the things I have always seen as part of the Martin Bryant story is that he was a good-looking lad. He was a handsome young man but that finished up being a problem because it raised expectations that he was never able to fulfil. The sloppy grin wasn't evil, it was Bryant caught unable to understand how to respond. He had a nasty streak, of course, but when you are bullied and rejected from such an early stage, it tends to make you nasty.

"Once you break it down you begin to see a terrible tragedy. What you get with Bryant is someone who did something evil. But, as a person, I'm afraid he is rather dim, rather silly, rather resentful and feels he was mistreated and despairs on life. You combine that with a fascination for guns and you've got a tragedy.

"Take the [father's] suicide out, and it wouldn't have happened. Without the money, it wouldn't have happened. Take the guns out, and it wouldn't have happened. Provide a little more effective care, and it probably wouldn't have happened."

The enormity of Martin Bryant's crimes mean he must die in jail. But according to Paul Mullen – and his world-renowned colleagues in Britain and Canada – researching what experiences and psychological events lead to violent acts like this young man's rampage may pave the way for timely intervention.

In future, understanding violence may help us prevent it and step in as a society – before it's too late.

CHAPTER 32
Beyond Bryant

Understanding the great beauty and potential of the human brain was once unimaginable, such is its vast, mysterious and infinitely complex nature. Now, not only is science starting to unlock the complex biochemical and physiological secrets of its functioning but we know too that the nature versus nurture argument is as redundant as a clunky old word processor or the early "mobile" telephones that looked and felt like house bricks.

The field of molecular biology has revealed that our genes do indeed play an enormous role in who we are and how we will respond to life. But whether these biological or familial predispositions will be expressed – if at all – has also now been shown to depend on a complex interaction between what we inherit and what we experience. This, in turn, also has the capacity to shape the wiring of our brain, our neurodevelopment.

One of the most significant finds of the past couple of decades has been the understanding that genetic expression or the triggering of predispositions to, say, a mental illness, can have a different effect on neural development depending on when they manifest during an individual's lifetime. In other words, it can also change how the brain grows and develops – and therefore will change how an individual will feel, behave or think.

Just as science is opening the doors to explain these pivotal processes, highly sophisticated imaging can now show us exactly where in our brain our emotions come from, where decisions are made, where thoughts are generated, our feelings of anger, love, sadness, cravings, addictions, why some people "see" colours when they smell different aromas, laughter – and white-hot fury.

We can also see what happens when the brain's "wiring" goes awry. Martin Bryant's expression of suicidal rage on that terrible day in Port Arthur was the product of just such a vast and complex interweaving – of genetic vulnerabilities inherited from both paternal and maternal sides of his family, and the life experiences that interacted with them.

Could anything have been done to help Bryant before he turned on a world he decided to hate? Can the past teach us about the future? Does society, the mental health or educational system, have a responsibility towards damaged young people like him, and could it have done more to intervene in his decline? Martin Bryant's wiring, his physiological make-up is probably, mercifully, unique. But the alienation and psychological upheaval he struggled with – and finally railed violently against – is not.

For Paul Mullen – and his colleagues in Canada, Britain and Australia – Bryant represents an extreme and thankfully rare example of why modern, industrialised nations need urgently to invest in research and management of mental disorders and aggression, both in early childhood and adolescence.

Had Bryant ended up in a mental health care unit receiving on-going treatment when he first developed his suicidal compulsions, it may well have dampened the catalyst that morphed violent fantasies to reality.

Mullen believes that in today's world such a patient might have been referred to the early psychosis unit but at that time in Tasmania there were no services for adolescents whom people feared were developing serious mental problems. "The help just wasn't there. If it had been, I suspect he would have been referred."

Mullen's colleague, Melbourne psychiatrist Professor Pat McGorry, is a world-renowned specialist in adolescent mental health, and has pioneered cutting-edge programs for 15- to 24-year-olds in Australia. Just as medicine has responded to heart disease and cancers by trying to pick up illnesses at the earliest possible point, McGorry and his colleagues have established a twin framework to identify and intervene to manage teenagers and young adults at the times in their lives when most serious illnesses such as schizophrenia tend to emerge.

"We do have significant amounts of evidence now that if we do pick up the early stages of these potentially serious illnesses then the trajectory of life can be changed dramatically and much more done in terms of recovery and social integration and that sort of thing," he tells us.

For McGorry, Martin Bryant developed neither as a monster nor a mystery but rather a child who had been identified to have serious problems as early as toddlerhood but who did not receive timely, individual help. "He is an extreme example but there are probably one in three young people who have manifested significant mental ill health by the age of 25 and obviously can be at risk – and at the time we can't easily tell the difference between the Martin Bryants and the ones who have problems that are more self-limited and will resolve.

"I definitely think [he could have been helped] ... even without any further advances in knowledge we know the risk medically of these at the sharp end ... you know [the dangers] when someone decompensates to that degree."

McGorry argues that the increase in mental disorders among young people in the developed world is inextricably bound up with the often toxic social and familial settings in which they are growing up. "That is why we are seeing higher rates of this in young people, because the environmental factors have got worse. The genetic risks have probably stayed the same but the likelihood of them being expressed may have increased. People have varying levels of intrinsic risk genetically ... but if you are trying to go through this period of life with lead in the saddlebags already and cumulative additional stresses because the way you are makes you more likely to be bullied, to be lonely, poor, disadvantaged, take drugs, get drunk ... all these things are increasing your risk of breakdown, of decompensation.

"For a guy like Martin Bryant, if he had more of the right sort of environment and less of the social disadvantage then the genetics might not have been so decisive, and certainly the final piece of behaviour ... well, you couldn't say that that was inevitable, that was purely because, I suppose, of how his life evolved."

Richard Tremblay, professor of pediatrics, psychiatry and psychology at the University of Montreal, has spent more than two decades studying and tracking more than 25,000 Canadian children aged five months to their mid-20s in a bid to find the roots of physical aggression. He is a world expert on violence prevention, and argues that children are at their most violent in their toddler years, and it is the familial and societal setting that "civilises" them.

In *Early Learning Prevents Youth Violence*, published in November 2008, he reported that a large longitudinal study in Montreal suggested that children who had greater difficulty controlling their aggressive behaviour than their peers when they entered kindergarten were more likely to persist with behavioural problems as they grew older, and that those who remained frequently physically aggressive during elementary school were much more likely to be violent during late adolescence. Similar results have been reported in other large samples in Canada, New Zealand and the United States.

Martin Bryant's behaviour, identified as disturbed when he was a toddler and later at school, would send warning signs today that might ensure his inclusion in early intervention programs.

Tremblay's work suggests that aggression in children is the "default" position, and it is the child's ability to learn to control themselves and their impulses that is learned from their environment and parental modelling. A wide variety of factors have been identified or linked with childhood aggression, including a history of physical abuse within the family and maternal antisocial behaviour.

In 2007, Tremblay presented work that suggested a genetic signature consistent with chronic violent behaviour at a meeting of the Royal Society, Britain's academy of science. It also suggested that genes may play a significant role in the acquisition of language and delayed development of communication skills – as occurred with Bryant – can contribute to increasing frustration levels in children, making them more prone to resort to violence as a tool to be heard. Ultimately, such research may not only help cover genetic profiles distinct to chronic aggression but allow researchers to identify children at risk and intervene earlier.

Children who fail to learn self-control can suffer consequences that spread outwards into all areas of their existence, from impaired schooling to loneliness and insecurity, that can last a lifetime. Overly aggressive children are also naturally rejected by their peers, and do not benefit from the normal socialisation that can occur through their better adjusted peers: they become loners, increasingly alienated and resentful. The converse can happen too when such children find each other and form groups and gangs in which aggressive behaviour is reinforced, often as a tool of survival.

Through the Montreal Longitudinal and Experimental Study, Tremblay and his colleagues have demonstrated that intensive interventions – targeting the child, his family and school environment at entry age – can change the long-term behavioural trajectories of aggressive kindergarten-age boys.

Pat McGorry, however, argues that Martin Bryant's case was even more complicated, having potentially fallen into a subgroup of kids who are dealt a double-whammy, with early neurodevelopmental vulnerability and a second surge of biological and social changes following puberty and continuing during adolescence.

These children's developmental pathways move away from normality early on in childhood but when puberty hits, they start to really run into trouble as the big changes in the brain that occur during adolescence butt up against their psychosocial vulnerabilities. "So there is that interaction between those things, the gene, the environment. You see, I think, it is a hugely important area for further understanding," he says.

"But we can't just wait for another 20 years until we have it all worked out. We have got to do something now, and there is a tremendous amount that can be done in terms of picking up kids who are clearly having problems and providing much better interventions, and at the moment, you know, even in developed countries, it is pretty pathetic in terms of the level of response."

Australia, like Canada, is one of the few Western nations that have begun to invest in researching and trialling programs designed specifically for young people. McGorry and his British colleague, Emeritus Professor John Gunn, and Professor Stan Kutcher in Nova Scotia, Canada, have all urged, lobbied and fought for governments to recognise that investment in adolescent mental health is a protective measure, one that could potentially save the public purse hundreds of millions in losses later.

It is estimated and accepted globally that 70 per cent of all major mental disorders emerge in people before the age of 30. And yet the vast majority of medical research – Kutcher estimates up to 90 per cent of the therapeutic work and research – focuses on adults over the age of 30.

"The biggest problem is that traditionally this has been based on the percolation model ... that is, we tried an intervention in adults, modified it and then we tried it on young people without understanding that the neural development and neural biology is completely different between adults and young people," Kutcher says.

"This is actually unconscionable in terms of its approach but is consistent with the way our society, the way politicians and leaders view young people and have failed to embrace the importance of early investment in this area."

Professor Gunn, a pioneer of forensic psychiatry in Britain, is now retired but his work over a lifetime has created a cornerstone of modern understanding of the links between mental illness and violence. His work spanned therapeutics, often with offenders in jail, epidemiology – including one of the first big studies on the prevalence of mental disorders in prisoners in England – and developmental psychopathology. He is a compassionate and powerful advocate for the academic study and research into understanding the social origins of violence. With his wife and fellow psychiatrist, Professor Pamela Taylor, he was the first to suggest links between schizophrenia and homicide.

Gunn says that he has long been puzzled by the fact that the period known for life's maximum disturbance – adolescence – remains one of the least of interest to both psychiatrists and government. "The neglect of adolescent psychiatry is a special form of self-harm undertaken by adult society.

"We spend a huge slice of our national expenditure on things like airplanes and guns and armies. We call it 'defence'. I'm not suggesting we shouldn't do that, but in ordinary terms, between wars, there are other things we have to defend ourselves from. The most important of those is violence, ordinary violence, and yet we know nothing about it.

"We spend no money on it and there is almost no research funds allocated to it yet, to most people, it is not as important as knowing they have armies overseas in Iraq or wherever. I've always found that disparity puzzling but I think it's due to stigma. Soldiers become heroes, warfare is grandiose and uplifting whereas people are appalled by ordinary violence, shy away from it and don't want to spend any money even if to prevent it."

Gunn echoes the calls from his colleagues in other continents for a rethink about resources for research. He says the money spent in Britain on his speciality is minuscule, and while the state builds institutions to house people who have committed crimes and recognise they need help, little is done to understand the origins of their behaviour.

"Society doesn't take ownership of people such as [Bryant] because he is seen as alien – [as if] he's not one of us and our society didn't produce him

... the very word 'evil' means it comes from outside, and isn't part of us. I understand that it isn't easy for us to accept that this kind of thing is part of our society, but it is.

"All the words like monster and evil produce political reactions. What the politicians fail to grasp is that while they think there are no votes in spending money on criminal lunatics – or whatever other awful phrase they choose to use – that there might be some mileage in saying, 'We are spending money on understanding how we can prevent crime.'"

Gunn is now working with colleagues to establish a charitable research fund to research aggression, mental disorders and the origins of violence. "Almost every other branch of medicine has quite big research funds; think about the huge advances in prevention of heart disease, cancer and so on, but this is also important. And yet it is difficult to persuade people that this is a good and charitable way of spending their money.

"Even psychiatry itself doesn't want to know anything about this area. Many of my colleagues are quite open when they're talking privately, saying they don't want this kind of image to stigmatise the rest of psychiatry. People are trying to get away as much as possible from violence and sex offences: those are the two big things."

Gunn says that despite media hysteria about rising violence in big cities such as London, there is no evidence to show this. "Nineteenth century novels suggest London was a fearsome, violent place. There are changing patterns of urban violence, and gang violence among London youth is an example. Yes, there is a rise in the last decade of gang fights with knives among boys ... but again there is very little research being done to see what this gang violence is all about, and why they use knives. They're all scared stiff, usually boys without hope and without a future who are living a feral life in many cases and looking after themselves, as they would see it. If we spend more time understanding the underlying issues then we could do more to prevent it."

Gunn is clear on the need for more knowledge. He argues that institutions to study criminology, forensic psychiatry and forensic psychology are urgently needed, and these sciences too must have their own "well-funded institutions".

"We have to accept that we are a very aggressive animal. It is also true that we are a very social animal. We live in incredibly intense communities in which we have to relate to other people, all of whom are aggressive, and keep our aggression and theirs in balance. I would agree with Tremblay that one of the things which is going wrong is learning those skills of social living. Most people who have done something terrible have had disastrous childhoods in terms of learning these social skills.

"It's almost impossible to find someone who has done something terrible who hasn't had a poor upbringing."

According to Kutcher, too, a big problem globally is that while we know that the environment and genetic expression are interwoven – and in turn affect the laying down of wiring, or neural pathways, in the brain – there is simply not enough rigorous research across the human life span. What is needed is a global study of a sufficient number of people to help science disentangle the complexities of the components.

"You know we are way past the point where we are looking at social determinants of health as explanatory models – that is old news. And we are way past the point where we look at genetics as the explanatory model ... it is too complicated for simple gene explanation. It is time to develop the capacity to go beyond this ideological model and to understand how they integrate," he argues.

"So what we need is large cohort studies of young people carried out from conception to the time of uterine development to early development through to early adulthood. They need to be incredibly well designed they need to be multinational and they need a huge cohort, hundreds of thousands of people, to allow us to sort these things out."

One of the greatest frustrations for mental health experts working with young people is that governments tend to respond to critical incidents such as Port Arthur or the US school shootings by making public health policy on the run rather than strategically and based on well grounded evidence.

In Australia, a federally funded program of care for young people with mental and substance use disorders was established in 2006 and there are now 30 "headspace" centres around the country where young people between 12 and 25 can self-refer themselves to gain access to a new style of mental health services. But even this initial stage of reform only reaches 10 per cent of the youth population, a kind of "base camp" with funding from government that is still not recurrent or guaranteed.

Says McGorry: "Other countries like Canada and the United States are beginning to recognise the huge problem. No other country has a regulated programmatic response to this. The Australian Government responded very positively. Evidence-based medicine is behind it and there is more capacity. Australia is ahead of other countries and has the best chance to forge ahead in this task of constructing appropriate and novel service environments."

"We all know how difficult adolescence is, and if you are trying to master those developmental tasks with a major genetic load or a vulnerability, whether it is for intellectual or emotional disorders – all of these things … who gets depression, who gets psychosis, who gets dependent on substances, all depends on gene/environment interaction."

McGorry says Martin Bryant's final journey was characteristic of most suicidal people in that he wanted to be stopped even as he drove to Port Arthur: "With all suicidal people there is a part of them that wants to be saved. That is why, if you can get to them, they have a chance. Someone who is depressed, who has suicidal thoughts or plans, if you can access them, it is always preventable."

Equally important, according to all the psychiatrists, is re-engaging young people in the workforce or schooling after they have emerged from a period of depression or other kind of mental illness. One of the most significant observations of Martin Bryant was his further isolation from society when he was deemed to be entitled to a lifetime on a pension and therefore stopped his odd jobs, gardening and little business ventures with his dad which gave him a working place in society.

Had he found a place where he felt useful, it might have changed his increasingly negative view of himself and the world.

"We see that a lot with the young people who come to us with potentially very serious illnesses like schizophrenia and bipolar disorder,"McGorry says. "One of our research projects published in *The British Journal of Psychiatry* shows that if you do re-engage and return people who are emerging from psychosis, if you return them to school or to work then they do incredibly well. We now get 90 per cent back to school and work compared to only 50 per cent before. This is a result of just a simple intervention of having an employment consultant working at the clinical service and connecting them and supporting them back to those environments, and it is so simple and it works.

"Otherwise, the main game was how to get benefits and how to get supported, and that just consigns them to continuing isolation."

Paul Mullen agrees:"Interestingly, they almost gave up on Martin Bryant ever having a chance of employment. In fact, he does have literacy and numeracy and he does have some qualities, and with the right influences, he might very well have been able to occupy a relatively menial task in open employment. He was physically able; in fact, he had a number of pluses physically."

Bryant was also failed by the system in the period after Helen Harvey and then his father died. His disintegration in the face of such loss is a normal human response let alone in an individual already so stressed and struggling emotionally in such a dramatic way."Once parents die or they can't cope any more, then they are completely marginalised, death rates are 20 years ahead of everyone else, just like Aboriginal people, the chronically mentally ill are in this situation,"McGorry notes.

Young men also appear to respond differently when psychologically vulnerable. Unlike young women, who tend to externalise and express their distress, young men are less likely to seek support or help and are much more difficult to engage and treat.

"They also exhibit offending behaviour. Just coming back to Martin Bryant, offending behaviour peaks between the 12- and 25-year age group so you get these synergistic/destructive interactions of offending and mental ill health. One is a risk factor for the other, and suicide rates are much higher in young men than young women ... so they are really in trouble. So of all people across the life span, young men really are the most in need, and we need much more effective preventative as well as treatment and care responses. Mental ill health is the key health issue for young people. Physical ill health is a relatively minor issue for young people these days."

Neuroscience has also revealed that the process of maturation in young brains, the development of the part of the brain that governs impulse control is a much longer process than was originally thought. There is now debate in some enlightened US states that the criminal law may need reform in light of new scientific understanding."That is a difficult concept because of society's punitive attitudes even towards the youngest offenders. But it is certainly true a lot of kids mature very slowly in terms of levels of responsibility, and the brain research shows that the degree of control of the frontal lobes over the limbic system and the deeper parts of the brain is something that is really not completed until somewhere around the mid-20s,"McGorry says.

"You can see that in people's behaviour but ... in research using brain scans and ... almost every psychological disorder you see has some sort of impairment of the relationship between the frontal areas of control and the deeper parts of the brain. It is definitely something that needs more discussion, but you are going to get a primitive response to that ... particularly from the shock jocks."

Pat McGorry does not speak from an academic ivory tower. He has three sons, one of whom has been the victim of two violent assaults in one year. Like his colleagues, compassion and understanding shapes his response: he does not lay blame, acknowledging simply that it may have been drugs or alcohol that exacerbated the immaturity and lack of impulse control in the young brains that dealt his boy the blows.

Similarly, Stan Kutcher believes the general public must be educated about mental health issues. It is incumbent on society to take some responsibility for the vulnerabilities of young people.

"I am appalled at the low level of the scientific literacy of the population generally and am particularly concerned at the low level of mental health literacy of the population. We are starting to see some changes in this, however – moving toward the positive. For example, Australia has started to make some inroads with their mental health first aid program but it is still very basic information that is being delivered. So much investment in mental health is now being driven by what I call distress as opposed to disorder.

"Governments and institutions find it easier to invest scarce resources in providing interventions of doubtful medical necessity for individuals who are distressed, and avoid investing in determining what works best for those who have mental disorders. In other words, let's provide psychotherapy for everybody who is feeling unhappy as opposed to providing the best research and therapy for people suffering schizophrenia.

"If we put that model to our public health system, it is a little like investing heavily in providing beds in hospital for people that have the flu and colds, and not providing hospital care for people that need urgent appendectomies. We feel good because we are investing in mental health problems whereas people with disorders are not being invested in at all."

Surprisingly for us, the experts all argue that an examination of Martin Bryant's life is both legitimate and could foster a more sophisticated public debate about mental health, violence and young people.

"I think it is wonderful that you are writing it up," McGorry insists. "And if I can make a suggestion in terms of the positive that can come out if it ... I have tried to do a fair bit of advocacy around this issue, and what I have found with people that can be useful – and it is a bit like advocacy in other areas like cancer or diabetes – is the public have to be a little bit ... look, 'frightened' is not the word but their anxiety level has to be tapped into to some degree.

"The terrible consequences of failed care and support for Martin Bryant could be repeated and, indeed, has been in many places since 1996. They have to understand that it might happen to them or it might happen to their kids or something like that. In the case of Bryant, it is society that is at risk."

McGorry cites the case of a 16-year-old boy he has seen at a headspace centre recently: "He had a very similar story thus far to Bryant. The young man is headed for jail unless he receives expert help, and has a long history of ADHD and conduct disorder. He wants help and the expertise is now available, however the specialist services are so under-resourced they cannot accept him due to large waiting lists. He is too complex for headspace even though he has never been treated. He needs a specialist team within the public mental health services.

"The message is that there can be more Bryants if something is not done about this issue. And positive things can be done and even with the present state of knowledge we have, it just requires the community and political will to actually do it."

CHAPTER 33
Behind Bars

Risdon Prison, modelled on jails built in the 1960s for the blazing hot conditions of the United States' deep south, is perched on a hillside on the outskirts of Hobart, a city often battered by the teeth-clenching winds from the Antarctic. For many years surrounded by bizarre pink cement walls, its open-plan, caged design focuses on the outdoors and is as ludicrous and incongruous as its nickname among locals: the Pink Palace.

For Maurice Bryant, Risdon jail loomed large in his darkest moments: Martin Bryant told inspectors Warren and Paine that his father had pointed to the walls on a drive down to Richmond and issued his only son a warning: "My dad said ... 'If you ever go over there, Martin, to that prison any time, I'm not gunna ever come and visit you. So stay away, stay out of trouble.'"

Bryant will never be released from Risdon, his sentence spanning 35 life terms with no parole. Justice William Cox made clear on November 22, 1996, that the gates of Risdon would never be opened to him: "I have no reason to hope, and every reason to fear, that he will remain indefinitely as disturbed and insensitive as he was when planning and executing the crimes of which he now stands convicted. The protection of the community, in my opinion, requires that he serve fully the sentences."

And yet Justice Cox also made a plea for some understanding and even compassion, a call which was not widely reported but which echoes the arguments of the world's most eminent forensic psychiatrists: "Without minimising the gravity of his conduct ... it would appear to me that the level of his culpability is accordingly reduced by reason of his intellectual impairment and the disorder with which he has been afflicted for so long, notwithstanding his parents' earnest endeavours to correct it. That the prisoner, through these handicaps, in combination with a number of external factors beyond his control such as the loss of stabilising influences, has developed into a pathetic social misfit calls for understanding and pity, even though his actions demand condemnation."

Today, Martin Bryant lives out his life enveloped in state-sanctioned secrecy, the only news of his welfare leaked out unofficially, sporadically and hardly ever verified. It is known that he has attempted suicide at least six times. He once tried to hang himself with bandages tied to his hospital bed while another time he swallowed a rolled-up toothpaste tube and took an overdose of the tranquilliser Rohypnol. Torn sheets tied into a noose were found on another occasion in his cell while the most recent, reported widely in March 2007, involved attempts to slash his own throat and wrists with a razor blade. The picture that has emerged through the handful of people who are allowed to see him – his mother, his psychiatrists and prison wardens – is of a man who has regressed dramatically, his lean good looks ravaged by middle age and ballooning weight bolstered by a reported ravenous craving for ice-cream and a lack of interest in physical exercise. Stories have also emerged of physical attacks on him from other prisoners as well as instances of bartering sex for privileges such as cans of Coca-Cola.

What is known is that profound loneliness has accompanied him to prison, the inability to socialise made worse than ever. His deterioration is in marked contrast to the first couple of years when a portrait of this most infamous of prisoners was permitted by prison authorities. The documentary by ABC radio journalist Ginny Stein was aired a year after the massacres and portrays a young man still obsessed with notoriety and desperate for acknowledgment of his terrible deed. Two chance encounters said much about him. As he wandered past the reporter who was interviewing the prison's security chief, Rod Quarry, Bryant noticed the microphone and wandered over: "You're busy talking away there? About me?" Bryant queried.

Quarry waved him away: "Not about you, cobber. You come next, some other time, maybe six months' time."

As he walked away, Bryant kept glancing back over his shoulder. Despite Quarry's denials, it was clear that he knew he was the subject of the conversation and, in those early years at least, continued to revel in his notoriety.

Risdon Prison staff, too, confirm the periodic requests by his mother to visit her son, and Bryant's increasing distance: "No, not this week," he would often say. Occasionally, there were meetings behind the omnipresent prison screens but even then, suddenly and without warning, he would simply stand up and walk away, leaving his mother alone, powerless as always. The tragedy of this loyal mother, sitting knee-to-knee with a son with whom she had always found it difficult to bond and cope, facing rejection decades later and even following such a terrible crime seems an additional cruelty. She is very much a victim of her son's crimes and still finds solace in conspiracy theories and denial. Fragile and yet strong in her faith, she lives a life tortured by the horror of what happened.

Rod Quarry, who was chief of Risdon Prison's security when Bryant was jailed, is one of the few people who have known him, and is happy to speak about him. He spoke to Stein and later to Mark Whittaker, a journalist at *The Weekend Australian*, on the 10th anniversary of the massacre. Thirteen years later, he happily agrees to have a chat with us, too. He left the prison long ago but his memories remain sharp. Quarry says his responsibilities at the time were made all the more complex because of the explosive community outrage – and inmate hostility – about Bryant's crime. All guards suddenly had to be screened to ensure there were no family or friendship connections with Bryant's victims. "My interest was about the situation he had created [for the prison] rather than Bryant himself but I watched him closely, I suppose, for two years," he says.

Quarry witnessed the young man's odd, little girl voice and watched as he went through a series of strange balletic exercises in his cell in the mornings. He saw Bryant destroy a TV set, and heard his continuing desire to relive his crimes, often wanting to be reassured that his world record for killing the most people as a lone gunman had not been broken. He would even ask prison staff, particularly women, about the welfare of their children, and appeared to revel in their discomfort. All this took place during the same period that lawyer John Avery and psychiatrists Paul Mullen, Ian Sale and Ian Joblin were working through their own assessments of Bryant's character, and the two police officers, John Warren and Ross Paine, worked to extract his confession.

Bryant pleaded not guilty at his first court appearance, which Rod Quarry believed was driven by his desire to relive his crimes in court and revel in public attention. This assessment turned out to be correct, as Avery's subsequent interviews with Bryant showed. What was more difficult to explain was his behaviour during the second appearance when he pleaded guilty. Then, Bryant grinned and broke out into fits of giggles as the charges were read. Quarry told Mark Whittaker: "He was looking at people, seeing who was looking his way. That was what he was about."

However, the then prison psychiatrist, the late Dr Wilf Lopes, saw it very differently and his explanation of Bryant's giggles and laughs had little to do with being cruel or callous but more about social ineptness. He told Stein: "Sometimes you see people laughing nervously or hysterically, laughing at a situation that's very serious. I would say this behaviour is akin to that; he does not realise that what he expresses outwardly is connected to the situation at hand. I think this is the main problem … if his IQ is at 11 years old, his emotional development is of a two-year-old."

Lopes said they had tried to retest Bryant's IQ but he would not co-operate. Why? "On the one hand he wants to show that his IQ is better than 11, but at the same time I think he's frightened that it might turn out to be true."

Lopes agreed with Mullen, but added: "Although psychiatrists have not been able to apportion to him a psychiatric diagnosis, it's quite obvious the way he thinks, the way he behaves, the way he relates, that it is abnormal. I would think he's probably closer to insane, particularly as his thinking has led to a behaviour which is totally unacceptable."

A few years later, Lopes gave another interview, this time revealing that Bryant had begun to reflect on his crime."I think he has some understanding of what occurred, some sort of remorse. The question is: How do you get him to express it? That is something that could be worked on to make his life worthwhile."

In November 2006, Bryant was moved from the old prison hospital to the newly built psychiatric wing next door, named the Lopes unit after the kind prison psychiatrist who died in 2004. As happens so often in such cases, the media reported that the move would give Bryant more "freedom", sparking outrage and a hostile community response.

Bryant's original legal definition as sane was again trotted out in the media amid suggestions that his incarceration in a medical facility would somehow lighten the load of his punishment because his welfare would be overseen by medical staff rather than prison staff.

Nevertheless, the move proceeded, driven by Tasmania's Director of Prisons, Graeme Barber, who signed the order: "I direct that prisoner Martin Bryant, who appears to be suffering a mental illness, be removed from Risdon Prison complex to the Wilfred Lopes centre, a secure mental health unit, on the following grounds: I consider it necessary to so remove the prisoner for his own health, wellbeing or safety, and for the protection of other persons. I also consider that appropriate treatment, care, rehabilitation or other services cannot be provided in the prison, or hospital, or [any other] institution to which the prisoner can be removed."

Martin Bryant had found a home.

In the search to answer why Martin Bryant went on his terrible rampage, the result and impact of his crime should not be forgotten. We include, based on the prosecution case, the following chapters which deal in detail with the violent events of that day. This account has been quarantined for those readers who may find it too harrowing.

CHAPTER 34
The Cafe

He stands at the door trying, incongruously, to balance in one hand a can of fruit and a cup of juice atop a plastic tray and in the other a long black bag hiding two assault rifles, 28 rounds of ammunition and sundry weapons. Martin Bryant asks two strangers, Carol Pearce and Carmel Edwards, who are entering the cafe with a tour group, to hold open the door for him while he manoeuvres past them and on to the front veranda of the Broad Arrow Cafe. The two women mean nothing to him, their instinctive courtesy irrelevant to what he is about to do. He mumbles something about having been surfing all morning as he finds a seat near the edge of the balcony.

It is just after 1.30pm on Sunday, April 28. The day is clear but has the fine chill that comes with the oncoming winter. Trade is brisk; the place is filling for a busy afternoon. At least 60 customers are spread through the old stone structure a few yards from the dark, glassy waters of the Port Arthur cove. Some are outside but most are inside eating, waiting to be served or browsing in the tiny souvenir section at the back of the shop.

Bryant has arrived at Port Arthur 10 minutes earlier, causing a commotion at the toll booth at the entrance when he refuses to pay the $25 fee and then objects to where he is told to park. He ignores the attendant, Ian Kingston, and parks his yellow Volvo among the coaches along the waterfront. Bryant is understandably cocky and aggro given that he has already murdered two people and is intent on killing many more. Just where it will happen is still undecided. He likes the idea of the Isle of the Dead where he can hunt at will as people get off the boat to walk around the cemetery. Instead he has gone to the Broad Arrow Cafe, perhaps because it represents past rebuffs but also because there is a crowd of people – targets.

He has gone inside and bought a meagre lunch, come back outside and sat down, anonymous among the throng, the only one by himself. It has been that way all his life, and now the time has come to right all the wrongs, real or perceived.

"There's a lot of wasps around today," he remarks casually in the general direction of one woman, a Mrs Sullivan, sitting at a nearby table. She hasn't seen any, she tells him.

Bryant is in the mood to converse. Did anyone have any parking problems like he had getting in? Nobody had. "Fuck him, I parked there anyway," he says of his confrontation.

Michael Beekman and Rebecca McKenna try to ignore him, although he is right about the wasps. The Melbourne couple have noticed them, too, but this guy is weird; talking to himself and muttering something about there not being many Japanese tourists around. He is hard to understand actually; jittery, eating quickly with fast hand movements and glancing back and forth between the door to the cafe and the car park. They watch him get up from the table, gather his tray and big black bag and walk back inside. Someone else holds the door for him. There is no end to the politeness here.

He is followed inside by Bev and Peter Kelly, who have finished their lunch and want to browse for souvenirs. They watch him walk through the cafe and place his bag on a vacant table near the north-west corner.

Inside the bag is a towel, a hunting knife and two lengths of sash cord rope. There is blood on the knife, which belongs to David Martin, who is lying dead on his bed at Seascape guest house, alongside his wife.

Bryant unzips his bag and draws out the AR-15 rifle, its magazine holding 26 cartridges, two having already been used on the Martins.

Michael Sargent had noticed Bryant when he walked in, particularly the way he stared at an Asian couple sitting at a table by the windows on the western side of the building. Bryant catches him watching and Mr Sargent holds his gaze just briefly before returning to the conversation around the table with his girlfriend Kate Scott, who is facing him across the table, and another couple, John Riviere and Carol Villiers.

Then come two shots in rapid succession – an ugly CHUNK, CHUNK – and Mr Sargent looks up to see the guy he'd been staring at holding a rifle. He's just shot the Asian couple – named later as Moh Yee Ng and Sou Leng Chung from Malaysia – and is now turning the weapon in his direction.

Instinctively, Mr Sargent dives forward to get under the table. The bullet creases the top of his head as he hits the floor. A second later, Kate Scott's body slumps next to his, the back of her head shattered by a fourth blast. Mr Sargent doesn't dare move as the shots continue. Instead, he shouts out blindly to other patrons to keep down. Some don't, others try but are found and killed anyway.

Mr Ng's body is slumped against a wall, table knife still in his hand as if he is about to take a mouthful. The shot has killed him instantly, striking him in the neck from within a few centimetres, the gun powder stippling around the entry wound, like a death tattoo. Many of the victims will be killed from a similar distance; from a few centimetres to a few metres – point-blank range, proverbial fish in a barrel. Ms Chung is hit in the left ear. The bullet continues to the base of the brain. She is dead before her head hits the window.

By now Bryant has already swivelled away from the two tables and is firing down the cafe, laughing to himself as he walks from table to table killing. It is easy. Like flies.

Anthony Nightingale is next. He was facing Bryant when the shooting began. As the gunman approaches, he stands and calls out in vain hope, "No! No! Not here." Bryant ignores the plea and shoots him in the neck. People outside the cafe who have heard the shooting watch his body slump against the window.

Ten members of one of the many tour groups are at the next table. Mervyn and Maureen Schadendorff, Maree and Gary Broome and John and Gaye Fidler have finished their meals and are waiting for the other four to arrive. Kevin and Marlene Sharp, Ray Sharp and Wally Bennett had entered the cafe behind Bryant and are standing with their backs to him when he opens fire.

Bryant, still laughing, moves from Mr Nightingale to the three men standing. He points the gun at Ray Sharp, who can only say, "That's not funny," before a shot drowns out his words. The bullet strikes him in the side of the head.

Wally Bennett is next. Bryant rams the muzzle up against Mr Bennett's neck and fires. The bullet passes through Mr Bennett's body and strikes the arm of his friend, Kevin Sharp, who is standing behind him. Mr Sharp is then shot a second time, through the left side of his face, killing him instantly. Gary Broome, who is at the table nearest the men, is hit in the face by a bullet fragment from the same projectile which killed Kevin Sharp. John and Gaye Fidler are also hit by shrapnel; he in the forehead, and she in the back.

Bryant turns again, towards a table where three people are sitting. Sydneysider Tony Kistan leaps to his feet and pushes his wife, Sarah, towards the door and out of harm's way. Andrew Mills is also standing, the horror unfolding so swiftly that he, like so many others, barely has time to react let alone flee. Mr Mills is shot in the head, behind his right ear; Mr Kistan in the left side of the head, from a range of two metres.

Two women sitting at a nearby table are struck by shrapnel from the two fatal shots to Mr Kistan and Mr Mills. Thelma Walker is hit in the head and ankle, and Pamela Law in the head and right thigh. Peter Crosswell, sitting with them, drags the women beneath the table to take shelter.

Patricia Barker, sitting at an adjacent table, is also hit by flying shrapnel, in the right arm, left hand and cheek, as she struggles to get down on the floor. She is sitting with seven others – Faye Richards, Carol Pearce, Fred Barker, Ron and Carmel Edwards and Robert and Alyece Elliott – who are crowded together beneath the table as Bryant stalks past. Another two members of their party, Lindsay Richards and Ken Pearce, are sheltering two tables away.

Bryant is moving constantly. He is now in the middle of the room, aiming towards the front door and a table where three people are finishing their meal and about to leave. Graham Colyer is putting his coat on when he is shot through the neck from two metres away. The bullet passes through his body as he slumps to the floor, almost drowning in his own blood. But he will survive as will Carol Loughton, who has been sitting with Mr Colyer and her 15-year-old daughter, Sarah.

As Bryant aims, Sarah runs towards her mother. The two women fall to the floor, Ms Loughton desperately trying to shield her daughter. It is all in vain. Bryant, in command, simply stands over them and shoots Ms Loughton in the back and Sarah in the head. The sound of the shot that kills her daughter ruptured Ms Loughton's eardrum. She will only learn of her daughter's death the next day after coming out of surgery for a gaping, 10-centimetre wound in her back.

The room is now in pandemonium as customers realise that the shooting is not some colonial re-enactment, as many initially believe. Amid the panic, Bryant swivels from where he has shot Mr Colyer and aims at Mervyn Howard, who is sitting with his wife, Mary, at one of two tables near the front doors. The bullet strikes Howard in the head, killing him instantly. He falls forward on to the table. His wife has no time to react as Bryant moves closer and fires, hitting her in the neck. She falls to the floor, injured but not dead. Bryant calmly leans over a pram parked by the adjacent table, places the muzzle of the gun near Mrs Howard's head and pulls the trigger.

The pram is empty. The baby, 15-month-old Mitchell Winter, is screaming in the arms of his mother, Joanne, who is hiding beneath the table with her father, Ron Fowler. Joanne's husband Jason Winter, is caught on the other side of the room when the shooting breaks out. He'd been returning trays and plates to the servery area, and now watches in stunned disbelief with others.

In the commotion, and despite the baby's distress, Bryant does not seem to notice Jason and the other onlookers as he turns his attention to the gift shop along the eastern wall of the building. An exit door is locked and cannot be opened without a key, which is held somewhere else in the complex.

As Bryant moves towards the shop where a dozen people are cowering in the tiny space, he crosses back past the table where Patricia Baker has been hit by shrapnel. Another member of her party, Robert Elliott, stands up. It is a moment of confusion that almost costs him his life, but there is simply no room beneath the table where a crush of petrified people are hiding, expecting to be the next killed. Realising his mistake, he tries to get to the stone fireplace but is cut down by two shots from Bryant, one striking him in the arm, the other in the head. Somehow he survives.

That sequence of events, from the moment Bryant begins firing to the moment he shoots Robert Elliott, has taken just 15 seconds. In that time, Bryant has fired 17 shots and killed 12 people. A further 10 lay wounded, either from direct hits or shrapnel. The sound of the shots thudding out across the green field beyond the window has been picked up by a video camera, one of four videos taken by brave bystanders in the confusion.

Police are later able to establish the timing based on the video tapes taken by tourists from outside the cafe, some hundreds of metres away. One tape by a Mr and Mrs Wilkinson, of Victoria, who had filmed from behind the cafe towards the penitentiary ruins, stops after 15 seconds. By that time Bryant has fired 17 times, the last at Mr Elliott. The second tape, by Barry Turner, was taken from the opposite direction, and records 21 shots in 25 seconds, the last four inside the gift shop.

At the gift shop counter, two staff members, Nicole Burgess and Elizabeth Howard, are standing, frozen. From several metres away, Bryant shoots Nicole where she stands, probably the longest shot he makes in the cafe. The bullet strikes her in the head and kills her instantly. Elizabeth Howard tries to turn away but is hit through the right arm and chest. Bryant stands over her body and fires again, then turns his attention to the customers now hiding as best they can in the confined area.

Like many others, Coralee and Dennis Lever and their friends Vera and Ron Jary thought the shooting was a re-enactment. Now they are hiding for their lives. Vera, Ron and Coralee have taken shelter with another woman, Jenny Moors, behind a hessian curtain that offers no protection from the gunman now standing above them other than a thin screen that obscures them from view.

But Dennis Lever is exposed. He has moved because there isn't enough room behind the curtain, and it costs him his life as Bryant shifts his sights from the dead women behind the counter and shoots him in the head. Coralee can see her husband where he lies but can do nothing without putting herself in danger.

Ron Neander and his wife Gwen are also in the gift shop. They recognise Bryant as the strange man they had seen in the queue for food a few minutes earlier. Now they have taken refuge behind a display table but it is not enough. Bryant spies them near the back wall and shoots Mrs Neander in the face.

Her husband may have been next except Bryant is suddenly distracted by a movement behind him in the cafe, near the fireplace in the centre of the room. He turns and moves back near the table where Mr Colyer and the Loughtons have been shot, firing as he goes, hitting and injuring Peter Crosswell, who is still under the table with Ms Walker and Ms Law.

The brief pause brings out another target. Dennis Olson and his wife, Mary, are hiding behind the fireplace with Jason Winter, who announces,

"He's gone," and begins to move towards his wife and baby son on the other side of the room. He realises his mistake as soon as he stands up: "No! No!" he cries out as Bryant fires twice. The first shot strikes him through his hand, raised in a desperate, pleading gesture, and enters his chest. The second hits him in the head, killing him instantly.

Shrapnel sprays and strikes Mr Olson in the hand, head, chest and left eye but Bryant has turned again and goes back to the gift shop area. He hasn't finished with those cowering in fear.

None of these shots require expert marksmanship, as a host of conspiracy theorists will naively claim later. They are fired from the hip, so close to the victims that little aim is required – cowardly, merciless and unfathomable.

Bryant finds five people crowded together at the locked rear exit door. They have no escape and no cover from the killer. Ron Jary makes the mistake of moving from behind the hessian curtain, probably because there is no room. Bryant shoots him through the neck. Pauline Masters, who has left her sister and mother outside while she looks at souvenirs, is shot through the right cheek. Peter Nash tells his wife, Carolyn, to get beneath him. He is protecting her when Bryant leans over and shoots him through the head.

Twenty people lay dead and a dozen or more injured by the time Bryant stops firing. Not because the carnage is finished. He has to reload.

Sandra Vanderpeer, an army major, is sheltering behind a display table with Bev and Peter Kelly. She recognises the telltale, hollow sound of the plastic magazine being changed. The empty 30-shot magazine is discarded near the servery counter. With that, Bryant leaves the cafe.

Bodies lie scattered through the room. Survivors will later talk of the lack of noise during the ordeal although the sound of the gunfire, heavy and robotic, would have drowned the screams of those unable to stay silent as they hoped to be missed by the gunman in his methodical hunt. The wounds are horrific.

The jigsaw of clues from witness accounts, video footage, sound bites and ballistic evidence estimate that Bryant was inside the cafe shooting for between 90 and 120 seconds. In less than two minutes, he has murdered 20 people and injured 12 more, either from direct fire or shrapnel. In all, he would fire 29 times, almost all from point-blank range.

And now he is outside with a fresh clip.

CHAPTER 35
The Car Park

Brigid Cook, kitchen manager at the Broad Arrow, feels confused. She and three other staff had fled the cafe when one of their colleagues burst into the kitchen and said a gunman was on the loose. They have escaped through a back door but now she doesn't know what to do. She hasn't seen any shooting so it might all be a false alarm. Then again if it is real, she should do something. Instead of running into the trees and safety, she turns and heads for the information centre, back towards probable danger, to warn others.

While she is telling others to get away, Bryant appears on the veranda of the cafe. He stands there in his three-quarter-length coat surveying the panic unfolding before him then, for the first time, raises the rifle to his shoulder, aims and fires across the lawn towards the ruins. All the shots inside had been fired from the hip. There had been no need to take aim but out here the shots were wild, indiscriminate, almost as if he were firing for the sake of it. The shots sound like a cannon as the sound reverberates in the lush green auditorium. Full metal jacket ammunition thuds into trees. Bryant walks swiftly from the balcony towards the car park.

Brigid Cook is moving towards the four tour coaches parked at the water's edge, warning others of the now obvious danger. She then hides with them behind a Trans Otway coach. Others stand between the Redline and Tigerline coaches, hoping Bryant won't come their way.

But he is coming closer. Bryant strides, almost jogging now, across the lawn down towards the front of the buses. He is hunting moving targets now. Royce Thompson, the Tigerline driver, is making his way cautiously down the passenger side of the vehicle, just as Bryant sticks his head around the side. He has nowhere to hide and Bryant blasts him in the back as he flees. Mr Thompson falls then manages to crawl to the back and roll beneath the bus, only to die from the massive wound which has shattered his chest.

Bryant continues across the front of the coaches to the Trans Otway coach, where Brigid Cook is sheltering with the others. She peeks out as Bryant appears. He fires from the length of the bus away and hits her in the right thigh. The bullet passes through one leg and lodges in the other but, using her apron to staunch the blood flow, she is able to make it to a guardhouse behind the buses where she collapses.

Bryant has moved on to the next bus where another knot of tourists are trying to get into the vehicle and lock the door. He is six metres from Winifred Aplin when he shoots her in the side of the head. She dies on the spot. He fires again, grazing the cheek of Yvonne Lockley as she scrambles for safety.

Neville and Janette Quin don't know where to run. When the warning first came they decided to head towards the jetty where the boat leaves for the Isle of the Dead. Then, when others shout that Bryant is moving along the water's edge, they double back towards the rear of the coaches, right into his sights. He fires and hits Mrs Quin in the right side. She falls almost exactly where Royce Thompson had fallen moments earlier.

It has become a deadly game of cat and mouse as groups of terrified people try to react to the sound of gunfire and ever-changing warnings yelled by others as Bryant changes positions and stalks his prey.

The passengers on the Trans Otway coach had begun to congregate as the shooting began, called together by the driver who was ready to leave the site. Doug Hutchinson and his wife Irene were among them but had become separated when the warning comes that Bryant is approaching. Mrs Hutchinson manages to get onboard but her husband is too far away. Instead he tries to get behind the bus but is hit in the arm and knocked off his feet. Most of Bryant's shots are now wayward, fired from distance against moving targets. Most of those hit are injured rather than killed although the wounds are horrific.

Martin Bryant doesn't pursue Mr Hutchinson. Instead, he suddenly stops and walks back to the yellow Volvo parked a few cars along from the line of coaches. Others watch from what they hoped would be a safe distance as he opens the boot. Is that the end? Is he leaving?

Their hopes are shattered when the tousled-headed figure, who has made no attempt to conceal himself and says nothing, just smiling as he kills, takes out another weapon. He's just changing guns.

Bryant loads a 20-round clip into the Fabrique Nationale semi-automatic .308 calibre rifle, another military weapon, and fires across the corner of the bay towards the wall of the main ruin. He is taking pot shots just like he used to as a teenager over in the next bay. But this is no air gun, and his targets are real.

Denise Cromer is near the boardwalk at the back of the ruin when she hears the shots. Gravel spits up a few metres in front of her and then a second bullet whizzes past her head. Her first thought is still that she is witnessing a re-enactment, such is the lunacy of the attack, but she puzzles about the genius of the technology that allowed a small explosive device to be planted in the pathway for effect.

Rodney Horrocks and his wife are sitting in their car having lunch at the other side of the cafe when Dennis Nudd bangs on the window and tells them to get out and hide. They can see Bryant standing at the boot of his car and realise the peril they are in as they sprint for the tree line. Bryant sees them, too – the movement catches his eye. A moving target; he aims and fires, missing the three and the high-calibre bullet slams into a tree, making it shudder with the impact.

Bryant shuts the boot, walks to the driver's door and sits behind the wheel of his car for a moment, as if weighing up whether to drive off or begin again. He chooses the latter, and walks back towards the coaches.

Pamela Sloane is inching along the foreshore with the injured Doug Hutchinson, who is nursing a shattered forearm but has managed to get to his feet. They are moving slowly, working their way from car to car as quietly as possible but Bryant spots them as he returns to the buses. He fires but misses. Janette Quin is not so lucky. Already injured and lying on the ground, Bryant walks back past, stops and shoots the stricken woman in the back.

It occurs to Bryant that he might find people inside the buses where they will be trapped and easy targets. He climbs aboard the Redline bus but no one is inside, but he knows there are some in the next bus – the Trans Otway – because he had wounded one woman as she climbed aboard. There are others, too.

He fires through the window, across the gap and into the side of the bus. It is indiscriminate but effective. Elva Gaylard is sitting next to Irene Hutchinson, crouched low, out of sight. Such is the power of this ammunition that the bullet slices through the coach's metal shell, through her arm and lodges in her chest. She is killed instantly.

Yvonne Lockley, who had been grazed by a bullet as she climbed into the bus, is hiding nearby with Gordon Francis and his wife. Mr Francis risks being seen by moving down the aisle of the coach to shut the door before Bryant can get inside. He feels a sharp pain in his left shoulder as Bryant fires again from the Redline coach. He collapses on the floor, his shoulder shattered.

Outside, Neville Quin has found his wife Janette, terribly injured, lying almost under the bus next to the dying Royce Thompson. She is barely conscious and terribly cold when he holds her. She has been shot twice, and unless he can do something quickly, she will certainly die in the car park.

As he kneels beside her, something makes him turn around. The gunman has just rounded the corner of the bus and stands there watching him before raising his rifle. Mr Quin can either stay and die or run and hope to come back to Janette later. He flees around the bus but as he does so realises the killer will probably try to cut him off the other way. He doubles back just as a bullet fizzes by his head, then another. He is by the door of the coach now and climbs aboard, hoping for sanctuary, but Bryant is younger and quicker, and he follows.

Mr Quin is sheltering behind a seat when he is found. There is nowhere to go. He is about to be killed. As Bryant raises the weapon, he utters his only words since the shooting spree had begun less than 10 minutes earlier:

"No one gets away from me," he says as he fires.

Mr Quin, who has defiantly faced his attacker, ducks forward instinctively as the gun roars. The bullet misses his head and buries itself in his neck. Bryant walks away, believing he has finished him off. But Mr Quin is still alive, albeit momentarily paralysed. He recovers and staggers back to his wife but it is too late. She dies beside the bus, in his arms, 15 minutes later.

For whatever reason, Martin Bryant decides he's had enough and it is time to make his escape. There is still confusion outside, not only with many people just beginning to realise the horrible truth of what has happened, but because of the echo of the gunfire through the natural amphitheatre, not knowing how many gunmen are shooting and where he or they are. Bryant can see the panic before him as he descends the steps of the bus; the figures squatting beneath cars or behind trees, some peering out from walls and others fleeing up the road to the main highway. Then he sees a man filming from the other side of the car park. James Balasko, an American tourist, has been recording footage of Bryant firing on the bus but, in doing so, has exposed himself. He is still focusing the camera when Bryant fires, hitting the car next to him.

He fires a few more shots, as if warning those watching not to follow. One flies at the cottage which used to house the prison commandant, and another across the water towards the ruins. He then jumps in his car, quickly reverses and is gone. Some say Bryant beeps his horn and waves as he goes; others say he is still firing out of the window.

Either way, he isn't finished.

CHAPTER 36
The Toll Booth

Of all those who escaped Martin Bryant's rampage, a foursome visiting from Victoria might consider themselves among the luckiest. John and Caroline Boskovic and their friends Peter and Pauline Grenfell had travelled together to Port Arthur, wandered around the site and had a quick lunch at the Broad Arrow Cafe. It was just after 1pm when they got up to leave. The three people waiting to sit down – Peter Crosswell and Carol and Sarah Loughton – would all be shot.

After the meal, the friends pause outside while Mrs Boskovic goes to the toilet near the information centre at the bottom of the entrance road to the main car park. Then the shooting starts, and she is dragged outside by Pauline Grenfell, excited by what others insist is a re-enactment. Some people actually move towards the noise, believing they are missing something, only to realise their mistake when they see those inside or near the cafe flee in terror. When the frightening reality dawns, they too run, ignoring their car and hurrying up the roadway towards the toll booth near the highway. Behind them comes the sounds of fear and the crack of gunfire as Bryant moves around the car park.

There are others around them, including Nanette Mikac and her two daughters, six-year-old Alannah and three-year-old Madeline. The Mikacs live at nearby Nubeena, and Mrs Mikac works as a ghost tour guide at the site but today she is just a visitor, there for a Sunday picnic with her daughters while husband Walter plays golf at a nearby course with friends. Now the day has turned dark and dangerous, and she isn't going to take any risks, carrying Madeline on her back so they can move faster and get to safety. Alannah runs to keep up. The trio is to the right of the Boskovics as the Grenfells fall in just behind. Mrs Boskovic can see the distress and overcomes her own by trying to calm the young girl as they climb the steep grade. It will be all right, they are away from the trouble. It is behind them. Her mother is also reassuring: "We're safe now, Pumpkin," she promises Madeline, the tollgate and highway are not far off. The child seems to relax.

Behind them the yellow Volvo drives steadily up the hill, the driver in no apparent hurry. It slides to a stop alongside the Mikacs. Nanette stops, puts Madeline down on the ground next to Alannah and walks them towards the car, believing it to be sanctuary.

Others watch in horror, including Mr Boskovic who had the same reaction but changes his mind when he sees the man open the car door. Bryant, who has changed back to the AR-15 rifle, gets out of the car, walks to Mrs Mikac and places his hand on her shoulder. She realises what has happened but by then it is too late. As others look on, helpless and transfixed by the horror unfolding before them, Bryant tells Mrs Mikac three times to get down on her knees. His voice is calm, in control.

"Please don't hurt my babies," she pleads as she drops to her knees.

John Boskovic grabs his wife's hand and runs up the hill, swinging to his right along a track further into the trees hoping to find cover. The Grenfells, caught behind, headed back down the hill and into trees. Behind them gunshots ring out – one, two, three, four, five then a pause for a few seconds before a sixth.

James Dutton witnesses it all. He and his wife, Joanne, were among those warned earlier by Brigid Cook. He looks over his shoulder as he runs for cover and sees Bryant kill Nanette Mikac with a single shot to the head. James turns away again, grabs Joanne's hand and hurries on to a dirt road, the shots continuing behind. As he glances back a second time, Bryant is advancing on Alannah.

Mrs Mikac dies instantly but Madeline is hit twice, first in the shoulder and then in the chest, and the second shot kills her. Alannah, terrified, is hiding behind a tree a few metres away. Bryant fires twice at her but misses. He then walks to the tree, finds the girl, presses the muzzle of the gun against the right side of her neck and fires. Clinical. The killings have reached a new level of inhumanity.

Bryant walks back to his car and continues up the hill towards the toll gate. It is only 100 metres or so. Anyone near the entrance has a clear view of what just happened. He pulls over on the verge behind a gold BMW. The owner is local resident Rose Nixon, who was showing the sights to three friends from northern NSW, Jim Pollard and Robert and Helene Salzmann. The Salzmanns are in the back seat while Mr Pollard drives. They have just pulled into the historic site, paid the fee and have driven about 100 metres down the hill when a man walking back up the road warns them to turn around. Mr Pollard does so, as does a red Holden Commodore behind, driven by Thomas Buckley, who gets out of his car to ask the toll booth attendant, Mrs Kingston, what is going on. He looks down the road to see Bryant shoot Mrs Mikac and Madeline, grabs his wife Debra and they run for their lives towards the highway. Keith and June Edwards have just turned off the highway and see the Mikac slaughter. They reverse out, wait for the Buckleys and then speed down the road towards Hobart as far as the Port Arthur service station where they stop to warn others.

Debra Rhodes doesn't notice the Edwards's car as she turns into the site. But she knows something is wrong when she is blocked by the BMW near the toll booth. Rhodes and her passengers, Frida Cheok and son, Nicholas, can see a woman in the front passenger seat of the BMW waving her hands frantically as if telling them to get away. Two men stand arguing near the back door of a yellow Volvo nearby. They watch as the younger of the two men pulls out a rifle, points it at the other man's head and pulls the trigger. Robert Salzmann falls, dead, on the road. Rather than drive away, Jim Pollard gets out of the driver's side and walks around to remonstrate with the gunman. Bryant answers by shooting him in the chest.

Another car pulls up behind Debra Rhodes's car, blocking her exit. Mrs Cheok signals frantically from the back seat, and the driver, seeing Bryant, responds by reversing and driving off. Rhodes does the same, and they flee as Bryant, ignoring their departure, walks up to the back door of the BMW, pulls Mrs Salzmann out of the car and shoots her in the neck. Rose Nixon is frozen in her seat as Bryant walks around the car, opens the door and shoots her twice as she cowers. The first bullet enters her right shoulder, perforating her neck and cervical spine, and the second enters her left shoulder and penetrates the left chest cavity. Bryant drags her body out of the car and dumps it on the road then decides he will take the car and begins transferring items from the Volvo, including the two guns, ammunition, two sets of Smith and Wesson handcuffs and a container of petrol.

As he does so, another car pulls in off the Arthur Highway. Graham Sutherland is with his wife, Stephanie, and two sons, Thomas and Stuart. Still 150 metres from the toll booth they can see three bodies lying on the ground. Thomas, sitting next to his father in the front seat, sees Bryant running back towards the Volvo where he grabs one of the rifles. He calls out a warning to his father who slams the car in reverse just as two blasts from a shotgun ring out. A hail of pellets shatters the windscreen, missing Mr Sutherland but spraying him with glass. A second shot penetrates the driver's door just above the door handle but somehow misses again as Mr Sutherland speeds off back towards Hobart.

Bryant is also on the move. Having taken what he wants from the Volvo, he drives back towards Seascape, looking for a hostage. But he has left a lot behind. Among the items discarded is the 12-gauge Daewoo semi-automatic shotgun fitted with a magazine containing nine cartridges, a cardboard box with 439 .38 calibre cartridges, 27 litres of petrol in two canisters and three packets of Little Lucifer fire starters. Inside a video camera bag, among other things, are six keys with tags marked Seascape.

Keith Edwards has been trying to flag down other motorists from the road outside the Port Arthur service station. Debra Rhodes joins him after pleading with George Laycock, owner of the photo shop opposite, to call the police. As they prepare to leave and head for Hobart, the gold BMW appears. The driver swerves on to the wrong side of the road, swings into the service station driveway and blocks the path of a white Corolla hatchback parked at the petrol bowsers.

Bryant leaps out of the car, gun in hand, wrenches open the passenger door of the Corolla and tries to pull Zoe Hall, who is sitting screaming in terror beside boyfriend Glen Pears, from the car. Those sheltering inside the shop watch as Mr Pears gets out and walks around the car and begins remonstrating with Bryant. They can't hear the words but he appears to be trying to placate the gunman or be offering himself as an alternative to his girlfriend.

Bryant's response is savage. He points the rifle at Mr Pears and shoves him to the back of the BMW where he opens the boot and forces the man to climb inside and kneel. After shutting the boot, he walks back around to the car door where Ms Hall was but she has scrambled to the other side of the car. Bryant raises the rifle and fires three times through the window, hitting her in the neck, arm and chest. She dies instantly. Bryant has what he wants – a hostage – and drives off at high speed back towards Seascape.

••••••••••••••••••••••••••

John Rooke is driving steadily along the Port Arthur Highway. He has a loaded trailer hitched to the back of his Datsun sedan, and isn't in a hurry but the bloke coming the other way sure is, swerving across the road and into the driveway of the Seascape guest house before slamming on the brakes and jumping out of the car. Then Mr Rooke sees the gun, a rifle of some sort. The gunman stands by the road, probably less than 10 metres away now, raises the gun to his shoulder and fires twice in quick succession. Mr Rooke is past the guy before he realises the shots have missed. He looks in the rear-view mirror, expecting to see the gunman firing at him. Instead, he hears two more shots and sees a car behind him get its windows blown out.

The four-wheel drive is being driven by Linda White from Melbourne. Boyfriend Michael Wanders is beside her. They have both seen the man by the side of the road holding a long gun but think he is waiting for the cars to pass so he can shoot at rabbits. They slow down as they pass, unintentionally giving Bryant an easier shot at them. He raises the gun and fires directly at Ms White. The bullet hits the bonnet and ricochets through the windscreen, showering her with glass. He fires again and again and again as the car passes by, smashing out the windows, somehow missing Mr Wanders but almost blowing off Ms White's right forearm. She brings the car to a standstill at the bottom of the next hill, out of sight of Seascape, and collapses in the passenger side while Mr Wanders tries desperately to start the car. One of the bullets has cut through the throttle cable, and he eventually gives up.

Behind them another car is approaching Seascape, unaware that the gunman is waiting. Doug Horne is driving a Ford Falcon sedan. His wife, Helen, is behind him, next to his sister, Faye. A friend, Neville Shilkin, is in the front passenger seat. He shouts a warning as they draw level with the driveway when he sees Bryant with the shotgun raised. "He's got a gun!" he yells but it is too late. Bryant fires and the windscreen blows out. Glass and shrapnel lacerate Mr Horne's chest and right shoulder, arm, elbow and forearm but none of the others are hit. He manages to keep driving and stops just past the car in which the injured Linda White lies. They take her and Mr Wanders and drive to safety at The Fox and Hounds a few kilometres up the road.

Anne Wardle is driving the Magna when she sees Bryant shooting at Doug Horne's car. She had three friends with her – Sylvia Riley, Mary Warburton and Joyce Maloney – and immediately begins reversing on the wrong side to avoid hitting any cars behind her. Bryant fires and hits the car but the damage is minimal. She drives several kilometres back towards Hobart before stopping to flag down dozens of cars on their way into danger.

One car she can't stop is a Ford sedan driven by Simon Williams, a Canadian Embassy official on holiday from Canberra. He and his wife, Susan, are admiring the view as they come over the hill towards Seascape. They don't see Bryant at first, rather the sight of a Magna sedan reversing on the wrong side of the road back up the hill. Then he sees Bryant firing from the driveway but Mr Williams has no choice but to keep driving past the property. As he draws level, Bryant fires again. The bullet shatters the passenger side window and shrapnel catches Mrs Williams in the hand, severing one finger, while glass lacerates her face. Her husband is also hit in the hand, causing serious injury, but he manages to keep driving to safety.

There are no cars after the Williams's. They've been stopped in both directions so Bryant gets back in the BMW and drives to the grassed area beside the cottage, alongside a bank of trees. He drags Glen Pears from the boot and takes him inside where the bodies of David and Sally Martin still lie on the bed. He handcuffs Mr Pears's wrists behind his back and uses the second pair to secure him to a post in the lounge room. Then he goes back outside, takes his guns and ammunition from the car, douses it with petrol and sets it alight.

The siege begins.

•••••••••••••••••••••••••••••

Carleen Bryant is strolling through a Hobart shopping centre when the first media reports of the massacre begin to filter through during the afternoon. Like so many others, she stops and watches the television screens in the electronics shop window, transfixed by the immediate horror as police try desperately to get a handle on the scale of the killings and the whereabouts of the gunman.

First it is a half a dozen dead, then a dozen, with a similar injury toll. The updates continue as media crews arrive and find survivors in a daze. The number jumps three or four with every update – 15 then 18 then 22, 25, 28. By nightfall it would be 30 with fears of more. Dawn would bring the tally to 35, with the dead outnumbering the injured.

Shopkeepers stand beside their customers to watch, business forgotten, and unaware that the killer's mother stands among them, her own life destroyed along with those of the many victims and their families. Slowly they disperse, drawn home to safety and their own television sets for updates as the gunman barricades himself inside the Seascape cottage, seemingly intent on a shootout.

Carleen Bryant leaves too, perplexed by early descriptions of the blond killer and instinctively worried about her son.

Where is Martin?